Nigeria and the Crisis of the Nation-State

Agenda for National Consensus

Published by
Adonis & Abbey Publishers Ltd
P.O. Box 43418
London
SE11 4XZ, United Kingdom
Email: editor@adonis-abbey.com
Website: http://www.adonis-abbey.com
Tel 0845 388 7248

Nigeria:
Adonis & Abbey Publishing Co.
P.O. Box 10546, Abuja
Email: editor@adonis-abbey.com
Website: http://www.adonis-abbey.com
Tel: 08165970458/08182006992

First Edition, January 2012

Copyright © Emeka Nwosu

British Library Cataloguing-in-Publication Data
A catalogue record for this book is available from the British Library

ISBN 9781906704896 (PB)/ 9781906704957 (HB)

The moral right of the author has been asserted

Cover Design: Asia Ifitkar

Nigeria and the Crisis of the Nation-State

Agenda for National Consensus

Emeka Nwosu

Table of Contents

Dedication

This book is specially dedicated to the memory of my late beloved mother, Madam Hannah Chinyere Nwosu who departed this sinful world on May 17, 2010 while the work was still in progress and to all lovers of democracy in our clime who believe that the Nigeria project is not irredeemable.

Acknowledgement

I want to thank the Almighty God for making this work a reality. I have always nursed the idea of putting my thoughts together in a book right from my days at the Daily Times in the 1990s as the Political Editor. My extra-journalism engagements in Abuja which saw me working at different times as the Special Assistant to the Senate President and Assistant Director in the Presidency caused me considerable distractions. I thank God that He still imbued me with the will to forge ahead with the project.

Some people played one role or the other in making this book a dream come true. It is only natural that they be acknowledged for their contributions. My special thanks go to Chief Uche Ezechuku, a veteran journalist, consummate intellectual and renowned author himself who gave me all the encouragement to proceed with this work. I must admit that the persistent concerns he showed in the progress of the work proved very motivational.

I cannot leave out Nick Hayes, the MD/CEO of Xavier Communications Ltd, a high-flying media and marketing consultancy outfit in Abuja. He is one person who believes that my writings are good enough to be preserved for posterity. I thank him for believing so much in me.

I must express my deep gratitude to Dr. Grant Ehiobuche, a top diplomat with the Nigerian Foreign Ministry who was of great financial assistance when I ran for the Ikwuano/Umuahia federal seat. As a serving diplomat in Nigeria's mission in Tokyo, Japan, he showed considerable interest in my political career. After the election, he kept encouraging me to continue to maintain my presence in the media.

Also not left out is Onyegbule Ukeje, a friend and brother who was with me in Umuahia during the electioneering. He was a major influence in my taking up a media column shortly after the 2007 election. I am deeply grateful to him for his encouragement.

I must also single out one of my kinsmen in Abuja, Christian Igodo, a young man who is so much in love with the written word. I would say that he is so addicted to my column in the Thisday newspaper every

Tuesday. He kept reminding me of the need to preserve my works in a book for which I gave him a firm promise. I thank him for reposing so much confidence in my intellectual abilities.

I cannot forget to mention Chukwudi Agwu, a progressive young man and vibrant banker, an avid reader of my newspaper column. He is one person who through his positive comments provided the inspiration for this effort. I thank him.

How can I forget Christian Amushie whom I met in the Daily Times in 1987? He has demonstrated true friendship and loyalty. I remain immensely grateful to him for his support.

I also thank Bright Aduku, my graphic artist who handled the initial draft of the work.

Finally, I want to thank my amiable and loving wife, Violet and our children, Nnanna, Nneoma, Emeka Jnr and Uju for being there for me. Without providing the needed stability at the home front, this book, perhaps, may have remained a pipe dream.

There are many others too numerous to mention for lack of space. I thank you all and plead for your understanding.

Above all, I take responsibility for any errors of omission and commission that may be contained in this book.

Emeka Nwosu, JP

Abuja, Nigeria
July 2011

Foreword

I have had the privilege of going through this book, *Nigeria and the Crisis of the Nation-State* written by an erudite journalist, Emeka Nwosu. I have known Emeka for over twenty years when he was engaged with the Daily Times as a Political Correspondent.

I followed with keen interest his journalism career especially when he became the National Chairman of the National Association of Political Correspondents (NAPOC), a very powerful grouping of all political correspondents in Nigeria.

As the Nigeria's Minister of Information in those sensitive days, I was closely associated with the group and Emeka. At the Daily Times, he occupied variously the positions of Political Editor, Editorial Board Member and Deputy Editor.

I read with relish his writings which were deeply analytical, incisive and refreshing. When I was reappointed Minister of Information in 2000 by President Olusegun Obasanjo, I did not hesitate to include Emeka in my team.

He was with me during the historic National Media Tour during which I led a delegation of Nigerian journalists, drawn from all the media houses in the country, on an on the spot evaluation of the impact of democratic governance across the country after two years of civilian rule.

In recognition of his proven literary competence, he was appointed into the Editorial Committee that produced a very seminal publication on the outcome of the National Media Tour. He discharged the responsibility with uncommon zeal and sagacity.

I am therefore not surprised that Emeka has come up with this book which is quite illuminating and stimulating. He has brought to bear on this work his highly analytical mind and lucidity of thoughts.

The primary focus of the work which is written in lucid and free-flowing prose is on the challenges of nation building and crisis of governance in Nigeria.

The author also writes passionately on other key areas of our national life which relate to such themes as the National Question, political leadership, media and national security, the electoral process, legislature, democracy, human rights and rule of law, power and politics, value systems, religion and inter-ethnic relations among others.

He makes the point clearly that the cultural diversity of Nigeria rather than be a draw back should be a source of strength. He strongly argued that for Nigeria to realize her manifest destiny there was the compelling need for her to draw from the collective strength of her diverse ethnic nationalities while de-emphasizing those divisive traits and stereotypes that have tended to constitute serious encumbrances to the process of nation building in the country.

A common thread that runs in all the issues treated in the book is the essence of building a united and harmonious society that is anchored on the principles of justice, equity and fairness. He further contended that national greatness is impossible in a plural society like Nigeria without forging national consensus amongst its peoples particularly the elite class.

What stands the work out is the simplicity of language, clarity of thought, demonstrable intellectual depth and logic of presentation. Given Emeka`s pedigree as a Political Scientist and an outstanding Journalist, I am hardly surprised at the quality of the work.

I must commend him for this singular contribution, coming at a critical period in the nation`s political history. The ideas canvassed in this book will serve as a veritable guide in the search for national consensus.

The book is a very useful contribution to the ongoing national debate on the way forward for Nigeria and will be of invaluable assistance to students of politics and diplomacy, law, international relations, public administration and social sciences.

It is also highly recommended to our policy makers in the Executive, Legislature and Judiciary and also the members of the general public.

The book is a major contribution to policy dialogue in our nation. I warmly congratulate Emeka for his efforts.

Professor Jerry Gana, CON
Former Federal Minister of Information; Cooperation and Integration in Africa; and Agriculture.

Introduction

This book is a product of an effort to preserve in one volume some of my writings in the media, particularly in Thisday newspaper in the last three years beginning from late 2007.

I had just returned to Abuja from Umuahia, Abia State in April 2007 shortly after an unsuccessful bid to represent the Ikwuano/Umuahia federal constituency in the House of Representatives. I was the candidate of the Action Congress (AC) in the 2007 election which was massively rigged across the country.

Having tasted the action as it were, I was encouraged by a lot friends and well wishers to take up a column in a national newspaper where I would share my thoughts including my experiences during the elections with readers nation wide.

I accepted the challenge and proceeded to contact the publisher of Thisday, Mr. Nduka Obaigbena, who graciously granted my request to keep a column in the newspaper. Following our discussions, I started writing every Tuesday. To the glory of God, I have sustained that column for the past three years.

What we have in this volume is essentially my thoughts on different aspects of our national life with prognosis for achieving national consensus and integration. The primary focus however is on the crisis of politics and governance in our country since the return to civil democratic rule in 1999.

I have titled the book, *Nigeria and the Crisis of the Nation-State: Agenda for National Consensus*. As the title suggests, the book is a collection of my writings on topical national issues ranging from the National Question, electoral process, political leadership and crisis of nation building, party politics, religion and other matters that have continued to agitate the polity.

As an emergent state from colonialism in 1960, Nigeria was immediately faced with the challenge of forging a united state out of her many ethnic and linguistic groups which habour deep suspicions about each other. The suspicions arose mainly from a mutual fear of domination and control especially among the three major ethnic groups of Hausa-Fulani, Igbo and Yoruba.

It had been argued that the British colonial masters who pursued the discriminatory 'policy of association' in their colonies in Africa including Nigeria did not make any conscious efforts to forge a common nation out of the disparate ethnic nationalities in the country. Not even the 1914 Amalgamation of the Northern and Southern protectorates would compel the British to reconstruct Nigeria as one harmonious entity.

Blinded by their greed for the exploitation of the material and mineral resources of the country, the colonial authorities aggressively pursued a divide and rule policy which saw the country being carved up into separate mutually exclusive enclaves.

The British colonialists never concealed their economic interests in the colonies. Ellen Thorp, a British author, in his book, Ladder of Bones, which is a reconstruction of the accounts of British involvement in the affairs of Nigeria from 1853 to 1953, clearly admitted that Britain benefited enormously from the West coast of Africa.

"To Britain, the importance of her West African Trade was immeasurable; without the raw materials which she obtained from the Coast she could not have survived the Second World War; and, equally important, the dollars which West African tin, cocoa, and palm oil brought into the British Treasury enabled her to solve some of her balance of payments problems".

Humphrey Nwosu, a professor of Political Science and former chairman of the defunct National Electoral Commission (NEC) who conducted the annulled June 12,1993 presidential election in his book, 'Laying the Foundation for Nigeria's Democracy', acknowledged the dubiousness in the approach of the colonialists to inter-ethnic relations in the country.

He wrote: "The British foisted on Nigeria their own preferred model of government albeit that they had neither sufficiently taught, nor had Nigeria's emergent leadership sufficiently imbibed the values and norms that make the tranquil operation of the system feasible" (Nwosu;2008:60).

Nwosu concluded by saying that: "Analysts of the neo-colonial and dependency schools of thought maintain that in Nigeria as in deed elsewhere in colonial Africa, the more fractured or inchoate the independence transition was, the more salutary the neo-colonialists gained firm grip for the continued control and manipulation of the political economies of these states by the metro poles in the post-independence period".

In other words, Nwosu is in complete alignment with the thesis that the interest of the colonial authorities was primarily economic and therefore self-serving. It could further be argued that the lack of interest of the colonialists in fostering inter-ethnic cooperation amongst the indigenous natives perhaps formed the foundation for the social mistrust and distrust evident in the relationships among the rival ethnic groups in the country even till today.

Perhaps the British colonial authorities feared that if the various ethnic nationalities were allowed to freely intermingle, they could forge a common understanding and brotherhood that might threaten their economic interests in the country. That was why the colonialists encouraged the policy of social segmentation in Nigeria, particularly in the northern part of the country.

This odious policy gave rise to the indigene-settler syndrome which has continued to pose the single most important threat to the peaceful coexistence of Nigeria. The policy of social segregation as encouraged by the colonialists resulted in the establishment of settler colonies known as 'sabongari' in Hausa language. The term refers to settlements of non-indigenes in the North.

In the Yoruba-speaking South West, the quarters for the settlers from the North were known as 'sabo'. And in the Igbo-controlled areas of the South East, such settlements were known as 'ogbe Hausa' or 'ama Hausa'.

This unfortunate bifurcation in social relations quite early in the history of our country had great consequences for the political stability of the emergent state. The policy of social segmentation which sought to minimize interactions and exchanges amongst the so-called indigenes and stranger elements within their own country was like a poisoned chalice which subsequently bred unnecessary tensions and instability in the polity.

In their work, "Conflict of Securities: Reflections on State and Human Security in Africa", Jamila J. Abubakar et al (2010:5) decried the bifurcation policy pursued in Africa by the imperial powers. They wrote: "Modern African states are essentially a creation of the famous Berlin Conference of 1886-1887. During this conference, the European imperial powers arbitrarily bunched together many heterogeneous and adversarial ethnic communities into disparate states. This colonial diktat was motivated by the economic and strategic interests of the imperial powers. The outcome is the continuing rejection and questioning of statehood by many African people, the perpetuation of pre-colonial inter-tribal feuds in more complex and implosive forms, and the extraversion of the post-colonial states to protect and advance the strategic interests of the Western powers that created these states. As a result of this situation, African states are contested and dysfunctional".

They further noted that the dysfunctional nature of the states in Africa has resulted in about 42 wars that had been fought on the continent since 1970, with vast majority of them within territorial boundaries.

Nigeria definitely is not the only pluralistic or ethnically diverse country that was colonized by an imperial power like the Great Britain. There are many others like that; except that in our case we have three dominant groups and over 250 smaller groups. But a close study of political developments in the post-colonial states in Africa clearly shows that the states administered by British colonial authorities compared to the ones colonized by France have recorded more cases of political crises and conflicts arising essentially from inter-ethnic misunderstanding. This perhaps has to do with the divisive policy of association or segregation pursued by Britain in her colonies.

Except perhaps in East Africa where former British colonies like Kenya and Tanzania, for long served as an oasis of stability within the conflict-ridden continent, the rest of the states administered by the British colonialists have suffered several conflicts which in many cases resulted into civil wars. The checklist includes Nigeria, Sierra Leone, Sudan, Uganda, Gambia, Ghana and Zimbabwe.

Until very recently, the former colonies administered by the French were relatively more stable than their Anglophone counterparts. This development had been attributed to the policy of assimilation pursued by France in her former colonies. By that policy, the French authorities sought to build African states that were basically the satellite extensions of metropolitan France.

Martin Meredith in his authoritative book, The State of Africa: A History of Fifty Years of Independence, noted the success attained by the French policy of assimilation in her African colonies. He stated: "In conducting their 'civilising mission' in Africa, they (France) had been highly successful in cultivating a small black elite to whom they accorded full rights as citizens on condition that they accepted assimilation into

French society and rejected their African heritage, family law and customs. In outlook, members of the elite saw themselves, and were seen, as Frenchmen, brought up in a tradition of loyalty to France, taking a certain pride in being citizens of a world power" (P.58).

The policy of assimilation neither fostered nor fed on the ideology of social segmentation and segregation. It is no wonder that for so long the Francophone countries remained socially cohesive and politically stable. In this group are Senegal, Benin Republic, Cameroun, Gabon, Guinea and Coted'Ivoire.

It must however be acknowledged that there are some Francophone countries that had been wracked by military conflicts, for most of their existence and therefore do not fit into our analysis. In this category are Chad, Niger, Central African Republic and Congo Brazzaville. The crises though partly ethnic, derived essentially from power play among the politically ambitious factions of the military elite.

It is my contention that for a proper understanding of the dynamics of the crises of nation building in Nigeria, we must take into account the historical circumstances surrounding her evolution from the ashes of colonialism. To do otherwise, would amount to embarking on a journey without any destination; a wandering of sort in the wilderness.

As we grapple with efforts to reposition Nigeria, away from the colonially-inherited divisive political order, her elites must come to terms with current political and social realities on the ground and embrace ideas that would guarantee equal rights to the citizenry and equitable access to power to all the ethnic nationalities in Nigeria.

In the chapters that follow, I have tried to share my thoughts on the engaging issues that have defined public discourse in our polity in the last three years. It is my expectation that you will find the content of this book very rewarding.

Chapter 1

Ogbulafor and Ekwueme Report

U pon his unanimous adoption as the National Chairman of the Peoples Democratic Party (PDP) at the party's national convention held in Abuja on 8th March this year, Prince Vincent Ogbulafor acknowledged the report of the Dr. Alex Ekwueme Reconciliation Committee as the road map to the future greatness of the party. He promised to implement the recommendations of the report, which many party faithful believe holds the key to fully transforming the party to a truly democratic institution in line with the aspirations of its founding fathers. For political observers and other interested Nigerians who have followed with keen interests the untoward developments in the party, particularly under the immediate past leadership, Ogbulafor's pronouncement was politically correct. The move by Ogbulafor, it is believed, holds the prospects of retrieving the party from the grips of a vicious cabal that had hijacked it and chased away its founding fathers in pursuit of selfish and inordinate political agenda.

The decision by the Ogbulafor-led National Working Committee (NWC) to zero in on the recommendations of the Ekwueme Committee as its take-off point has been widely acknowledged as a right step in the right direction which is capable of strengthening and repositioning the party for future challenges.

The Ekwueme Reconciliation Committee, it will be recalled, was set up following widespread complaints by party members who were either sidelined or forced out by the restrictive and punitive policies pursued by the Ahmadu Ali-led exco under the superintendence of former President Olusegun Obasanjo. Under the infamous era of Obasanjo's suzerainty in the party, many prominent members including the founding fathers who were opposed to the self-succession agenda of the former President were, through an ingenious process of membership revalidation, deregistered from the party which they had contributed immensely in building up from the formative stage.

The idea and philosophy then behind the so-called membership revalidation was to weed out elements in the party who were perceived as stumbling blocks to the realization of the unfolding evil third term agenda. A major casualty of the evil scheme was former Vice President Atiku Abubakar. He and his numerous supporters who were the main target of the membership revalidation plot, subsequently moved out of the ruling party to form the Action Congress (AC).

During this era, all the structures of the party that were meant to guarantee internal democracy were willfully subverted. Imposition and mindless substitution of candidates became the order of the day.

Also within this period, following the defeat of the third term agenda in the National Assembly, Obasanjo and Ali hatched and successfully executed another plot which sought to make the former President the life chairman of the Board of Trustees of the PDP. At a kangaroo convention, presided over by Ali, the constitution of the party was amended through the process of affirmation to allow Obasanjo take over the chairmanship of the Board, which at that material time was being occupied by a former acolyte of his, Chief Tony Anenih. One of the key recommendations of the Ekwueme Committee was the amendment of the party's constitution with a view to returning the ownership of the PDP back to the people to whom it truly belongs. The report was categorical in its call for re-visiting the reconstitution of the chairmanship and membership of the Board of Trustees and reverting to status quo.

I have had the privilege of going through the Ekwueme report. Other salient recommendation of the committee was the abolition of the title of Leader of the Party at national and state levels. The idea of the President or Governor being the Leader of the party at the national and state levels respectively was seen as antithetical to the effective functioning of the party. With such practice, the tendency had been for either the governors at state level or President at national level to appropriate and seize control of the party, sometimes to the alienation of those elected to run the affairs of the party. This kind of situation breeds instability within the system.

Apart from calling for the readmission of all the estranged founding leaders of the party who were forced to quit, the Ekwueme Committee further recommended that all party meetings and activities henceforth should be held at party secretariats and not at the personal homes of well-to-do party members or Government Houses. The argument was that party members who were not in the good books of such party bigwigs were hardly allowed access to such restricted venues.

The Committee further observed that the party lacked internal democracy, arguing that it could not give what it did not have. It therefore recommended that all the structures in the party that are meant to promote internal democracy must be re-invigorated and strengthened.

The whole range of recommendations contained in that report are quite apt and salient. If well implemented, they are capable of transforming the party as a formidable political institution. The incisiveness and quality of the recommendations, however, are not surprising given the caliber of people that served on the Ekwueme Committee. Apart from the erudite Dr. Ekwueme, a former Vice President and founding father of the PDP who was the Chairman of the Committee, other members include but not limited to the venerable Mallam Adamu Ciroma, the late Professor Emmanuel Ossamor and the ebullient Professor Jerry Gana.

In underscoring the importance his leadership attaches to the Ekwueme report as a veritable road map for the PDP, Ogbulafor, in a politically sagacious move, set up a committee under the chairmanship of the party's Deputy National Chairman, Dr. Mohammed Haliru Bello to review the report with a view to advising and guiding the National Working Committee on the implementation of the report.

The major challenge before Ogbulafor and his NWC is to muster the requisite political will and capacity to pursue with single-minded energy the reform measures as clearly articulated by the Ekwueme Committee. His leadership must remain focused and refused to be intimidated by some powerful elements within the party whose privileged positions may be adversely affected by the implementation of the Ekwueme Committee recommendations.

If the party has any hope of re-inventing itself, the Ekwueme report seems to provide the way forward. Ogbulafor must therefore not shy away from rising up to the occasion. Given his political pedigree and some imaginative decisions so far taken by his leadership in purging the party of some infamous legacies, there is every assurance that Ogbulafor will bell the cart. I wish him and his National Working Committee the best of luck.

ThisDay, May 20, 2008

Chapter 2

Abuja's Motion Without Movement

Abuja, as a Federal capital of Nigeria was conceived by the administration of the late Gen. Murtala Mohammed in 1976 as a center of unity in which every Nigerian, irrespective of tribe or religion, would have a sense of belonging. As at the time the decision was taken, Lagos, the then capital city of Nigeria, was becoming increasingly choked up on account of population explosion and mounting pressure on the limited land that was available for development.

As Lagos continued to witness congestions and chaos, the need became imperative to move the seat of power away to a more central location where land was abundantly available for future development.

The Akinola Aguda panel that was subsequently set up to recommend a suitable location for that purpose settled for Abuja, describing the choice as " secure, centrally located, easily accessible from all parts of the country and a true symbol of unity".

Since that decision was taken, Abuja, beginning with the administration of President Shehu Shagari, has witnessed phenomenal growth and development. The pioneering works were done during the presidency of Shagari with John Kadiya from Plateau state presiding as the first Minister of the Federal Capital Territory. He was ably assisted by Mark Okoye from Anambra state who was then the Minister of State.

Under Shagari, Abuja began to take shape with the springing up of critical infrastructure such as the Airport, State House (Aguda House), residential quarters and network of roads. Ever since, the various successive administrations had, for good or bad, left their imprints and footprints on the geographical landscape of Abuja.

Some of the past FCT Ministers discharged their mandates with a sense of mission and purpose while a few others performed quite below average. Among those widely adjudged as outstanding Ministers, beside the pioneers, were Mamman Vatsa, Bagudu Mamman, Mamman Kontagora, Gado Nasko and Mallam Nasir el-Rufai, who served in the immediate past administration of Olusegun Obasanjo.

In the course of its development, however, the master plan of Abuja as originally conceived has witnessed some grave distortions with serious implications to the orderly development of the city. Most of these distortions, which had almost blighted the capital city, occurred under some of the past military administrations. The worst culprit is said to be the reign of Gen. Jerry Useni under the dictatorship of the dark goggled General, Sani Abacha.

The retrieval of the original master plan of Abuja as envisioned by its founding fathers was the preoccupation of the immediate past Minister, el-Rufai, who did quite a lot to correct the distortions and return Abuja to the path of sanity. I am not a fan of el-Rufai on account of the sectionalist bent of some of his policies and the disdain with which he treated court orders. Again, the recent revelations at the just-concluded public hearings on the FCT by the Senate have clearly shown that there were so many things which el-Rufai did wrong. Nevertheless, one thing that he would never be accused of was lack of vision and clarity of thought.

In spite of the overzealous manner with which he carried out his duties which, in many instances was offensive to public psyche, el-Rufai was quite a competent officer who understood his brief very well. No matter whatever grudges one may hold against him, his era was a legacy of achievements. But for the diminutive former Minister, Abuja would, by now, have become a huge urban jungle. The decision to rid Abuja of illegal settlements was quite painful, but he had to do it to save the city from transforming into a slum. Today, both residents and visitors alike are proud of the greenery and orderliness of Abuja, thanks to the vision of el-Rufai.

The exit of el-Rufai saw the emergence of Dr. Modibbo Umar, who was the Minister of Commerce in the Obasanjo administration. Under Modibbo, it would appear that innovativeness and vision have taken a flight from Abuja. He has not taken the city beyond where el-Rufai left it.

The only visible thing we have seen is the erection of traffic lights on every available road junction, even where they are not necessary, thereby generating traffic jams all over the place.

The same lack of vision has manifested in the policy of the Modibbo administration to ban smoking of cigarettes and consumption of alcohol in the FCT. The question on the lips of many residents of Abuja is, is this the least of our problems? Chasing after smokers and beer drinkers, is that what the Minister was asked to do in Abuja?

It is already one year that President Umar Yar`Adua`s administration had been in power. Sadly enough, the whole one year in FCT has been that of motion without movement. And it is said in the scriptures that "my people perish for lack of vision". It is becoming glaring that the current state of directionless ness and rudderless ness is as a result of lack of vision and mission. We cannot continue with this kind of sorry situation.

Somebody should tell the current FCT Minister to wake up from his slumber. If he is having problem of funding, he should let Nigerians know. One year period is enough a time for any focused and imaginative leader to make a mark.

Our former Head of State, Gen. Murtala Muhammed, whose portrait today adorns the nation`s currency note recorded impressive achievements within only six months in office before he was felled by assasins` bullets. One of those achievements is the creation of Abuja which Modibbo is privileged to be at its helms at the moment.

A leader must have a clear vision, a sort of roadmap on how to discharge the burden and challenge of leadership. It's such a vision that propels him to impact positively on the lives of the people and leave meaningful legacy behind.

Modibbo, after one year in office, is yet to demonstrate that he has any blue-print on how to take Abuja to the next level. I don't see any justification whatsoever for the apparent non-performance of the current FCTA under his watch.

In his present enterprise to rid Abuja of cigarette smokers and beer drinkers, he should be careful not to give the impression that "shariah" is being smuggled into Abuja through the back door. I don't think that cigarette smoking and beer drinking is the problem of Abuja residents.

Abuja, as a growing Federal capital territory, faces the critical challenge of infrastructural development, insecurity of lives and property, unemployment crisis etc. These are the issues that should constructively engage the attention of Modibbo and not the current shadow chasing that is going on.

ThisDay, June 3, 2008

Chapter 3

Turaki's Elongation Campaign

ormer Governor of Jigawa State, now distinguished? Senator of the Federal Republic of Nigeria, Alhaji Saminu Turaki, recently tried to assault the sensibilities of the nation by exhuming the ghost of the vexatious "tenure elongation" otherwise known as "third term agenda" which was long dead and buried by the 5th Senate. Turaki, who is currently facing charges by the Economic and Financial Crimes Commission (EFCC) for money laundering and embezzlement of public funds, was recently widely reported in the media to be canvassing for the elongation of the tenure of the current President, Alhaji Umar Musa Yar'Adua.

He said that the Senate would, during the forthcoming constitutional amendments, consider a two term of 7 years each for President Yar'Adua with retroactive effect from May 29, 2007, meaning that Yar'Adua should be in office for 14 years instead of 8 years, assuming he wins a re-election in 2011. His puerile argument is that the tenure extension would enable the President to oversee the faithful implementation of his Vision 2020.

The Vision 2020 policy initiative which Turaki is now talking about was not even formulated by Yar'Adua. It was one of those fantasies of former President Obasanjo who never saw anything good in the economic initiatives of his predecessors in office such as Sructural Adjustment Progrmme (SAP) of Ibrahim Babangida or Vision 2010 of Sani Abacha.

The Vision 2020 aims at placing Nigeria amongst the most developed and industrialized countries of the world by the year 2020. This is no doubt an ambitious project. I don't know how this goal can even be actualized with the current and indeed deepening state of darkness in Nigeria.

Turaki, in his unsolicited campaign for the elongation of the tenure of Yar'Adua tried to justify his thesis in the following words. "Yar'Adua wants to make Nigeria the hub of petrochemicals in Africa. He has really worked out and analyzed the Vision 2020. ...Each term of the two terms can be amended to seven years each. This is to allow Nigerians to really benefit from a particular government. From what I observed as a former governor who did eight years, if you don't finish your programme within the period, the next man will come and change it. So, I will prefer two terms of seven years…So, Yar`Adua should stay till year 2021"

My initial reaction to this bizarre proposal was that of disbelief and shock; disbelief and shock in the sense that a person who calls himself a distinguished Senator could embark on such an unholy mission having being in this country and witnessed how the third term plot by Obasanjo almost pushed Nigeria to the edge of the precipice.

Although one is not surprised at the current scheme of Turaki, given the lead role he performed in the failed tenure elongation plot of the Obasanjo administration, it is unbelievable that the same man who claimed to have funneled the N30 billion that he is being accused of embezzling by EFCC into the Obasanjo third term project, is coming up again with another devious plot.

It is very apparent that Turaki`s motive is self-serving, given the fact that he is currently standing trial for misgovernance of his poor rural state, Jigawa. The possibility exists that he may be jailed if convicted on any of the countless charges against him. So the recourse to clamouring for Yar`Adua to stay forever in office may be a smart move on his part to ingratiate himself to the President and possibly secure a reprieve from the law.

On both counts, he has failed because it has been proven with the defeat of Obasanjo`s third term agenda, that Nigeria cannot be a banana republic. Even if Turaki is presumed to be flying a kite for any faceless interest group, our political history has clearly shown that efforts at self-succession, self-transmutation or tenure elongation by past leaders no matter their benevolent disposition or otherwise have always met with failure and frustration.

General Yakubu Gowon after being in power for nine years, reneged on his pledge to return Nigeria to civil rule in 1974. The following year, while he was attending a summit of the then Organisation of African Unity (OAU) in Kampala, Uganda, his government was toppled in a bloodless coup.

In the case of General Muhammadu Buhari who came to power in December 1983 following the overthrow of President Shehu Shagari`s administration, he was removed in August 1985 before he could even unfold any political agenda, if at all he had one, to return the country to civil rule.

The succeeding Babangida administration that embarked on a convoluted but deceitful political transition programme with a disguised intention to remain put in office after being on the saddle for eight good years, was stopped in his tracks, hence he had to "step aside".

General Sani Abacha who took over shortly after Babangida's forced exit, worked tirelessly towards self-transmutation, but before he could realize his ambition, he was "arrested" by the cold hands of death. Given these developments which have become part of our national political history, it should be clear to Turaki and those who may be behind him that his current enterprise is an exercise in futility.

Nevertheless, Nigerians must be vigilant and prepared to stop the likes of Turaki and his ilk wherever they may be from creating confusion that may plunge this country into avoidable and needless political crisis.

It is however reassuring to note that some of Turaki's compatriots in the Senate had condemned his outbursts and dissociated the Upper legislative chamber from this perfidy.

The Chairman, Senate Committee on Media and Information, Senator Ayogu Eze, who spoke on behalf of the Senate lashed at Turaki in no uncertain terms for his embarrassing comments. His words: "He (Turaki) is completely on his own; it was an embarrassing statement from the Senator. It was an unguarded statement; it was unfortunate and not expected of a senator who is also a member of the Constitution Review Committee. He has no mandate from anywhere to make such statement for the Senate; it is undemocratic calling for tenure elongation for Yar'Adua; it is a recipe for confusion; it is an attempt to truncate our democracy and it is condemnable".

In a similar vein, the man representing the President's constituency in the Senate (Katsina Central Senatorial District), Senator Ibrahim Ida has condemned Turaki, saying that the Jigawa Senator's remarks were personal to him, representing neither the stand of the Senate nor that of the North.

Much as reassuring as these comments may be, the Senate should go a step further by censuring Turaki and withdrawing his membership of the Constitution Review Committee so as to send strong signals to the public that the forthcoming constitutional amendment process is not intended to achieve a pre-determined agenda.

The Presidency should also come out with a categorical statement dissociating itself from the misguided campaign of Senator Turaki.

Anything short of that, the tendency is for people to believe that Turaki is not acting alone, afterall that was how Arthur Nzeribe started with his infamous Association for Better Nigeria (ABN) that eventually truncated Babangida`s political transition programme. Enough of this confusion!

_____

ThisDay, June 10, 2008

Chapter 4

Investigating Aviation Sector

Troubled by the poor performance and consistent harvest of tragedies after tragedies by the vital aviation sector of the national economy, the Senate, sitting in plenary on Wednesday, 7th May, 2008, passed a resolution, directing its Committee on Aviation to undertake a wholesale investigation into the sector with a view to providing a veritable road-map that would assist the nation in arresting the decline.

It will be recalled that between 2005 and 2006, Nigeria suffered three major air crashes in which many innocent souls and prominent citizens were painfully dispatched to their early graves. There was the Bellview incident that occurred in October 2005 in Lisa near Abeokuta in Ogun State, which claimed the lives of the cream of our society.

One year after, a passenger plane belonging to Sosoliso airline recorded a very devastating crash at the Port Harcourt International Airport, with the pupils of Loyola Jesuit College, Abuja as the major casualties. The Port Harcourt incident was immediately followed by the crashing of the ADC airliner in Abuja shortly after take-off. The then Sultan of Sokoto, Alhaji Muhammadu Maccido was among many illustrious Nigerians whose lives were prematurely terminated in that incident.

Following these serial tragedies, there was a general outcry in the whole country with widespread calls for a drastic overhauling and sanitization of the aviation sector. Former President Obasanjo summoned some stakeholders` meeting which resulted in the setting up of the Air Marshal Paul Dike Committee to undertake a comprehensive appraisal of the state of affairs in that sector.

Following the recommendations of the Dike Committee, a princely sum of N19.5 billion was disbursed to the Aviation Ministry to enable it beef up facilities and modernize the nation`s airports with a view to securing the safety of our airspace.

As at today, the N19.5 billion intervention fund has become a subject of controversy with many allegations of misappropriation and misapplication of the fund flying in the air. The allegations became intensified following the disappearance of a Beechcraft 1900D with all the crew members on board around Obudu mountains earlier in the year.

All these developments provided the background for the current intervention of the Senate, which is worried like other Nigerians that in spite of the huge capital investments in the aviation sector, not much progress has been recorded.

The Aviation Committee, chaired by Senator Anyim Ude, a renowned journalist and bureaucrat, was subsequently mandated in that resolution to carry out a public hearing on the disbursement and utilization of the N19.5 billion Intervention Fund released by the Federal Government in 2006 for the rehabilitation and development of infrastructure in the aviation industry.

The Committee has since swung into action in line with the resolution of the Senate as it begins today the public hearing into the aviation sector. Preparatory to the hearing, it had been reliably gathered that the Committee Chairman and members have been receiving threats to back off the assignment. There are also reported moves by the agents of the cabal that misapplied the fund to infiltrate the committee. But all the efforts had come to naught as the Chairman of the Committee is such a man of impeccable integrity that cannot be compromised.

These threats and moves are believed to be coming from the agents of some entrenched mafia in the system whose interests may be jeopardized by the investigations. The cartel and their godfathers would want the investigative hearing halted so that they could continue with the pillaging and pilfering of the scarce national resources which are meant to salvage the aviation sector, a critical segment of the economy.

The committee has demonstrated political and unbending resolve by proceeding with the investigations, the threats notwithstanding. The Chairman and his members owe this nation a responsibility to follow the investigations to a logical conclusion. The national experience with the aviation sector in Nigeria, over time, has been quite unsavory and unpleasant. The Committee has a rare opportunity to etch its name in gold by re-writing the story for the better.

The Committee Chairman, Senator Anyim Ude, a no-nonsense personality has already given an indication that no stones would be left unturned to ensure that the investigations live up to public expectations. This is evident in the meticulous and painstaking planning that has gone into this public inquiry.

Given the copious list of individual and corporate actors who have been lined up to appear before the Committee, it would seem that Senator Ude and his colleagues are determined to get to the roots of the matter.

There is no doubt whatsoever that this current investigative hearing into the aviation sector enjoys the support of the entire people of Nigeria who want to see an end to the frequent calamities associated with the aviation industry in the country.

There is no doubt that given the steely resolve of the Committee to get to the roots of the rot in the sector, the nation may yet have an opportunity to salvage the aviation industry and restore the sagging confidence of the traveling public in the sector.

The Committee must therefore go the whole hog in this national assignment to unravel all the circumstances surrounding the disbursement, deployment and management of the N19.5 billion Intervention Fund. It is indeed regrettable that, after injecting such a huge amount of money into the sector, the story of non-performance, negligence and corruption continue to be the norm.

The Committee has a bounden duty to unmask the entire rapacious clique in the industry that has been bleeding this nation to death. No person shoud be spared no matter how highly placed.

ThisDay, June 24, 2008

Chapter 5

Soludo and the AFC Probe

The sinister campaign in some sections of the media by some faceless primordial groups to get the Governor of the Central Bank of Nigeria (CBN), Professor Chukwuma Soludo out of office at all cost is still being pursued with vigour. Some of the media houses that have been recruited into the campaign to rubbish the hard earned reputation of the CBN Governor, are coming out almost on regular basis with highly tendentious materials with a view to securing his conviction in the court of public opinion over CBN`s investments in the African Finance Corporation (AFC), a strategic initiative of Soludo.

Only last week, a Northern-based national newspaper, carried a screaming headline on its front cover titled: '$480m AFC Probe: Panel wants Soludo to step aside". In what was purely a speculative and obviously sponsored report, the newspaper in question, quoting anonymous sources, gleefully disclosed that the investigative panel probing the AFC matter has recommended that the CBN Governor should step aside from his position to enable it "carry out its investigation unrestrained" This sounds logical. Isn't it?

This proposition which is already in the public domain is supposedly a proposed recommendation to the authorities that set up the panel in the first place. If the panel does not habour any pre-determined agenda, why would it first go public on its findings and recommendations when the Government that set it up is yet to be availed with such information? If the panel is not up to mischief and playing a script, why was the anonymous source to which the story was attributed described the AFC initiative as a "scandal"?

Without holding brief for any body, what is unfolding with the so-called AFC probe seems to me as an attempt by rapacious and ravenous elite, driven by primordial considerations, to re-assert its hegemonic influence, believed to have suffered some setbacks in the immediate past dispensation, in all important segments of our national life.

Perhaps, this powerful shadowy group, perceived to be very influential in this current dispensation, with this ongoing campaign to subjugate Soludo, does not want to leave any one in doubt as to the potency of its political connections and networking capacity. I believe that by taking on Soludo, it has misfired.

From all available accounts in the media so far, it has not been in any doubt as to the propriety of Soludo's action in the formation of the AFC and the $480 million investment in it. It has been proven that the initiative was backed by a presidential approval and followed all necessary procedures, with relevant Government agencies discharging their roles in line with the legal instruments setting up the body.

For instance, the Attorney-General of the Federation at the time, Chief Bayo Ojo and his counterpart in the Ministry of Finance were part of an inter-ministerial committee that ironed out all the necessary papers that related to the initiative. The issue is why is that Soludo is being singled out for persecution for a noble initiative that was the collective responsibility of the government that was then in power?

It is clearly out of the question that Soludo should on his own, without the relevant authorization; go out of his way to commit such huge funds into the AFC without the backing of the former President. The Soludo that the nation knows and who has demonstrated uncommon competence and brilliance since he mounted the saddle at the Central Bank of Nigeria is wiser than that.

From every indication, the Soludo that we knew from his undergraduate days at the University of Nigeria, Nsukka (UNN) has not changed from the circumspect of mind and stubborn belief in ethical principles for which he was renowned. We were all contemporaries at the UNN and its Students' union politics. He was known to have always demonstrated high moral principles both in academic and extra-curricular affairs while we were on campus as undergraduates. And those principles have never departed from him.

He brought those sterling principles to the national arena when through his ingenuity; he transformed the banking sector to the enviable status it has attained in our country today. The banking consolidation which boldly bears the imprimatur of Soludo is one of the amazing economic revolutions of our time.

Today, as we speak, the banking sector is one of the most vibrant sectors of our national economy. It was in appreciation of his unrivalled achievement in the banking consolidation that a grateful nation awarded him Commander of the Order of the Federal Republic, CFR, one of its highest national honours.

Why would some people want to pull the man down, in spite of his contributions? Some of his critics often accuse him of intellectual arrogance. Even if it were so, when has that become an offence under the laws of the nation, if we may ask?

If Soludo should go because of assumed intellectual arrogance, those who are currently lobbying actively to take over the CBN, should have exercised little patience. Under the CBN Act, he has 5-year tenure to spend. And since he was appointed in 2004, it means that he still has one more year to complete his tenure. If for any reason that he is not reappointed by the current President, the mandarins who are after the job can then have a field day.

They don't need to put Soludo down before they can achieve their ambition which legitimacy I concede to them. It is said in the scriptures that a prophet is without honour in his community. It is an irony of life that the man we are trying to bring down is paradoxically being toasted and celebrated on the international financial circuit.

This kind of destructive campaign that is going on is nothing but a sad commentary on our collective efforts at nation building. No matter the opinion which his critics and antagonists may hold to the contrary, the truth of the matter is that on any scale Soludo is weighed, he is a success story. We don't gain anything by heating up the system. Let's give peace a chance.

ThisDay, July 1, 2008

Chapter 6

Aviation's Contract Bazaar

Two weeks ago on this page, I undertook an appraisal of the impending investigative public hearing by the Senator Anyim Ude-led Senate Committee on Aviation and the explosive issues the Committee was to contend with. It is important to note that the hearing was in response to the resolution of the Senate on May 7, 2008, which mandated the Committee to investigate the application and utilization of the N19.5 billion Intervention Fund released by the Federal Government in 2006 for the rehabilitation and development of infrastructure in the Aviation industry.

The Intervention Fund was initiated by the Obasanjo administration in response to the series of air crashes that occurred between 2005 and 2006 in which the nation lost over 400 of her citizens including innocent pupils of Loyola Jesuit College, Abuja.

The Fund was to be disbursed as follows: Replacement of obsolete control tower equipment at Lagos, Abuja, Kano and Port Harcourt airports…N6.5 billion; Severance Benefits for disengaged staff of Federal Aviation Authority of Nigeria (FAAN)…N2 billion; Rehabilitation of infrastructure at the nation's airports…N11 billion.

The one-week public hearing had just been concluded. I happened to have followed the proceedings from the beginning to the end from a vantage position within the Senate Hearing Room 1, venue of the investigative hearing. It was one week of intensive and rigorous inquiry, during which passions were occasionally inflamed and tension reaching a crescendo. The disclosures at the hearing had been quite revealing and shocking.

In the exercise of its mandate, the Committee did not leave anything to chance. It ensured that all those who had anything to do with the application and disbursement of the fund appeared before it to state their roles. Similarly, the Committee also encouraged individuals who had useful information that would help it to unravel the actors behind the misapplication and misappropriation of the fund to come forward to render evidence.

The personalities that appeared before the Committee included two former Ministers of Aviation who actually administered the fund, Prof. Babalola Borishade and Chief Femi Fani-Kayode. Others were the current serving Ministers of Transportation, Mrs, Diezani Allison-Madueke and Mr. Felix Hassan Hyat. The Chief Executives of Aviation Parastatals, both serving and retired were all on hand to say what they knew about the Intervention Fund. Also in attendance were both foreign and local contractors who handled some specific projects covered by the Intervention Fund.

The most contentious of the projects was the Safe Tower contract executed at the princely sum of N6.5 billion which the Committee has been able to establish through its Technical Consultant, Capt. Dan Omale, was outrageously inflated to tune of N5.5 billion. Omale, who presented a pictorial and detailed analysis on the status of the N19.5 billion Intervention Fund, disclosed that the quotation for the replacement of control tower equipment at the four designated International Airports obtained direct from the manufacturers of the equipment in Canada at a 100 percent marked-up price was N2 billion. But the contract was awarded by the former Aviation Minister, Prof. Borishade to an Austrian firm, M/S Avsatel at the whooping sum of N6.5 billion.

To rub salt into injury, the Head of M/S Avsatel in Nigeria who secured the mouth-watering contract, Mr. George Eider disclosed that their tender for the contract contained neither a bill of quantities nor any pricing list whatsoever. When he was asked whether he followed due process in getting the job, he, in a most arrogant manner, said it was not his business but that of the Ministry of Aviation. According to him what mattered was "stopping planes from falling from the Nigerian skies and coffins of school children".

It was a most irresponsible and insensitive posturing.

The same Eider was asked whether there was a due process mechanism in Austria, to which he answered in the affirmative, stressing that it was very stringent in that country. The Committee was able to conclude that he took advantage of the Nigeria situation, acting in collusion with some Nigerian collaborators. He could not justify the colossal contract sum for which he had collected N6.4 billion out of the total contract value of N6.5 billion. Even though the outrageous sum is for the four International Airports in Kano, Lagos, Abuja and Port

Harcourt; as at date, work has only been completed in three, remaining Kano. Meanwhile, the man has been fully paid.

When Prof. Borishade appeared, he could not convince the Committee on why the safe tower contract was awarded to Avsatel at such prohibitive cost when there was a bid of N1.2 billion for the same project. He could also not proffer any convincing reason why the contract was awarded without complying with due process requirements like the bill of quantities and pricing list. In the opinion of the Committee, the safe tower project, though well-intentioned, has been used to defraud the country.

There were also some Ministerial approvals that were clearly meant to siphon out public funds budgeted to improve critical infrastructure at our airports. How else can one justify an approval by a Minister for the sum of N506 million to be paid as consultancy fee for perimeter fencing of the nation's four major airports? Not for the actual execution of the job!

From the gory details that were disclosed at the investigative hearing, it was really apparent that the Intervention Fund was like a bazaar in which those entrusted with the responsibility of administering it, were helping themselves to it in a most audacious manner. Payments were made from the Intervention Fund for activities that were quite outside the scope of the Fund. An example is the sum of about N34 million that were expended by the Aviation Ministry on Ministerial Committees carrying out routine assignments.

The heart bleeds at the level of profligacy and looting that goes on in high places in this country. In the past, people stole public funds with some measure of moderation and trepidation. Today, the story is different. People now steal public funds entrusted in their care with impunity and scant regard to public feelings.

A situation where contractors would collect mobilization fees, abandon work and disappear from sites without being called to account, is responsible for the kind of impunity we have seen in the Aviation sector with this investigative hearing. Indeed, how can the nation be able to meet the Millennium Development Goals if our system continues to permit such high level of graft in the public sector?

The Senate Committee on Aviation led by Senator Anyim Ude has done quite a good job by trying to get to the root of the rot in the Aviation sector without compromising its integrity. The investigative hearing was conducted in a most forensic manner and with utmost sense of fairness and objectivity.

The Committee members demonstrated knowledge, competence, depth and sheer brilliance in the way and manner they handled even complicated and complex matters that were raised in course of the investigation.

Although some arrests have been made following disclosures at the hearing, Government must call for the report of the Committee when it is put together and go ahead to implement it to the letter.

ThisDay, July 8 , 2008

Chapter 7

Remembering Mko Abiola, icon of Nigeria's Democracy

Its exactly 10 years since the legendary Moshood Kashimawo Olawale (MKO) Abiola exited this mortal plane to immortality under controversial circumstances. Given the unfolding events and developments in our country recently, Abiola's memory remains evergreen in the collective consciousness of our nation.

In spite of unrelenting efforts by political revisionists and renegades to blot out the place of this historical figure and his standing from our national psyche, his image, more than ever before, has continued to loom large to the discomfiture of the conspirators who worked tirelessly to scuttle the pan-Nigerian political mandate given to MKO Abiola on June 12, 1993.

At the head of this group is the former President, Olusegun Obasanjo, who for the 8 years he was in power, deliberately refused to accord Abiola his rightful place in our national history. In spite of entreaties and representations that were made by various interest groups and Non-Governmental institutions in Nigeria, calling on Obasanjo to honour the memory of Abiola, the then President, for inexplicable reasons remained obstinate and indifferent.

The Senate of the Federal Republic of Nigeria under the leadership of Chief Ken Nnamani even passed a resolution calling on former President Obasanjo to immortalize the late Chief MKO Abiola. That resolution was treated with ignominy, as the Government never took any step to accord any honour to the man variously seen as the martyr of our democracy.

Yet, the bitter truth that cannot be wished away is the fact that without the annulled June 12, 1993 Presidential election which Abiola won fair and square, there would not have been anything like the second coming of Obasanjo to the national political scene. Obasanjo's disdain and contempt for Abiola was hardly disguised. This was clearly reflected in the dismissive comments credited to Obasanjo in far-away Harare, Zimbabwe at the height of the struggle for the revalidation of the annulled mandate, to the effect that Abiola was not the messiah Nigerians were waiting for.

Obasanjo has since left office in circumstances that were anything but edifying. But against the wish of his likes, Abiola has remained the issue in Nigerian politics, several years after his mysterious death in Government custody. On this occasion of the 10th remembrance anniversary of the late political icon and business tycoon, I join millions of Nigerian compatriots and lovers of democracy to pay tribute to the memory of Abiola.

One specific lesson we have learnt from the Abiola trajectory is that no matter how long and much we try to suppress the truth and falsify history, the truth like the Northern star remains constant. Again we are reminded that truth is an open wound which only conscience can heal.

Today, all the truth that was suppressed to deny Abiola and the people of Nigeria the rare opportunity to chart a new and refreshing political direction, away from the divisiveness and bigotry of the past, is bouncing back forcefully to the national stage. After being in self-imposed confinement for 15 years, the man who conducted the June 12, 1993 Presidential elections, adjudged the freest, fairest and most credible in the history of Nigeria, Professor Humphrey Nwosu, has broken his silence, though belatedly, on the outcome of that election.

Professor Nwosu in his account of the conduct of the June 12 election, contained in his book which was released recently stated how his Commission was trying to navigate the legal obstacles placed on its way by the agents of the military, to enable it pronounce the results which Abiola had won before the annulment took place. On page 304 of the book, he wrote and I quote: "It is important to note that all the parties affected in this landmark legal procedure including MKO Abiola knew the position of NEC. It had completed a compilation of the results of June 12, 1993 Presidential Election. It had also verified the same and determined that MKO Abiola was the winner. NEC was walking through a tight rope to remove the obstacles placed on its path in order to declare MKO Abiola, the winner when suddenly those who opposed the conduct of the election caused the annulment of the election on June 23, 1993"

It will be recalled that Professor Nwosu, in his position as the Chief Returning Officer in that election had already announced results from 14 out of the existing 30 States then, when he was stopped midway from releasing further results by the ruling military junta led by General Ibrahim Babangida. Prior to that wicked act, all the results from the States, except Taraba that was being expected, had all come in to the headquarters of the then National Electoral Commission (NEC). It was common knowledge to everyone that Abiola had been returned with a huge mandate that defied both religious and ethnic barriers.

Given the scuttling of that mandate by the enemies of democracy, and given the fact also that the full results were not officially announced, media reports had continued to refer to Abiola as "presumed winner" or "acclaimed winner" or the man "widely believed to have won the election". Now that Professor Nwosu has removed the veil on the military conspiracy, the correct position is that Abiola, until his death in Government custody was the President-elect of the Federal Republic of Nigeria.

Based on this truth, the Government of President Yar`Adua must commence forthwith the process of national healing and reconciliation by first acknowledging the victory of Abiola in that election. The official recognition of Abiola as the President-elect by the Government will then set the stage for the payment of the necessary restitution and subsequent immortalization of the man.

History will be kind to Yar`Adua if he takes this very important step to put behind us, a very ugly chapter of our national political history. If what the former Governor of Lagos State, Senator Bola Tinubu, was reported as saying at a recent event in Lagos to commemorate the 10th anniversary of Abiola`s death is anything to go by, then there is a silver lining in the horizon. At the event, he was quoted as saying that President Yar`Adua had promised to accord the late political icon due recognition in due course. The nation is waiting as history beckons on Yar`Adua to break the jinx.

Obasanjo had the opportunity to do so but for petty politics and ego, he refused to act. Yar`Adua, therefore, cannot afford to miss this historic opportunity to write his name in gold by upholding that pan-Nigerian mandate and honouring the memory of MKO Abiola, the martyr of our renascent democracy.

ThisDay, July 15, 2008

Chapter 8

Failure of Governance in Nigeria

I must confess from the onset that the inspiration for this piece came from my personal observations and experiences on a trip last week from Abuja to the Eastern parts of the country by road. The state in which the roads currently exist is very horrifying to say the least.

When we were passing through the stretch of road from Lokoja, the Kogi State capital to Ajaokuta, which hosts the moribund largest steel complex in sub-Saharan Africa, a lot of questions were racing though my mind. What has happened to governance in Nigeria? Why have our governments at all levels abandoned their constitutional obligations to guarantee and promote the welfare and security of the citizenry? Of what meaning is representative politics in Nigeria?

While I was pondering over these questions, my thoughts quickly went to my days at the University of Nigeria, Nsukka where we were introduced to the teachings of the Social Contract philosophers such as John Locke, Jean Jacques Rousseau and Thomas Hobbes who variously posited that governance or power is a collective trust held and exercised by the Leviathan or Sovereign on behalf of the people who have voluntarily submitted their power of self help in exchange for an ordered political community. The essence of the people surrendering their power to act individually to the Leviathan or Sovereign was to avoid chaos and to secure for every body in the community the common good. The Sovereign was expected, in return, to promote the good of the society.

It is this mutual covenant in which the people willingly and voluntarily submit to the authority of the Sovereign or Leviathan in exchange for the guarantee and promotion of their collective well-being that is referred to by the philosophers as "social contract".

One of the most prominent of the social contract philosophers, Thomas Hobbes, had argued that without the social contract, the society would be mired in a state of nature in which life was "brutish, short and nasty". The deduction arising from this philosophy is that once the masses have given their mandate to the government, they should expect, in return, the goodies of governance or what are popularly known in this clime as the dividends of democracy.

Thomas Hobbes, in propagating the social contract philosophy, went further to enunciate "the concept of rebellion", which he argued must be applied by the people as a control measure in the event of any default by the Sovereign to discharge his responsibilities to the community.

I am not saying, by inference, that we should be up in arms against non-performing government in the country. Rather, from the theories of the social contract philosophers on which modern day governance is predicated, the people have the right to question, upbraid and complain about a deviant government. In Nigeria, under the 1999 Constitution, the electorate is invested with the "power of recall". Under this constitutional provision, the people have the inherent powers to sack any government that is incompetent or found wanting in the discharge of its constitutional obligations to the governed.

After all, it is stated in Section 14 (2) (b) of the 1999 Constitution that "the security and welfare of the people shall be the primary purpose of government". From what we encountered on the road on that trip to the East, what we have on our hands in the country today regrettably is nothing but the failure or flight of governance. The social contract which enjoins government to uphold the security and welfare of the citizenry is clearly being observed in the breach.

Or how else can the horrible and scandalous state of that road and by extension other roads in the country be rationalized in this new millennium? What passes for a road in the stretch between Lokoja and Ajaokuta is, for short of appropriate qualification, an unqualified disaster. That road, like the case of the notoriously bad Shagamu-Ore-Benin highway and Enugu-Port Harcourt express way, is a complete write off, a national disgrace.

Any government that believes it is in power at the behest of the people cannot justify such a criminal neglect of that vital national link that bears heavy traffic in persons and goods between the northern and southern parts of Nigeria. The scandalous nature of that road clearly exemplifies the failure of governance in the land.

From our investigations, both the Kogi State and Federal Governments have shared responsibilities on that road. They should immediately wake up to their constitutional duties and do justice to that road and save the nation the horrendous incidents that are recorded daily on that route.

Such terribly bad sections of the nation's highways usually provide safe havens for unfettered and seamless operations by men of the underworld. The highway robbers most often lay ambush for their victims who must, of necessity, slow down at those bad spots on the road.

Many innocent motorists and passengers alike have met their untimely deaths at such places. A recent example is the incident that happened on a bad spot very close to Ninth Mile Corner on the Nsukka-Enugu highway. The robbers took advantage of the poor state of the road and lay siege there, robbing, maiming and killing innocent travelers who were unfortunate to be on that road that morning

As the robbers scurried away from the scene on the approach of a police highway patrol, they left in their trail, deaths, destructions and devastations. If that portion of the road had been fixed, perhaps, that tragedy would have been avoided. So, the death of those innocent citizens in the hands of men of the underworld is the price the people have to pay for failure of governance. For how long are we going to contend with poor governance in our country?

I am aware that the resources available to government are very scarce with so many needs competing for them. Such an imperative compels governments world-wide to prioritize their needs and pursue them with single minded energy.

This perhaps explains why the Yar'Adua administration reduces its priorities into a 7-point agenda with infrastructural development, food security and energy ranking high on the agenda. For government to make any positive impact, on the people, the areas that have been identified as national priorities ought to be pursued with all the urgency they deserve. Sanctimonious preachments would not do.

The people of Nigeria deserve a better deal. Making the roads motorable is the least the people expect from their government.

ThisDay, July 29, 2008

Chapter 9

Freedom of Information Bill and Challenge of Democracy

The issue of the freedom of the press, if I may recollect correctly, has remained a major item on the national political agenda for a very long time, starting from the colonial era through the immediate post-colonial period to now. Even as at the time I formally joined Nigerian journalism in 1987, the clamor for press freedom and democratic governance had been relentless and continued to echo around and beyond the nooks and crannies of this country.

In the count down to independence in 1960 and immediately thereafter, the nationalist press at the vanguard of the agitation for political freedom led by the West African Pilot owned by Dr. Nnamdi Azikiwe waged a titanic battle with the British colonial authorities on the need to transfer political power to the indigenous people of Nigeria. The colonialists who were bent on deepening their stranglehold on Nigeria saw in the bourgeoning local press a major irritant that should be contained at all cost.

For the colonial masters, the Nigerian press in its relentless agitation for self governance constituted a great threat to the political and economic interests of the metropolitan power hence the over-riding need to checkmate its excesses. The nationalist press, in its avowed determination to reclaim the country from the impostors would not give up, in spite of many draconian legislations such as the Official Secrets Act and the laws on sedition which were formulated and put in the way of the press to hamper it in its patriotic duty to hold government accountable to the people.

This asymmetrical relationship which had its origin in the mutual suspicion between the press and the colonial powers clearly marked the beginning of the conflict that had continued to characterize the relationship between the press and government in our country till date.

This brief excursion into the political past of the country is perhaps necessary for a better appreciation of the current dialectics as it concerns the on-going quest for freedom of information and the difficulties being experienced in that regard. Much have been written and said on the desirability of probity in the conduct of our public policy since the

Freedom of Information Bill was formally tabled before the National Assembly for consideration and passage into law.

It is disheartening to note that this all-important bill which essentially seeks to promote openness and transparency in governance and in all facets of our public life is being mischievously misconstrued by those who should even know better. I have followed with considerable interest the arguments on both sides of the debate. I have also deeply reflected on the fears of those opposed to the bill. In all of these, I have not seen anything either in the letter or intent of the bill that seeks to place the media above the rest of the society.

In their bid to shoot down the bill, many of our Distinguished Senators and Honorable Members have variously dressed it in false garbs, to the extent that they had succeeded in creating the erroneous impression that the FOI bill is a media bill that is designed to give absolute immunity to the pen fraternity. Nothing can be further from the truth!

It is however gladdening to observe that the National Assembly as presently constituted is not short of journalists amongst its members to drive the process of actualizing the Information bill. I can identify the likes of Senator Anyim Ude who has had an eventful career as a broadcast journalist of repute; Senator Smart Adeyemi, immediate past President of Nigeria Union of Journalists (NUJ); Senator Ayogu Eze of the Newswatch fame; Senator Osita Izunaso who had a stint with the now defunct Satellite newspaper; Hon. Abike Dabiri of the NTA Newsline fame; and Hon. Eziuche Ubani, a former Political Editor of Thisday newspaper.

Some of these media personalities in the National Assembly have done well in conscientizing some of their unyielding colleagues on the desirability of the FOI bill. But some of them are yet to register their names on the positive side of history as the debate rages on. We are all watching and taking note.

I am worried at this continued demonization and emasculation of the press by our own indigenous elite who in the Political Science parlance we refer to as the comprador bourgeoisie. It is not the intention of this piece to join issues with any one on this matter but rather for our elected representatives to see the nexus between the clamor for corporate governance and freedom of information.

It is absolutely impossible for us to achieve transparency and openness in the conduct of public policy without the press and the people of Nigeria having the legal capacity to access information that is within the public domain. The FOI bill does not seek to confer any special advantage on the media, contrary to the claims by the opposition. Rather, the bill is seeking to strengthen the existing constitutional capacity of the media to hold government accountable at all times to the governed; a huge responsibility which is guaranteed under Section 22 of the Constitution of the Federal Republic of Nigeria, 1999.

In deed, under the FOI bill the discharge of this onerous responsibility is being shared by the media and the people for whom government exists in the first place. The concerns on the reckless abuse to which the bill may be deployed if it becomes an Act of Parliament are genuine and quite appreciated. However, those concerns are not sufficient to warrant the strangulation of the bill. For any excesses on the part of the media, enough laws exist in our legal codes to deal with such issues as libel, defamation, slander, sedition and even treason.

What should be of paramount concern to every Nigerian irrespective of our present stations and status in life is whether the FOI bill as conceptualized is for the good health of the nation or not. Will it promote corporate governance? Will it deepen our democratic values? Will it eliminate the culture of secrecy which is anachronistic and inconsistent with democratic governance?

I think the bill answers all these questions in the affirmative. The bill, in my view, will ensure an unfettered flow of information, a major pillar on which modern day democratic governance is erected. Similarly, the ability of the media and citizenry to access public records in public interest will be enhanced by the bill if passed into law. This will also help to check the rampant cases of rumor mongering and peddling of falsehood which have become the characteristic hallmarks of our politics.

It is in deed gratifying to note that the stiff opposition the bill had faced in the National Assembly is melting down. Receiving a delegation of Nigerian Guild of Editors (NGE), led by its President, Gbenga Adefaye, in his office recently the Senate President, Senator David Mark, was reported as saying that the FOI bill would serve the cause of our society very well. He said: "I have always maintained that the Freedom of Information Bill is a bill that will be beneficial to every body. It will be beneficial to you (journalists) in your profession and it will be beneficial to us as politicians".

He however, expressed objections to any demand for unlimited latitude by the media and subsequently called for the criminalization of libel as a condition for the passage of the bill by the Senate. The Senate President as a concerned Nigerian and public office holder is entitled to his opinion. The truth of the matter is that there is no need to single out the press for vilification. Enough laws, as noted earlier, already exist in our legal codes to deal with libel and other sundry matters. If such laws exist, why make the criminalization of libel a precedent condition for the promulgation of the FOI bill into law?

The media people amongst the members of the National Assembly have a duty as much as the NUJ and NGE to dissuade their colleagues from their present stand point which to me does not appear helpful. If we must practice corporate governance, the enactment of the FOI bill is a desideratum.

ThisDay, October 14 , 2008

Chapter 10

Yar'Adua's Incoming Cabinet

After a lack-lustre performance by a poorly rated cabinet, President Umar Musa Yar`Adua in his current reworking of the Federal Executive Council seems determined this time to give focus and verve to his administration. This optimism is hinged on the caliber of personalities on the widely speculated list of presumptive Ministerial nominees which was last week submitted to the Senate for screening.

On the list are prominent Nigerians with impeccable public records of achievements in their various callings. They include the following amongst many others: Prof Dora Akunyili, the great Amazon who had proven her mettle as NAFDAC boss, Alhaji Shetima Mustapha, a former Minister in the Second Republic and a man endowed with the power of introspection, Dr. Sam Ominyi Egwu, a former University don and immediate past Governor of Ebonyi State, Chief Achike Udenwa, fomer Governor of Imo State, admired by many for his level-headedness and Alhaji Ibrahim Lame, who until his nomination was the Secretary General of the Dr. Abubakar Olusola Saraki-led Northern Union.

Also on the list are Prof. Babatunde Osotinmehin, the long serving Chairman of National Agency for the Control of Aids (NACA), Dr. Rilwan Lukman, a Petroleum Engineer and past President of OPEC, and Dr. Olabode Agusto, a technocrat who served in the immediate past federal administration as Director-General of the Budget Office of the Federation.

Even for the most implacable critic of President Yara`Adua, this list, it must be admitted, is very impressive by any standard. These fellow Nigerians who have been penciled down by Mr. President as Ministerial nominees, I believe, are among our best and brightest. I have no doubt whatsoever that such a remarkable team will greatly assist President Yar`Adua to make a great difference in the life of our country men and women.

As at press time a total of 13 names of nominees had been submitted in the first batch to the Senate for consideration as Ministers of the Federal Republic of Nigeria. The Presidency is expected to submit the second batch of the nominees in the next couple of days to bring the number to 20 which was the exact figure that was weeded out of the cabinet about a month ago.

Some of the personalities expected in the second batch and who as at press time had undergone security screening reportedly include the following: Chief Ufot Ekaette, former Secretary to the Government of the Federation, who served in that capacity under the immediate past federal administration for eight good years and Alhaji Kashim Imam, former governorship candidate of the ruling Peoples Democratic Party (PDP) in Borno State. More names of very highly qualified Nigerians are expected to make the final list.

Given the caliber of personalities being proposed as Ministers by the President and their impressive credentials, there is no doubt that Alhaji Yar`Adua is very determined and poised to give the nation a new lease of life and a sense of direction.

As the nominees are being weighed to determine their suitability for the tasks ahead, it has become clear that the President is responsive to the feelings of the public. Many of the Ministers who were relieved of their portfolios actually had no business being in the cabinet as they made little or no impact for almost two years they were on board. It is gratifying to note that some good fresh hands are coming up to strengthen and fortify the cabinet in response to public outcry.

However, it had been expected that the President should have made a clean sweep of the cabinet to make room for more professionals and technocrats who would assist him to speed up governance and deepen the gains of the democratic process. Alas, this is not to be because there are still a good number of the old rumps that do not deserve retention in the cabinet. The saving grace, however, is the new crop of achievers that is making the cabinet this time around.

Many of the new people coming on board have the requisite experience, competence, and capability to deliver on the President`s Seven-Point Agenda. Let's take for instance the likes of Akunyili, Osotinmehin, Lukman, Agusto, Egwu and Ekaette. These are very solid Nigerians with well-known track record of performance.

Prof. Dora Akunyili has distinguished herself as a go-getter and achiever of high distinctions. Her high-flying performance in NAFDAC has attracted encomiums and accolades from far and near. Her relentless crusades against fake and counterfeit drugs have recorded huge successes. Akunyili, without mincing words, is a pride to the nation.

There is no doubt that she would bring into the cabinet the same zest and panache with which she approached her job as NAFDAC boss.

Prof. Babatunde Osotinmehin is another eminent Nigerian who has acquitted himself creditably in the struggle to prevent and checkmate the spread of HIV/AIDS in our country. As the Chairman of NACA over these years, he has done very well in terms of public sensitization and creating the necessary national awareness on the dreaded scourge. It is undoubtable that he will be an asset to the cabinet.

Although Lukman has been severally recycled by successive administrations in Nigeria, it cannot be doubted that he is a man of proven competence. In the past, he has had to hold sensitive portfolios like Petroleum, Foreign Affairs and Power at various times, and he did distinguish himself in those positions. No wonder he is one of the people on whose experience the President is counting upon to deliver on the Seven-Point Agenda.

The immediate past Governor of Ebonyi State, notwithstanding what opinions his critics may hold against him, is an erudite scholar who will be a round peg in a round hole as a federal Minister going by the visible achievements he recorded in his eight-year stewardship in the State. With every sense of responsibility, it can be safely concluded that Dr. Egwu is the father of modern Ebonyi, given the trail he blazed in the infrastructural transformation of that young State. Among his contemporaries in the Eastern States, his performance stood him out as a lone star in the firmament.

His sterling performance in office was not surprising given his antecedents. He was a University don and former Commissioner for Education in his State before being elected as Governor. If his pedigree is anything to go by, there is no doubt that he should be able to give a good account of himself.

Chief Ufot Ekaette, is another nominee whose nomination has gone down well with a wide spectrum of our society. He has a reputation as a bundle of integrity, competence, knowledge and wisdom. These rare qualities were prominently on display within the last eight years of the Obasanjo administration in which he served as the Secretary to the Government of the Federation (SGF). Strong indications have emerged that he will be in charge of the newly created Ministry of Niger Delta, the vessel through which President Yar`Adua intends to tackle the huge developmental challenges in the ever restive and volatile Niger Delta region.

We are confident that these nominees will have easy passage in the Senate as they go through the rituals of confirmation hearing. With such an assemblage of stars in his cabinet, President Yar'Adua has no excuse to continue or remain on the slow lane. He must now move on a faster pace as he goes into his mid-term. The Seven-Point Agenda must now be put on a full throttle for the collective benefits of the citizenry.

ThisDay, December 9, 2008

Chapter 11

Collapse of Values in Nigeria

When will Nigeria be in the news for the right reason? Put differently, why are we always in the news for the wrong reasons? And when will good news that will delight the rest of the world emanate from Nigeria? Is this country that has remained potentially great cursed? When will this vicious cycle of bloodletting, hatred, animosity and killings come to an end in this country?

The recent mayhem in the ever restive Jos, Plateau State capital in which over 500 people, most of them innocent souls were prematurely dispatched to the world beyond is one grievous incident that is too grave to comprehend. One shudders at the relative ease with which people resort to wasting of precious human lives at the slightest provocation or even for no tangible reasons.

What happened in Jos in the last few days which resulted in such staggering death tolls is not only baffling but defies every human imagination. In a country where we profess to be one people with one destiny, one is yet to come to terms with the exhibition of such extreme hatred and animosity that could provoke the level of human slaughter that was witnessed in the Plateau State capital.

No matter whatever explanations that may be offered for the tragic occurrence in Jos, there cannot be any justifications for the senseless shedding of blood of innocent Nigerians including women and children. The actions of the hoodlums and their financiers who took laws into their hands by willfully destroying lives and property in such an unprecedented scale in the city of Jos are not only despicable and unacceptable but also downright reprehensible.

These recurrent killings in Northern Nigeria must be of concern to every right thinking citizen of this country, including the authorities. And in all the crises that we have witnessed, without exceptions, the killings always take on ethnic or religious coloration even when the issues in contention are primarily political. The latest wanton destruction of lives and property in Jos is one too many if it is recalled that only seven years ago the same Plateau erupted in an orgy of sectarian violence that claimed over one thousand lives. In 2004 a repeat of such senseless killings was done to the consternation of the nation. It is hard to believe that so soon after, the same Plateau would relapse into another wave of human disaster.

In all of these, official inquiry was conducted and recommendations made on how to stem future occurrences. But here we are today, going through the same bitter route of waste and destruction. The deduction is very clear. We have learnt nothing and we have forgotten every thing. Otherwise, how can this type of carnage be visited on the Plateau again when the victims of the past crises were yet to recover fully from those unfortunate incidents.

As for me what has happened and still happening on the Plateau is simply the collapse of our previously cherished values and ethos in this country. It is certainly not peculiar to Plateau State. It is a terrible syndrome that has become a part and parcel of our heritage of late.

The societal values that place premium on the sanctity of life, good neighborliness, tolerance, entrepreneurship and peaceful co-existence have been grossly eroded, no thanks to globalization and other harmful foreign influences. If not for the total collapse of our value system, how can people take delight in shedding innocent blood of their fellow citizens for whatever reasons? If not for the collapse of our cultural values, how else can supposedly rational beings loot property of fellow citizens and burn down sacred places of worship in the name of religion or ethnicity?

In a recent interview with a national newspaper, a well known scholar and motivational speaker, Professor Pat Utomi underscored the centrality of social and cultural values in the advancement of any society. He lamented the gradual erosion of our values over time, blaming the situation for the tragedy that our country has become. His words: "I have been convinced for a long time that the reason why Nigeria is not making progress is the collapse of culture....Unless we can change our values, this country won't go far." I cannot but strongly concur with Utomi. Unless we change our current values which place much emphasis on crass materialism at the expense of our common patrimony and humanity, the journey to nationhood will remain a mirage and pipe dream.

It must be admitted that we have had inter-ethnic and communal clashes in the past starting with the 1953 Kano riots in which the Hausa-Fulani was squared against the Igbos, resulting in the loss of lives and property. The regularity of these ethno-religious clashes ever since, particularly in the Northern parts of the country is becoming very worrisome. Something must be done by the authorities to stem this dangerous trend.

I have a feeling that the way we are going, with less emphasis on human lives, we may indirectly be singing the nunc dimitis of this country that has remained potentially great. The only way to pull this country back from the precipice is for the Government of the day to conduct a wholesale inquiry into the current crisis with a view to unraveling the remote and immediate causes.

The result of the investigations should be able to reveal the perpetrators of the evil plot and their motives. The Government should thereafter go further to apply the full weight of the law on those found culpable in this macabre drama. This will serve as a deterrent to those who might wish to toe this infamous path in the future.

I strongly believe that one of the reasons why there had not been any let up in this recurrent harvest of tragedies in parts of Nigeria is because the Government has not been able to demonstrate an iron resolve in dealing with the organizers of these criminalities and their sponsors in high places. It is the general expectations that, this time, the Government must spare no efforts to unravel the circumstances and motives surrounding this latest tragedy on the once peaceful Plateau. Anything short of a judicial commission of inquiry will not do. The commission must be empowered to undertake a wholesale investigation with a view to unraveling the causes and the culprits behind the dastardly acts. Such identified culprits should be severely punished. The commission should also come up with far-reaching recommendations that will help Government in preventing a re-occurrence. The nation has shed enough blood of innocent souls on the Plateau. This is the time to say enough is enough.

It must however be acknowledged that President Yara`Adua`s prompt and decisive intervention helped to prevent the escalation of the mayhem. This is in sharp contrast to the tardiness exhibited by the authorities in Plateau State who were very slow in responding to the emergency.

We must also commend the Governors of the South Eastern States for rising swiftly to the occasion. If not for their timely response and appeal, there would have been a possible backlash in several cities in the South East, particularly Aba, Umuahia, Onitsha, Owerri, Okigwe, Abakaliki, Awka and Enugu which boast of substantial Northern populations.

We have had enough of ethno-religious crises. If we must secure our future as a nation, this is the time to put a stop to all this nonsense.

ThisDay, November 25, 2008

Chapter 12

Stemming the Tide of Bestiality

A s we gradually get to the end of the year 2008, it would seem that the Armageddon which was long predicted in the Holy Scriptures has finally descended on our country, Nigeria. The terrible tragedies and unconscionable level of criminality and depravity being inflicted on the nation, at random and of recent, by agents of Satan across the land seriously call for concern.

The echoes of deaths and cries of agony, occasioned by the recent sectarian crisis in Jos, Plateau State capital, are still resonating across the entire geographical landscape of Nigeria. Eye witness account of what transpired in Jos described it as the worst inter-ethnic and inter-religious violence ever recorded on the Plateau. It was further described as a "tragedy of monumental proportions", which might take the State over twenty years to recover.

But for the direct victims of the crisis, life can never be the same again. The innocent lives that were lost cannot be brought back to this world. Those that were permanently maimed are going to live with such injuries and their scars for life. Those who lost all their life possessions and property will continue to bemoan the fate that befell them as they begin life anew.

While the nation is grappling to come to terms with the recent human disaster in Jos, other sections of the country are mired in one form of criminality or the other. In the South Eastern part of Nigeria, criminal gangs are on the loose, abducting and kidnapping innocent Nigerians for ransoms.

In this new but dangerous enterprise, no community, town or individual is immune. As at the last count, several villages and towns have suffered one casualty or the other with security agents making little or no progress to infiltrate and smash the various syndicates. Now, people live in perpetual fear, as no one knows who the next victim will be.

Residents in the affected States, today, find it difficult to move freely while foreign investors and visiting tourists avoid the endemic States like a plague. The implications are quite obvious. They are evident in the loss of foreign investments and jobs and human capital flight.

The situation in the South East today is very grim and palpable. Citizens of those areas living outside the region, no longer find any attraction in visiting their homes. Such a situation can only result in the perpetuation of poverty and underdevelopment.

In the South West, armed robbery gangs have laid siege on most of the cities making lives cheap and unbearable. From Lagos through Ibadan to Oshogbo, it had been a tale of woes as armed bandits rob freely from one bank to the other, looting and killing in the process.

Available statistics showed that in the last three months several banks in Ibadan, Oyo State capital have played hosts to armed robbers. They include Skye Bank, Union Bank, UBA, Intercontinental Bank and Oceanic Bank. In the process of the on-going rampage by men of the underworld, innocent staff and customers of the banks and ordinary citizens who were unfortunate to be caught in the cross-fire, fell to robbers' bullets.

The situation had gotten so bad that the Banks had lost confidence in the capacity of the Nigeria Police to protect them. The Banks, in order to register their anger and protest, shunned a recent meeting called by the Assistant Inspector-General of Police in charge of the Ibadan Zone, Mr. Tunji Alapini and the Commissioner of Police in the Oyo State Command, Mr. Bashiru Azeez to seek a way out of the crisis.

The banks were said to have been miffed at the indifference and inability of the Police to rise to the occasion, a situation that had reportedly emboldened the robbers to continue the serial raids of banks operating in the Oyo State capital, Ibadan. The same scenario is also playing out on the ever busy Lagos-Ibadan Expressway.

Only recently it was reported that a six-man robbery gang laid siege at the Ibadan end of the Lagos-Ibadan Expressway, robbing, maiming and raping their victims in the process. Luck was later to run out against them, when some Police detectives, acting on a tip-off, besieged the robbers and engaged them in a gun duel, resulting in the arrest of one of the bandits. Others reportedly escaped with bullet wounds.

On interrogation, the apprehended robber said he and his comrades in crime were on the road to collect their own share of Sallah gifts from the traveling public. This is rather unfortunate and further goes to show the level of bestiality to which this country has sunk.

On this score of rising criminality in the land, no part of Nigeria seems to be spared. As the nation contends with recurrent crises in the North, bordering on religious zealotry and fundamentalism, in the South-South of Nigeria, criminal militia groups have high-jacked the struggle of the people of Niger Delta for resource control and self-determination.

Criminal elements in the region, masquerading as freedom fighters have taken laws into their hands by directly challenging the sovereignty of the Nigerian State. They seize the water ways and perpetrate all kinds of heinous crimes against the people they profess to be fighting for. They engage in illegal bunkering of crude oil. They engage in kidnapping and abduction of both Nigerians and foreigners alike for ransoms.

These criminal elements attack and destroy oil facilities owned by multi-nationals prospecting for oil in the area. The worst part of it is that they have now graduated to a dangerous situation where they now hijack and raid ocean going vessels, thereby giving this country a very bad image within the international community.

Given their nefarious and despicable activities, they have unwittingly taken the sail out of the wind for the agitation of economic empowerment of the Niger Delta. No one is any longer taken in by their so-called agitation for the emancipation of the people of the region. There is no doubt that they are only "emancipating their pockets".

The time has come for the people of Nigeria to come together in a genuine forum, conference or by whatever name called to address in a frank manner the National Question. Of course the National Question deals with the issue of inter-ethnic and inter-religious relations and power sharing amongst the constituent groups in the country to ensure peaceful co-existence.

The raging crises in the country, whether religious, ethnic or social, if not controlled could snowball into a major national conflagration with disastrous consequences for the unity of the country. And like Blaine Harden noted in his book, 'Africa: Dispatches from a Fragile Continent', "there are sound reasons to fear catastrophe. Like Sudan, Nigeria is rent by religion. It is divided north and south between Muslims and Christians, and economic hard times have ratcheted up religious tension. Religious riots are common and could spill over into civil war".

Harden knows what he is talking about, having served on the continent as the Correspondent of the highly influential Washington Post for several years in the 1980s. The current administration in Nigeria led by Alhaji Umar Musa Yar`Adua must seize the initiative by leading this country into a genuine national dialogue for us to fashion out how we want to live as a nation and the terms of the union.

This is necessary in order to avoid the predictions of people like Harden about Nigeria from coming true. A stitch in time saves nine. If the unimaginable things that are currently happening are allowed to continue unchecked, we may have no country we may call our own.

ThisDay, December 16, 2008

Chapter 13

2007 Elections In Retrospect

In the last couple of days, the Chairman of the Independent National Electoral Commission (INEC), Professor Maurice Iwu has been talking too much without exercising any discretion at all. Given the scandalous elections he conducted in 2007 which brought this country into disrepute and dishonour within the comity of civilized nations, one would have expected Iwu to show some penitence and seek the face of God. Rather, on the contrary, he has remained ever garrulous and remorseless.

I am therefore constrained to comment on what I consider regrettable acts of indiscretion on the part of this man who was given a life time opportunity to break a national jinx, but instead chose to walk on the path of infamy and ignominy. I had been very restrained from baring my mind on Iwu since after the elections in which I was a direct victim of INEC's manipulations and brigandage for obvious reasons.

I chose the most civilized way out for venting my anger by going to the Election Petitions Tribunals sitting in Umuahia, Abia State capital to seek redress in the manner in which Iwu's INEC conducted elections into the Ikwuano/Umuahia Federal Constituency seat in which, without being immodest, I was a viable candidate on the platform of the Action Congress.

I don't intend to dwell much on the open daylight robbery that took place in the name of elections with the active connivance, support and endorsement of the so-called INEC. It is a matter for another day. But suffice it to say that even when we approached the tribunal for justice, a lot of roadblocks and obstacles were mounted on our way by INEC to forestall our chances of getting justice.

To secure a Certified True Copy of the fake result the electoral body announced to enable my counsel file our election petition, was a Herculean task. The officials in custody of the document insisted on their palms being greased before they could do their jobs. Even when we had succeeded in filing our petition, it took threats and cajoling before my legal team would be allowed access to the cooked-up documents that

INEC used in arriving at the pre-determined results pursuant to a ruling of the tribunal that ordered INEC to make available relevant materials used in the election to me.

I have had to comment on my personal experience as a key player in the 2007 elections in order to underscore the fraud, farce and charade that was organized by INEC in the name of elections.

Against the background of the wholesale fraud and corruption that characterized the 2007 elections as attested to by neutral international election monitors, one would have expected Iwu to accept the fact that the election he organized was a farce and genuinely seek the forgiveness and understanding of the Nigerian people. Instead, he has been confronting and attacking any person or group that dared condemn the elections.

Only recently, he has taken on two eminent Nigerians namely, Professor Wole Soyinka, the Noble Laureate and Senator Ken Nnamani, the immediate past Senate President, for scoring INEC low in the conduct of the controversial 2007 elections.

Professor Soyinka in a recent interview had described the 2007 elections conducted by INEC as the worst in the history of Nigeria, demanding that former President Olusegun Obasanjo under whose presidency the fraudulent election took place and Iwu should face public trials to give account of their roles in the exercise. Iwu did not hesitate a second in responding to Soyinka in a most vile manner.

As a democrat, I concede to Iwu his right to respond to allegations against him. But in doing so one would have expected him to show some discretion by addressing the issues raised instead of chasing shadows.

In his response, couched in a most uncouth language, he had accused Soyinka of playing to the gallery and seeking newspaper headlines. He did not stop there. He went further to make insinuations on Soyinka's leadership of the Federal Road Safety Corps (FRSC) during the Ibrahim Babangida era. I am not a spokesman of Soyinka. And it is not my intention to do so here. Soyinka, an international icon is more than capable of defending himself and his role in the FRSC.

My position is that the extraneous issues raised by Iwu in response to Soyinka's press interview were uncalled for and totally diversionary. It is also inconsistent with the standard of behaviour required of an academic of Iwu's status. Iwu as a Public Officer should learn how to properly conduct himself. He must learn how to take criticisms in good faith.

Resorting to hurling personal abuses and trading insults with those who disagree with him can neither help matters nor wish away the fact that he conducted a grossly flawed election.

His recent attack also on Senator Ken Nnamani would seem to be in line with what is now emerging as a trend in INEC. For daring to criticize the way and manner the 2007 elections were conducted, Iwu did not waste time in carpeting the former Senate President, accusing him of nursing a hidden agenda.

Nnamani in a recent press interview had rated the 2007 elections very poorly, noting that he would have arrested Iwu and put him on trial for violating the Electoral Act of 2006 if his tenure as Senate President had not elapsed. Iwu was very swift in his response which as usual was very vitriolic. Again, instead of addressing the issues raised by the former Senate President, Iwu descended to the level of imputing motives for the position of Nnamani.

According to a statement issued by INEC, Iwu claimed that Nnamani lobbied him to halt the election to enable him (Nnamani) take over government as interim President after Obasanjo's tenure would have expired.

The statement went further: "Deploying the most pitiable appeal to base sentiments, Chief Nnamani reminded the INEC Chairman that both of them come from the same part of the country and his (Nnamani) being President of an interim government of Nigeria will benefit "our people". The statement concluded: "It was, however the gentle but blunt refusal of the INEC boss to grant the unconstitutional request that pitched the former Senate President against Iwu".

Somebody should call Iwu to order. Every body cannot be wrong and only Iwu is right.

Iwu's belated disclosures on Nnamani, as far as any discernible mind is concerned are outrightly pedestrian and childish. Assuming but without conceding that the disclosures on Nnamani were true, why has it taken him close to two years after the said elections to make his revelations? This is a very cheap propaganda that cannot fly in the face of reason. Iwu should have chosen a better tale!

Prof. Iwu must come to terms with the fact that he conducted the most perverted election in the history of Nigeria and seek a way of making restitution so that he can secure the forgiveness of his country men and women. Talking tough and adopting a fire-for-fire approach can only earn him further contempt and derision from the populace.

This is what the European Union Observer Mission (EUOM) said of the elections Iwu conducted: "The 2007 State and Federal Elections fell far short of basic international and regional standards for democratic elections. The elections were marred by very poor organization, lack of essential transparency, widespread procedural irregularities, substantial evidence of fraud, widespread voter disenfranchisement at different stages of the process, lack of equal conditions for political parties and candidates and numerous incidents of violence". Can Iwu be proud of these observations? How come that Iwu is still strenuously defending such a farcical election that has been so endorsed by neutral observers?

If he had gotten it right, there would be no ground for any one to lampoon Iwu. Take the case of Ghana that had just conducted internationally acclaimed presidential and parliamentary elections in which the opposition won. The chairman of Ghana's electoral commission, Kwado Afari-Gyan had been receiving accolades from both the winning and losing parties including international observers.

In endorsing the outcome of the elections in Ghana, the same EU observer Mission that scored Iwu's INEC poorly gave kudos to Kwado Afari-Gyan, noting that "Ghana's Electoral Commission had worked competently and transparently". This is a food for thought for Iwu and his co-travelers in INEC.

ThisDay, January 27, 2009

Chapter 14

The Crisis of Constitution Amendment

The on-going face off between the Senate and House of Representatives over the methodology for the review of the 1999 constitution has become a matter of serious national concern. Like a joke, what was thought to be a minor difference bordering on show of ego and pride has finally degenerated into an impasse with each of the chambers getting more entrenched in its trenchant positions and not shifting any grounds at all.

The consequence is that the decision of National Assembly to undertake a joint review of the Constitution has become a mirage. As the impasse deepens, with no hope and sign of any reconciliation between the two warring chambers in sight, the possibility strongly exists that the current attempt, after previous attempts in the immediate past, to review the constitution may once again become an exercise in futility.

The immediate cause of the current crisis is traced to the walk-out staged by the 44 members of the House of Representatives at a Retreat in Minna, Niger State organized by the National Assembly Joint Committee on the Constitution Review (JCCR) to set the tone and parameters for the constitutional amendment process.

The 44 members of the House of Representatives are part of the 88 member-committee jointly raised by the two chambers to carry out the responsibility of reviewing and amending relevant sections of the 1999 constitution. The other 44 members were appointed by the Senate. As was the practice in the immediate past, the Deputy Senate President, Senator Ike Ekweremadu was designated the Chairman of the JCCR while his counterpart in the House of Representatives, Hon. Bayero Nafada was assigned the portfolio of Deputy Chairman of the JCCR.

This was the subsisting situation or rather the understanding before the JCCR members set out to Minna. In Minna, the JCCR members who are drawn from the House of Representatives demanded that the Deputy Speaker, Alhaji Bayero Nafada, earlier designated as Deputy Chairman should be made the Co- Chairman of the JCCR.

The demand was naturally resisted and rejected by the Senators on the grounds that the Senate was the upper chamber and the House of Representatives, the lower chamber. They saw the action of the House members as an affront to the constitution which according to the Senators confers superior status on the Senate over the House of Representatives.

In justifying its sudden volte face in Minna, the aggrieved House members said that they took the action in order to safeguard the independence and autonomy of the House as guaranteed by the constitution. They further argued that by accepting the position of Deputy Chairman of the JCCR, it would amount to the House playing a second fiddle to the Senate. This, according to them, was unacceptable as it was not in line with constitutional provisions.

They further argued that the two chambers were equal and co-ordinate, and as such the idea of upper or lower chamber was alien to the constitution, insisting on according the House equal status on the consideration of the review of the constitution.

The House members hinge their arguments on Sections 9,58,60 and 62 which expressly and by inference grant autonomy to each chamber of the National Assembly. Section 9 deals with the mode of altering or amending the provisions of the constitution. And this grants the power jointly to the National Assembly, consisting of the Senate and House of Representatives. This section also grants the power of concurrence to each of the House before any proposed amendment could become law.

Section 58 on the other hand deals with the mode of exercising the legislative power of the federation. The section in sub-section (1) states as follows, "The Power of the National Assembly to make laws shall be exercised by bills passed by both the Senate and the House of Representatives and, except as otherwise provided by sub-section (5) of this section, assented to by the president".

The sub-section of Section 58 states inter alia, "Where the president withholds his assent and the bill is again passed by each House by two-thirds majority, the bill shall become law and the assent of the President shall not be required".

Section 60, on the other hand grants to each of the chambers the power to regulate its own procedure. This, according to House members gives them the authority to function as an autonomous and alternate chamber to the Senate; hence the issue of the alleged superiority of the Senate does not arise.

Section 62 enjoins the two chambers to appoint a joint committee on Finance or any other joint committee as they deem relevant. It is perhaps on this basis that the Joint Committee on Constitution Review (JCCR) was set up.

The Senate has however countered the arguments of the House, describing them as an after thought. Spokesman of the Senate, Senator Ayogu Eze had informed the nation at a press briefing that the JCCR at its maiden plenary last December passed a resolution in which the Deputy Senate President was endorsed as the Chairman of the JCCR while the Deputy Speaker was adopted as the Deputy Chairman. He noted that sensitive documents sent to Embassies in relation to the Minna Retreat were signed by Hon. Nafada in his capacity as Deputy Chairman. He was wondering why he and House members did not protest at that time, only for them to do so belatedly in Minna.

He also stated that there cannot be any co-Chairman as Section 53 emphatically grants the Senate the pre-eminent power of chairing any joint session of the National Assembly. The section in sub-section (2a) states as follows:-

"At any joint sitting of the Senate and House of Representatives, the President of Senate shall preside, and in his absence the Speaker of the House of Representatives shall preside"

To further buttress his points, he made references to some constitutional powers exclusively granted to the Senate such as powers of confirmation of Ministers, Ambassadors and other high-ranking officials of government. He also referred to past constitutional amendment processes in which the various Deputy Senate Presidents served as chairmen and Deputy Speakers, as vice-chairmen. He said the protest could not be for any altruistic motive. Thereafter he threw a bombshell. He said that intelligence available to the Senate showed that some fifth columnists had infiltrated the House with a view not only to torpedo the constitution review but also to scuttle democracy in Nigeria.

Since after his submissions, it has been a war of words by both Houses. The latest outbursts came from the spokesman of the House, Hon. Eseme Eyiboh who described the Senate as a satanic chamber where Senators operate under satanic influence. The House has since passed a resolution, endorsing the walk out by its members. From available indications, the House, it would seem, may want to undertake a separate review of the constitution.

The dimensions the altercations between both chambers are taking are becoming very worrisome. Urgent national efforts must be taken to douse the brewing tension, otherwise it is capable of not only truncating the constitutional amendment process but also undermining our fragile democracy.

However, I do not believe that the best way of solving the crisis is by pleading with House members to return to the JCCR. No! If we succeed in bringing the House members back through making entreaties to them we have not solved any problem in the long run.

Since the House Members are raising their objections on constitutional grounds, even if those objections were an after thought, it will do the nation a lot of good if this matter is settled once and for all through the interpretation of the judiciary. The truth of the matter is that the position of the House is strengthened by section 4 of the constitution which vests the legislative powers of the Federation in the National Assembly consisting of the Senate and House of Representatives. The power is not given exclusively to any of the chambers. It is a power that is jointly shared by both Houses. To that extent, the House remains an independent and alternate chamber to the Senate.

Again, the fact that Section 53, grants the president of the senate the power to chair a joint sitting of the National Assembly is not sufficient enough to extrapolate that section to other areas in which the constitution is silent. The issues that need judicial interpretation now are:

For the purpose of amending the constitution of the Federal Republic of Nigeria, 1999, does the same constitution envisage a joint committee? If the response is in the affirmative, who is legally qualified to chair the Joint Committee? These issues must be conclusively dealt with so as to clear the way for an unimpeded constitutional amendment process, free from unnecessary bickering and grandstanding.

ThisDay, February 3, 2009

Chapter 15

Senate`s Aviation Probe Verdict

After many months of intriguing politicking, the Senate last week mustered enough courage and political will to take action on the report of its Committee on Aviation which probed the utilization and application of the N19.5 billion Intervention Fund. The Committee led by Senator Anyim Ude, representing Ebonyi South in Ebonyi State was severally commended by both the leadership of the Senate and Senators who commented on the report for a thorough and comprehensive report.

The Committee, based on its findings made very far-reaching recommendations. Almost all the sixteen recommendations made by the Committee were adopted with minimum amendments. The highlights of the report include the indictment of two former Ministers of Aviation, Dr. Babalola Borishade and Mr, Femi Fani-Kayode, found guilty of official graft and abuse of office.

In the case of Borishade, he was indicted for the inflation of the Safe Tower project to the tune of N5 billion. The safe tower project was meant to equip the nation`s four major international airports to enhance the safety of Nigeria`s airspace, which at that time was considered very unsafe following serial air crashes in the country which claimed the lives of many innocent souls.

The report, accordingly urged the Federal Government to use the EFCC and Police to recover the inflated sum. It further recommended the prosecution of Borishade and others indicted on the misuse of the fund. The report noted that the safe tower project, though well intentioned, was used to defraud the country.

With regard to Fani-Kayode, the Committee found him guilty of irregular awards of contracts and undue interference in the management of the parastatals under the Ministry. The report recommended a ban on him from holding public office for five years.

The Senate, however, could only note these recommendations because the issues were already a subject of litigation in the law courts.

The Committee was able to establish that fake due process certificates were used by fraudulent contractors and their collaborators in Federal Aviation Authority of Nigeria (FAAN) to fleece Government funds. It subsequently directed that the source of the fake certificates be probed by security agencies. The recommendation was unanimously adopted.

Also adopted was the recommendation that the Federal Government should set up a contract review panel to review all the contracts awarded with the Intervention Fund with a view to recovering all monies on inflated contracts.

It is important to note that the probe into the Aviation sector was in response to the resolution of the Senate on May 7, 2008, which mandated the Committee to investigate the application and utilization of the N19.5 billion Intervention Fund released by the Federal Government in 2006 for the rehabilitation and development of infrastructure in the Aviation industry.

The Intervention Fund was initiated by the Obasanjo administration in response to the series of air crashes that occurred between 2005 and 2006 in which the nation lost over 400 of her citizens including innocent pupils of Loyola Jesuit College, Abuja.

The Fund was to be disbursed as follows: Replacement of obsolete control tower equipment at Lagos, Abuja, Kano and Port Harcourt airports…N6.5 billion; Severance Benefits for disengaged staff of Federal Aviation Authority of Nigeria (FAAN)…N2 billion; Rehabilitation of infrastructure at the nation's airports…N11 billion.

The Committee undertook a one-week public hearing in which all those who knew anything about the application of the Fund was summoned to give evidence. It was one week of intensive and rigorous inquiry, during which passions were occasionally inflamed and tension reaching a crescendo. The disclosures at the hearing were quite revealing and shocking.

The most contentious of the projects was the Safe Tower contract executed at the princely sum of N6.5 billion which the Committee had now found out to have been outrageously inflated to the tune of N5 billion. The contract was awarded by Dr. Borishade to an Austrian firm known as M/S Avsatel.

It will be recalled that during the investigative public hearing by the Anyim Ude-led Committee the Head of M/S Avsatel in Nigeria who secured the mouth-watering contract, Mr. George Eider disclosed that their tender for the contract contained neither a bill of quantities nor any pricing list whatsoever. When he was asked whether he followed due process in getting the job, he, in a most arrogant manner, said it was not his business but that of the Ministry of Aviation. According to him what mattered was "stopping planes from falling from the Nigerian skies and coffins of school children".

It was a most irresponsible and insensitive posturing which the Committee captured in its report to the Senate.

It is not surprising that Eider has been indicted alongside Borishade by the Committee and recommended for prosecution by security agencies.

One of the most glaring cases of abuse of office which was established by the Committee was the lopsided recruitment into FAAN by Fani-Kayode in flagrant violation of federal character principles as enshrined in the Constitution of the Federal Republic of Nigeria. Out of a total work force of about 8,000, a total of 4,397 staff representing about 60 percent of the entire work force of FAAN come from the South West geo-political zone, with about 90 percent of this coming from mainly Ogun, Ondo and Osun States.

The Senate decried the situation and subsequently adopted the recommendation of the Committee to the effect that FAAN must observe federal character principle in its staff recruitment. Accordingly, the Senate also approved the right sizing of the bloated work force.

One significant thing about the Aviation Committee report is the level of thoroughness and professionalism that were clearly evident. No wonder it was difficult to sweep it under the carpet despite what some insiders described as spirited attempts by some powerful forces to kill the report. The Committee members demonstrated a unity of purpose. The report was signed by 10 out of 11 members. This is considered a major feat in the Senate.

It was therefore not surprising that the Chairman of the Committee and his members received a lot of accolades from the entire Senate for a job well done during the consideration of the report by the upper legislature.

The outcome of the Aviation probe has once again brought unto the national stage the quantum of rot in our system. The heart bleeds at the level of profligacy and looting that goes on in high places in this country. In the past, people stole public funds with some measure of moderation and trepidation. Today, the story is different. People now steal public funds entrusted in their care with impunity and scant regard to public feelings.

A situation where contractors would collect mobilization fees, abandon work and disappear from sites without being called to account, is responsible for the kind of impunity we have seen in the Aviation sector. The Senate Committee on Aviation led by Senator Anyim Ude has done quite a good job by trying to get to the root of the rot without compromising its integrity.

The ball is now in the court of the Federal Government, in line with its due process posturing, to go ahead and implement the report without any hesitation.

ThisDay, February 17, 2009

Chapter 16

Assault on Human Rights in Zamfara

It is unbelievable that in this time and age, free citizens of Nigeria within Nigeria are being subjected to untold persecution, harassment and intimidation by agents of the state for holding independent political opinion. In Zamfara State, located within the North Western axis of the country, it is being alleged that Governor Mahmuda Aliyu Shinkafi, who recently crossed over from the All Nigeria Peoples Party (ANPP), the platform on which he was elected as governor of the state, to the ruling party at the centre, Peoples Democratic Party (PDP) has foisted a regime of fear on the citizens of the state, using coercive instruments of state to forcefully move the ANPP structure to his new party (PDP) against the will of the people.

Those who, in exercise of their constitutional right to freedom of association resisted this perfidious act are being held in police and prison custody on trumped up charges. The atmosphere is said to be charged and tensed following this unwarranted assault on human rights in the once peaceful and serene state that is noted for the agricultural productivity of its citizenry.

The Governor claimed that he dumped the ANPP which made him a Deputy Governor for eight years and returned him as governor in 2007 in exercise of his fundamental right to freedom of association. It is instructive to note that Alhaji Shinkafi was the only serving Deputy Governor in the whole country that was returned by any party as a substantive governor.

Now that he has found it politically expedient to jump ship, he should concede to others their own rights to freedom of association as guaranteed by the constitution.

It is not our intention here to question the propriety or otherwise of his action in decamping to another party, even though there is everything opportunistic about it. The matter is before a court of law as the ANPP is asking him to resign as Governor since he had left the party that brought him into power.

In a full page statement issued in one of the national dailies recently, a Kaduna based human rights body, Human Rights Monitor, catalogued all the allegations bordering on infringement on the rights of the people, high-handedness, overbearing dictatorship and intimidation. The body led by Human Rights Activist, Mr. Festus Okoye further accused Governor Shinkafi of setting up an illegal security outfit which his government had been using in terrorizing ANPP supporters unwilling to play along with the Governor.

Investigations conducted by Festus Okoye and his organization showed that "the Zamfara State Government in concert with the Security Agencies, the Attorney General and some sections of the Judiciary have unleashed a wave of terror, intimidation and persecution of some elements within the state who have refused to switch allegiance and party with them".

The report further alleged: "Some hired thugs have since the defection of Mahmud Aliyu Shinkafi to the PDP been removing the posters, banners and logos of rival political parties and affixing their own. This has led to clashes in Gusau, the State capital and other neighbouring local governments".

The most pathetic of the revelations made by the Human Rights Group is the case of illegal arraignment and detention in prison of a woman activist who was alleged to have publicly stated her resolve not to leave ANPP for PDP. Permit me to quote the report in full so as to bring forcefully to the public domain the type of atrocious acts that are being currently perpetrated in a 21st century Nigeria.

"On 21st January, 2009 at about 1700hrs, one Kabiru Samaila of Mortgage Area Gusau, reported at Central Police Station Gusau that on 17th January, 2009 at about 23.30hrs, he met you Aisha Mohammed alias Noble of Ungwan Toka Area of Gusau at Rogo Supermarket, Gusau with your friends and overheard you telling people that you will not be in PDP because all the party members are homosexuals. Such attitude can cause breach of the peace in the state. You are hereby suspected to have committed the above mentioned offence.

"On the 23rd day of January, 2009 the chief Magistrate Court 1, Gusau remanded her in prison custody even though he lacks jurisdiction to try the offence. However, on the 28th day of January, 2009 the Chief Magistrate transferred the matter to Sharia Court 2, Tudun Wada, Gusau for lack of jurisdiction. The Divisional Police Officer for Tudun Wada

Station, Abubakar Shika apparently acting under instructions mobilized three trucks of policemen to court.

"The Upper Sharia Court Judge, Kanwuri, Alhaji Mohammed Sani heard the matter at 5pm, denied her bail and ordered that she be remanded in prison custody till the 16th day of February, 2009 when he would rule on the application for bail. It is instructive to note that the offence of defamation under Section 392 of the Penal Code carries a maximum of 2 years imprisonment and is ordinarily bailable".

It is indeed inconceivable that a Nigerian citizen and for that matter a young woman is being made to go through this kind of ordeal for holding an independent political view. The report as presented by Human Rights Monitor is very revealing. And it at once exposes the high level of political intolerance and repressive tendencies of Governor Mahmud Aliyu Shinkafi and his cohorts.

There should be an urgent intervention from the Judicial and Police authorities in Abuja to halt the Shenanigans that are going on in Zamfara. Such level of abuse of power and office should not be tolerated in any way. Under the laws of the land, it is not an offence for individuals to hold contrary political opinion to those of the Establishment. In deed Section 40 of the Constitution of the Federal Republic of Nigeria guarantees the individual the right of freedom of association. Against this background therefore, no Nigerian, no matter the circumstance, should be compelled or cajoled into joining a particular political party as doing so amounts to a gross violation of the fundamental right of the individual.

All men of goodwill should take more than a passing interest in what is going on in Zamfara at the moment. It is clear to every discernible mind that danger is lurking in the state. If the government does not retrace its steps, the situation may spiral out of hand and snowball into a major social conflagration with the potential spill-over effect on neighbouring states.

What is going on at the moment is a dress rehearsal for an impending titanic struggle for the soul of Zamfara politics between the Shinkafi group and his estranged godfather, the immediate past governor of the state, Alhaji Sani Yerima, still considered a major political force in the state.

Close watchers of Zamfara politics predict that it may be an uphill task for Shinkafi to deliver this ANNP stronghold to PDP, his incumbency notwithstanding, given the pervasive influence of Sani Yerima in the state. Resorting to forceful conversion of people to a party other than their natural choice cannot be a better strategy at political realignment in the state.

If Shinkafi wants to succeed in altering the political balance in the state, he must show some level of imaginativeness and creativity in his politics. Above all, he must make a difference in office so as to convince the people that his political choice is the best for the state. Even with all this, it is not a guarantee that the entire state would follow him sheepishly into PDP.

He should forthwith put paid to the present regime of terror and persecution in the state. In line with constitutional provisions, individuals should be allowed to exercise their rights to freedom of association and expression as they deem fit. The regimentation of people on account of their contrary political views by the Shinkafi government is a panicky measure that can only inflame the polity.

We urge for caution and restraint. This democracy is still very fragile. Anything that would heat up the system in any way should be seriously avoided. It is against this background that we join Festus Okoye and his group in urging the Inspector General of Police to order the immediate disbandment of the illegal security outfit being funded by the Zamfara State government and which has become a terror weapon against opponents of the regime.

It is in the interest of the government in Gusau to allow a level playing field for all political actors in the state. Let the people freely make their political choices. It cannot be by coercion and intimidation.

ThisDay, Febuary 24, 2009

Chapter 17

Oluwole Rotimi's Diplomatic Gaffe

The diplomatic row currently playing out between Nigeria's Foreign Affairs Minister, Chief Ojo Maduekwe and General Oluwole Rotimi who, until recently was Nigeria's Ambassador to the United States is not only scandalous given the treasonable comments credited to the Ambassador but also raises fundamental questions on the continued corporate unity of this country.

Oluwole Rotimi, prior to his sack by the President, Alhaji Umaru Musa Yar'Adua was reported to have been having a running disagreement with Maduekwe over issues bordering on policy, protocol, hierarchy and management of Nigeria's Mission in Washington. The altercations which were said to have started since last year reportedly resulted in exchange of series of correspondences between the Minister and the Ambassador culminating in a letter written by the latter in which he called Maduekwe a tribalist and made other unprintable remarks about him.

General Oluwole, who could not control his temperament, was reported to have made very inciting, disparaging and explosive comments about the ethnicity of Maduekwe who is his boss by virtue of his position as the Honorable Foreign Minister of Nigeria. He was quoted as saying: "I have dealt with people like you (referring to the Minister) in the past. I was the Adjutant General of the Nigerian army that thoroughly defeated your rag-tag Biafran army"

It is sad and regrettable that 39 years after the end of the Nigeria-Biafra civil war, a high ranking Government official and some one who participated in the war to keep Nigeria one still harbors such deep seated hatred and animosity against Ndigbo, a major component group in this country. From such treasonable and arrogant outbursts credited to Oluwole Rotimi, it seems clear to me that we still have a long way to go in forging a united and harmonious country.

Unless the likes of Oluwole Rotimi and his ilk in our society (and there are many of them) are weaned of such arrogant mentality, our claim to building a united and prosperous Nigeria will remain pretentious and a lip service.

It is not my intention to hold brief for Maduekwe. He is more than capable of defending himself. Nobody is perfect. It is only God that is infallible. To that extent Ojo has his own short comings. But one thing you cannot accuse Ojo of is tribalism. Ojo, had in recent past incurred the wrath of his kinsmen because of unpopular positions he took in defence of former President Olusegun Obasanjo, who incidentally shares the same ethnicity with Oluwole Rotimi.

It will be recalled that some time in 2001, at the height of Igbo clamor for the presidency of Nigeria, Ojo Maduekwe who was then the Minister of Transport berated the Igbo aspiration as "idiotic". He was subsequently declared a persona non grata and enemy of Ndigbo in the whole of Igboland for that provocative and ill-advised statement. It took a high level intervention by many well meaning and respected Igbos and personal apology by Ojo for him to be forgiven by Ndigbo. It does not therefore make any sense to describe such a fellow as a tribalist. Oluwole`s allegation can only be seen for what it is.....a cheap propaganda that cannot fly in the face of reason and logic.

It is in deed tragic for this country that some one with such a mind set, full of ethnic hate, could rise to the level of a General in the Nigerian army and also attain the level of an Ambassador in our diplomatic service. A man with such contempt for a constituted authority does not deserve to represent this country in any capacity whatsoever.

With the insensitivity demonstrated by Oluwole Rotimi, he showed that he does not have either the requisite temperament or capacity to run our most important diplomatic mission in the world. Ojo Maduekwe was therefore right in his assessment which resulted in the sack of the Ambassador.

He told Mr President thus: 'This man (Oluwole Rotimi) has no temperament to be an ambassador of Nigeria in our most important mission. This is a strategic assessment of the situation. Anyone who has such a disposition may not be able to handle the Nigerian embassy in Washington, which is deemed in Nigerian diplomatic circles as a strategic and sensitive mission. The recommendation that he be recalled has to do with his capacity to run the place'.

The President was convinced, more so when the provocative letter of Rotimi was attached as an evidence of his unsuitable temperament in Maduekwe`s brief. He acted swiftly and ordered the sack of this

Ambassador whose irresponsible and treasonable comments had ruffled a lot of feathers here in Nigeria.

The authorities should not just stop at the recall of Oluwole Rotimi from his Washington duty post. He must be made to apologize to Ndigbo and in deed all Nigerians for making such divisive comments and bringing the country into disrepute.

His reference to a defeated rag tag Biafran army is undiplomatic, insensitive, arrogant and totally out of context. It amounts to reopening an old wound which is already healing. He should be sanctioned for making such reckless and unguarded statements.

The umbrella socio-cultural organization of the Igbo ethnic group, Ohaneze Ndigbo, must demand for an apology from the Federal Government for this mindless assault on the collective psyche and sensibilities of Igbo people of Nigeria. Why would an underperforming Ambassador who believes that he cannot defer to his boss because he is an Igbo whose 'rag-tag Biafran army' was defeated by Oluwole Rotimi be left in Washington to continue to embarrass the nation with his unacceptable behavior. His recall is therefore very appropriate.

The Igbos between 1967 and 1970 fought a war of survival. Whether any one likes it or not, it is a credit to their resilience and fighting spirit that for three solid years they were able to endure what has been described as the most ferocious and atrocious war ever witnessed on the continent of Africa in which all the superpowers in the world worked against their interest. Ndigbo had, since after the unfortunate civil war, been working more than hard to contribute their quota to national development. We have no apologies to offer for defending ourselves against possible extermination by the enemies of Ndigbo as exemplified by the likes of General Oluwole Rotimi.

By immediately ordering the recall of the Ambassador from Washington for his diplomatic misconduct, President Umaru Musa Yar`Adua has proven himself to be a patriot who genuinely believes in the unity of the country and oneness of her people irrespective of our cultural and religious differences.

The action of the President is timely and has the potential of soothing wounded nerves. What has emerged from this whole episode is that in future those being proposed for top government positions must be ascertained to be worthy in their character, social conduct and above all, temperament.

Nobody appointed by his or her nation to render service in any capacity can be greater than that nation. In deed it is a privilege to be called upon in a nation of 140 million people to render service. It will therefore be a great disservice for any one so favored to abuse with impunity such trust and privilege.

As a nation, we must at all times emphasize those things that unite us as a people rather than those issues that dwell on our differences. I, for one, am confident that this country called Nigeria has the potential and capacity of attaining greatness if only we can act with the oneness of purpose. We cannot realize our manifest destiny by playing the ethnic cards all the time.

ThisDay, March 3, 2009

Chapter 18

Crisis of Elections in Nigeria Union of Journalists (NUJ)

Penultimate weekend, Nigerian Journalists in their numbers assembled in the Federal Capital Territory, FCT, Abuja, to participate in the Triennial Delegates Conference of their Union, (NUJ). As it was the practice in the past, the occasion was to afford members of the pen fraternity the opportunity for stock taking and self appraisal of the performance of both the Union and the Journalism profession in the last three years.

The Delegates Conference was also supposed to present practicing Journalists in Nigeria the platform to appraise the state of the nation and the performance or otherwise of its leadership. And finally, all the talk shops were usually followed by an election in which new set of leaders were elected or the mandate of serving officials was renewed.

Regrettably enough, the Abuja Delegates Conference failed to achieve any of the stated objectives because of the crisis of confidence and primitive politicking that became the order of the day. To say that what happened at the International Conference Center, venue of the event, on Saturday, 27th March, 2009, was a show of shame, is to play down what was clearly a huge national embarrassment. It was in deed a big disgrace never witnessed in the history of the NUJ.

In a determined bid to ensure that the outgoing leadership was returned at all cost, the former President, Mr. Ndagene Akwu and the Credentials Committee appointed to organize the elections, perfected a strategy in which elders and even past leaders of the Union and non-delegates who are normally accorded observer status were cleverly locked out at the entrance gate of the International Conference Center.

In all my activist years in NUJ, this was the first time such an ill-conceived agenda was being devised by those in whose shoulders were entrusted the responsibility to provide direction and leadership to the Union. It was such an embarrassing spectacle to behold the presence of hundreds of journalists, most of them senior members of the profession, being refused entry into the venue of the conference on the instructions of the outgoing President, Mr. Akwu, who was also seeking re-election.

This untoward development gave an early indication that there was a grand conspiracy by some vested interests to manipulate the proceedings and the eventual outcome. And part of the strategy was to ward off as much as possible many leading lights of the profession whose interventions and wise counsel may not serve the best interests of the incumbents. This is clearly a great departure from what used to be the norm in the past where former leaders and elders of the Union including friends of the NUJ and leaders of the approved affiliate associations were invited to participate at the opening ceremonies.

I recollect with nostalgia that at the Delegates Conference of 1992 in the serene city of Calabar, the capital of Cross Rivers State where Alhaji Sani Zoro was returned unopposed, all practicing journalists who found their way into the Canaan city as Calabar is popularly known, were allowed access into the Cultural Center, venue of the conference, during the opening ceremonies. Goodwill messages were taken from past leaders of the Union, Nigeria Labor Congress (NLC), other friendly Trade Unions and specialized Associations affiliated to the NUJ. It was in this regard that I, in my capacity then as the National Chairman of the National Association of Political Correspondents (NAPOC) addressed the Calabar Delegates Conference in session.

In spite of the tension that was generated by the declaration of Alhaji Ladi Lawal of the Lagos State Council to challenge Sani Zoro for the Presidency, the Calabar conference was concluded successfully with no incidents. Incidentally, Zoro himself was equally a product of the Lagos Council as he was then of the defunct Concord Newspapers, Ikeja, Lagos. Journalists at the conference proved to be mature politicians as all contending issues were amicably resolved.

At the next Delegates Conference held in Sokoto, the seat of the Caliphate, we similarly had a peaceful election which was hotly contested by Ladi Lawal and Bonnie Iwuoha. Ladi won, but he was to lose it later on technical grounds, paving the way for Iwuoha to assume the Presidency. But in all these situations, the conferences and elections were effectively and competently managed.

What we are seeing in our great Union today is totally different. It would appear that desperation and brinksmanship have taken over. This, we must resist. We, as the watch dog of the society, often times, take delight in pontificating or sitting in judgment over the affairs of others, particularly in the light of our statutory obligations under Section 22 of the 1999 Constitution. Is it not shameful that at this age and time, we cannot put our house in order? Is it not also disappointing that we cannot organize free and fair elections to pick our leaders? Must we manipulate an election so that a favored candidate can emerge at all costs?

We have a noble past we can look up to, to guide us. Election must not be a do or die affair even though a former President of Nigeria would wish otherwise. I remember that at the Delegates Conference held in Ibadan, Oyo State capital in 1996, an incumbent President, Iwuoha, organized an election in which he lost to Lanre Ogundipe of the Oyo State Council. The Union did not cease to exist thereafter. The same fate also befell Ogundipe when he organized an election in which Smart Adeyemi emerged. I have cited all these instances to prove that the NUJ is bigger than any one of us. Those who contrived the present crisis must give peace a chance.

It is unfortunate that thousands of Journalists came from all over the country to Abuja to elect their own leaders and at the end of the day, for no fault of their own; they were unable to exercise their franchise.

Although the abrupt termination of the conference may have cast the NUJ in bad light, the decision of a section of the Abuja Council to stall the elections should be accepted as a counter strategy to checkmate arbitrariness and dictatorship in our Union. It is our belief that when eventually journalists gather again in Abuja to finish the unfinished business, sanity, civility and decorum will prevail.

In my estimation, there is no doubt that the election will be a key contestation between Madam Funke Fadugba, a former Chairman of Lagos Council who creditably acquitted herself on the seat, Garba Mohammed, former Deputy National President and Wahab Oba, the current Chair of Lagos Council. With the permutations that are currently on ground, Fadugba is widely tipped to emerge as the first female President of the NUJ. We are eagerly looking forward to seeing history being made as we re-assemble in Abuja to complete the unfinished business.

ThisDay, April 7, 2009

Chapter 19

Issues in Nigeria`s Re-Branding

Since the Minister of Information and Communications, Professor Dora Akunyili, made public the intention of the Yar`Adua administration to re-brand the image of Nigeria, the issue has generated a lot of mixed reactions. But in spite of the differing positions, there is the unanimity of opinions on the image problem of the country and the imperative need for cleaning it up. The differences would seem to dwell more on the appropriate strategy for going about it.

Most public commentators who had commented on the issue believe that the entire project is diversionary and ill-conceived. The kernel of their arguments which make a lot of sense is that you don`t need to embark on a propaganda campaign for Nigeria to project a better image abroad. Rather, it is the satisfactory performance of Government in the discharge of its Constitutional obligations to the citizenry that defines the way and manner the country`s image is perceived abroad. The case of Lagos State under Governor Babatunde Fashola who has done tremendously well to give Lagos a huge lift is cited as re-branding in action. This is more so as the stellar performance of the ebullient Governor has attracted massive media attention both from within and outside.

Not long ago such global media networks like CNN and BBC beamed their spotlight on the transformative developments that are taking place in Lagos under Fashola. These influential global media institutions were attracted by the infrastructural revolution going on in Lagos and not seduced by any meaningless propaganda campaign. The Information Minister, however, shares a different view. She does not believe that the re-branding campaign is diversionary or wasteful. In her maiden presentation at a ceremony at the Shehu Musa Yar`Adua Center, Abuja, she showed a lot of passion and even emotions on the issue of re-branding the image of Nigeria. She expressed the resoluteness and commitment of the Government to pursue the image re-branding project to a logical conclusion.

She had observed: "The perception of Nigerians overseas is even worse, partly because of the way we present ourselves. Most of you must have experienced being asked to stand aside in the airports because we are suspected to be criminals. I am even getting more worried because this phenomenon is becoming life threatening. People have been attacked and even killed outside this country just because they are Nigerians or suspected to be Nigerians". Against this background, therefore, I wish to concur that the initiative to re-brand the corporate image of Nigeria can hardly be faulted. Aside from the poor and bad image that we have outside; internally, the attitude of our leaders and the led to the Nigeria project has been anything but satisfactory. That is why many social critics and other well meaning Nigerians have often insisted that any lasting solution to our image problem has to come from within first.

In a situation where our leaders do not emerge through a credible and transparent process but are instead foisted on us against the will of the people, the manifest destiny of our country can hardly be realized. In a situation like this, it becomes difficult for the average Nigerian to demonstrate that patriotism and nationalism that can galvanize Nigeria to a truly great and respected country.

The people have seen their leaders breach the laws, subvert the Constitution, loot the treasury, engage in immoral and unethical practices without the law taking its course. They have seen a situation where a convicted Governor who stole his State blind would be let off the hook through corrupt plea bargain process. The same ordinary Nigerians have also witnessed a situation where a Police chief would be sentenced to only six months imprisonment after being convicted of fleecing his organization billions of funds meant for the welfare of his officers and men. Situations like this cannot elicit the best and right conduct from the citizenry. We have seen our leaders with their escorts drive against traffic, beat traffic lights and terrorize innocent Nigerians on the highways for "their Excellencies" to have free passage. We have also witnessed situations in the country where the lives of the flying public are put at extreme risk because of a "VIP movement". Such unfortunate Nigerians whose lives are considered to be of no consequence have often been made to hover dangerously in the air for hours because of such "VIP movement". Such actions that treat the ordinary Nigerian as inconsequential and irrelevant can neither inspire any confidence nor elicit any nationalistic fervor from the people. Like globally renowned literary giant, our own Professor Chinua Achebe noted in one of his works, we as Nigerians must strive to know where and when the rain started beating us.

It seems too obvious that if we are to make any impact in terms of sprucing up our battered national image, we must begin from home by addressing key challenges like poverty, ignorance and disease. Any re-branding process that does not address these fundamental challenges of existence misses the point. It is good to note that Akunyili recognizes the need for the re-branding project to be home grown. According to her, "My team and I know that we cannot successfully re-brand Nigeria without the support and buy-in of Nigerians…This is because we want Nigerians to take ownership of this initiative from the outset. The re-branding of Nigeria needs to be home grown and people-centered".

However, for this project to succeed, we must begin to change the unproductive ways we have been doing things in this country. Government should forge a new covenant with the people that is based on truth and trust. The leadership of this country must be by example. There should be no different set of laws for the leaders and the led. We must be governed by the same set of laws which should be no respecter of any body. Above all, the Government must begin to creatively address the problem of economic hardship in the country which has forced many Nigerians abroad as economic refugees. Many fraudulent Nigerians whose activities have brought so much harm and damage to the image of the country often cite the harsh economic environment at home as the motivating factor. In spite of the global financial meltdown, Nigeria is enormously endowed by nature to the extent that any Government that strives a little can make a difference in the lives of Nigerians. It is really regrettable that after several years of being awash with petro-dollars, Nigeria is still ranked amongst the poorest countries in the world. The reason can only be because of official corruption and mismanagement.

If we must get it right this time, we should break away from the vicious cycle of corruption, mediocrity and ineptitude. Our aspiration to a better Nigeria should transcend mere sloganeering.

ThisDay, April 14, 2009

Chapter 20

The Clamour for Second Term

It just started as a whispering rumor until Chief Tony Anenih's curious prayers at Shehu Musa Yar'Adua Center, Abuja, blew open the agenda. While giving the closing prayers at the 12th Memorial Anniversary of the late General Shehu Musa Yar'Adua, a former Chief of Staff, Supreme Headquarters and foremost Political tactician who died in Abacha's gulag twelve years ago, Anenih had prayed that God should grant President Umar Musa Yar'Adua good health to complete his remaining six years in office.

It was neither for any vain reason nor could it have been by sheer happenstance that this prayer request was made in the presence of some ambitious politicians who were known to harbor aspiration to the Presidency in 2011, particularly Alhaji Atiku Abubakar, the immediate past Vice President in the last administration.

From the "take or leave it manner" Anenih made his point, he did not leave any one in doubt that a second term in office for President Umar Musa Yar'Adua was a foreclosed matter. And that seemingly innocuous prayer was the signal that many political jobbers were waiting for to go to town with a second term sing song for Yar'Adua.

Ever since the Abuja event, the floodgate would seem to have been thrown open with all manner of characters joining the fray. It does not even matter that the Yar'Adua administration that is being urged to go for a second term is yet to complete a second year out of its first term of four years.

It also does not matter whether President Yar'Adua has delivered on his Seven-Point Agenda or not. And it would also not matter whether the country under Yar'Adua is making progress or not. For the pro-Yar'Adua campaigners, what matters is for the President to remain on the political saddle willy-nilly.

Anenih, the wily old political fox is adept at the "politics of second term". Since his infamous "no vacancy at the Villa" statement in 2001 under Olusegun Obasanjo, Anenih would seem to have acquired an oracular reputation in matters of this nature.

It is equally this same Anenih who, in the heat of the Igbo clamor for the Presidency in 2001, told Ndigbo to wait till 2015 as the North would do eight years after Obasanjo`s eight years before power could rotate to the South East. I must add that the Igbos will need to work extra hard to make it in 2015 as the South South is very poised to spoil the fun for them.

Having known Anenih for what he is and represents politically, it is hardly surprising that many opportunistic groups and individuals who do not wish to be left behind have taken up the gauntlet to push for a second term for Yar`Adua. Among them are Alhaji Adamu Aliero, FCT Minister; Dr. Haliru Bello, Deputy National Chairman of PDP; PDP Governors` Forum; a section of the Nigerian Senate and some other shadowy groups.

At the risk of being misrepresented, I would like to state in a most categorical term, that I am neither against a second term for Yar`Adua nor those leading the agitations. As a sitting President, Alhaji Yar`Adua is entitled to a second term in office. Like the Spokesman of the Senate, Senator Ayogu Eze said the other day, "Yar`Adua would be entitled to the option of first rejection" as an incumbent when the time for party nomination comes.

Nevertheless, what is of concern to many Nigerians and they should include the admirers of Yar`Adua is the timing and morality of the campaign. I strongly believe that it is not only early but also diversionary to be campaigning for a second term now when the administration is barely two years old in office and yet to deliver on its mandate as symbolized in the Seven-Point Agenda.

It must be quickly admitted that President Yar`Adua has not openly stated that he would go for a second term. On this face value, it would be extremely judgmental to conclude that he is nursing a second term ambition. But his studied silence amidst the raging campaign can be interpreted to mean a tacit endorsement of the proposal.

Like I noted earlier, there is nothing absolutely wrong for an incumbent to seek a second term in office. It is constitutional and legitimate. But such an aspiration must be based on several factors including, most importantly, performance and concrete achievements within the first term and stable health condition. The verdict of social critics as Yar'Adua reaches the mid-term of his first four year tenure is that of non performance, inaction and purposelessness. The Government cannot be identified with any remarkable or outstanding achievements within the last two years even within the context of the much touted Seven-Point Agenda.

The extremely poor performance of the 2008 Federal Budget is one clear indication of the purposelessness of the administration. That budget did not attain more than 15 percent implementation, a situation that resulted into the return to the treasury of billions of naira appropriated for projects otherwise meant to bring democratic dividends to the door steps of the people.

The Number One item on the Seven-Point Agenda, power supply, has remained very elusive. President Yar'Adua, had on assumption of office, pledged to declare a state of emergency to address squarely the problem of epileptic power which had been the bane of our national development. The magnitude of the problem is such that many industrial and manufacturing concerns have been forced to close shops on account of low capacity utilization with the attendant job losses.

With only two years to the end of the first tenure of YarAdua, the state of emergency as pledged by the Government is yet to be declared. Apart from mounting and conflicting excuses as to why Government has not acted, there is even nothing on the ground to show that the emergency may be declared as promised. The only reasonable conclusion that can be reached in the circumstance is that the enormity of this singular problem appears to be very daunting and too overwhelming for the President.

Every where across the length and breath of Nigeria there is so much despair and despondency. In the midst of ravaging hardship and poverty in the land, the Government appears helpless and diffident.

Never in the history of Nigeria had the citizenry been so demoralized and dejected on account of a Government that seems very clueless and visionless, in spite of abundant good will that greeted it on inception.

It is therefore irritating that some political jobbers should be campaigning for a second term for Yar'Adua when Nigerians were yet to feel the impact of his administration. Much as second term is legitimate and constitutional, it should be earned.

It is not just enough for second term to be thrust on the shoulders of an incumbent simply because it is his right to so aspire. A second term for any incumbent should be a function of many variables, chief of which is stellar performance in office.

Those who are agitating for second term for the President should allow him a breathing space so that he can remain focused and use the remaining two years of his Government to deliver on the Seven-Point Agenda. The clamor for a second term now is an unnecessary distraction that the country can ill-afford.

_____

ThisDay, April 21, 2009

Chapter 21

Balance of Power in the South East

The shape of things to expect in the political terrain of the South East in 2011 is already firming up, given the flurry of partisan activities, with wide ranging implications, which had taken place in the area recently. The antecedents of the political space that is today known as the South East geo-political zone are well known to political pundits, that it would be needless to beggar the question here.

Although the people are highly republican and individualistic in their approach to politics, they have, however, always seen the need to operate under a common political umbrella. A dispassionate appraisal of this tendency has shown that it had less to do with a clannish political orientation than it had more to do with a craving for forging national political consensus.

Whether it was in the First Republic, Second Republic or the ill-fated Third Republic or in the first half of the Fourth Republic, the people of the South East have always shown an inclination towards a common political value.

In the First Republic, the entire Eastern Region consisting of South East and South South geo-political zones of today came under the common political platform of the Dr. Nnamdi Azikiwe-led National Council of Nigerian Citizens (NCNC). In the Second Republic, most of the area particularly Igbo speaking communities also came under the control of the Nigerian Peoples Party (NPP) led by the same indomitable and indefatigable Dr. Nnamdi Azikiwe.

The same political pattern was to be repeated in 1991 when the entire Igbo speaking States with the exception of Anambra, voted massively for the defunct National Republican Convention (NRC). With the return to partisan politics in 1999, all the five Eastern States, again without any exception, came under the political orbit of the Peoples Democratic Party (PDP). The trend continued until 2007 when the powers that be at the center, acting in collaboration with some political renegades otherwise known as Abuja politicians, tried to impose their narrow political will on the populace. The effort met with stiff resistance, leading to the political balkanization of the zone.

This unfortunate development has resulted in a situation where today, the five States in the South East are controlled by three different political parties, thereby laying to rest the politics of consensus in the area. As at today, the Orji Uzor Kalu-led Peoples Progressive Alliance (PPA) is in control of Abia and Imo States even if the hold on Imo is tenuous; the All Progressives Grand Alliance (APGA) is the ruling party in Anambra State while the PDP is in charge in Ebonyi and Enugu States.

Never in the history of the South East have the people been so politically fragmented and segmented. The immediate interpretation of this very unusual phenomenon is that the people of the South East could make alternative political choices in the face of injustice and oppression.

Again, with the political turn of events in the South East in 2007, the people, through the choices they made, resoundingly repudiated "garrison politics" as defined by the ruling PDP at the center at that time.

As 2011 draws closer, there seems to be an effort in the direction of political re-alignment in the zone. If this becomes a reality, it will not be out of sync. Rather, this will be consistent with the political character of the zone.

If the event organized by the PDP in Enugu, prior to the just concluded National Convention of the party in Abuja, is anything to go by, the entire South East geo-political zone may be moving to one political direction, unless the opposition political parties redouble their efforts.

At a zonal rally organized by the PDP, many key politicians, including some founding leaders of the party who left the party for one reason or the other, staged a return and were warmly received by the National Chairman, Prince Vincent Ogbulafor, who happens to be a son of the soil.

Prominent among them were Dr. Okwesilieze Nwodo, its founding National Secretary; Commodore James Aneke and Navy Captain Anthony Ogugua, two of them former military governors and Prince Nicholas Ukachukwu and Chief Ikechi Emenike, former PDP stalwarts who left to run as the gubernatorial candidates of the rival ANPP in Anambra and Abia States respectively. Others were George Muoghalu, former National Secretary of the ANPP and Dr. Offia Nwali, a Second Republic Senator from Ebonyi State.

The list further included the former Deputy Governor of Imo State, Engr. Ebere Udeagu who decamped to DPP and ran as Vice Presidential running mate to Alhaji Dalhatu Bafarawa and Chief Chris Anene, the founding Chairman of PPA in Anambra State.

Earlier, the likes of Senator Jim Nwobodo, a founding leader and Presidential aspirant on the platform of the party who were forced out by some of the reigning champions in the party including former Governor Chimaroke Nnamani some time in 2003 had returned back to the PDP fold following the resolve of Ogbulafor to implement the recommendations of the Dr. Alex Ekwueme Reconciliation Committee. With the regrouping of the PDP in the South East, the opposition parties face real threat of annihilation unless they redefine and reposition themselves as attractive alternative political platforms with enough potential to take the people to the Promised Land.

The PPA and APGA, given their growing clouts in the zone, can give the PDP a good run for its money. However, the two parties appear to be structurally weak to contain the rampaging influence of a re-invigorated PDP.

The internal contradictions in APGA which are already playing out in Anambra where the second term aspiration of its only Governor, Mr. Peter Obi, is being challenged by the son of Obi`s deputy, Dame Virgy Etiaba, show that the party may not present a united front against a determined PDP. Again, the intractable and the never ending legal tussle between Chief Umeh and Chekwas Okorie over the leadership of APGA may further undermine the capacity of the party to make the desired electoral impact.

With the way things stand now in the South East, it would seem that the only party that has the potential to checkmate the PDP is the PPA. Given the relatively good performance of its two governors in Imo and Abia, the PPA led by the irrepressible Orji Kalu may make some inroads into neighboring States like Anambra and Ebonyi while seeking to consolidate on its gains in Imo and Abia.

In the light of the foregoing, the two parties to watch in the South East are the PPA and PDP. But the pressure will be more on the PPA to sustain the current balance of power in the zone.

The problem that I see in the East is this politics without character or for want of a better phrase, political opportunism. This, however, is not peculiar to the East alone. It is some thing that appears to be our political heritage in this country. Nevertheless, the time has come for us to begin to give meaning and value to our political beliefs. And that is where the admonition of Barack Obama to his country men some time in 2005 becomes instructive for us here in Nigeria.

He said: "If we are to shine as a beacon of hope to the rest of the world, we must be respected not just for the might of our military, but for the reach of our ideals". Can we vouch for the ideological content of our politics? This is a food for thought as we watch events unfold.

ThisDay, April 28, 2009

Chapter 22

Ekiti: Shame of a Nation

Ekiti State in the South West of Nigeria has been in the news for obvious reasons. And the issues arising from the deadlocked supplementary gubernatorial election, in which former Governor Olusegun Oni of the Peoples Democratic Party (PDP) and Dr. Kayode Fayemi of the Action Congress (AC) are the main combatants will, for a very long time to come, continue to dominate national discourse.

It is sad and regrettable to note that almost two weeks after the conduct of the re-run election ordered by the Appeal Court in Ilorin in some wards located in ten local government areas of the Sate, uncertainty, confusion, chaos and anarchy pervade the entirety of Ekitiland.

The Appeal Court, ruling in a petition brought by the AC candidate, Dr. Fayemi, challenging the declaration of Engr. Oni as the winner in the April 14, 2007 gubernatorial election, had upheld the results in six local government areas whilst ordering the repeat of the election in 62 wards spread in ten local government areas, where the polls were marred by violence and malpractices. The successful outcome of the re-run election in these ten local governments was expected to determine who truly the rightful Governor of Ekiti State is.

But sadly enough, the election had become deadlocked on account of conflicting reasons in which one is not in a position to authenticate. However, the truth on the ground was that election had been concluded in nine out of the ten local government areas, with the exception of Oye, where the polls could not take place because of violence.

Up to the time things went awry with the elections, results from five local government areas had been officially released. They include Gbonyin, Ekiti South West, Ise-Orun, Ijero and Irepodun. The results showed that the two candidates were running neck to neck, but the AC candidate still had an advantage of 11000 votes from the April 14, 2007 elections endorsed by the Appeal Court.

The situation had since taken a new and dangerous turn with the reported resignation of the Resident Electoral Commissioner (REC), Mrs. Ayoka Adebayo. In her letter of resignation forwarded to President Umar Musa Yar`Adua, the REC raised very grave issues that verge on the integrity and sanctity of the electoral process in Nigeria.

In the resignation letter she noted as follows: "In accordance with the rule of law, the on-going election in Ekiti State was supposed to be the election that will enhance the image of INEC, electoral process in our dear country, Nigeria and the whole black race. Unfortunately, the circumstances changed in the middle of the process; therefore, my conscience as a Christian cannot allow me to further participate in this process."

The issues raised in the letter have once again put the sincerity and commitment of President Yar`Adua to bequeath to the country a legacy of credible electoral reforms on the spot.

Prior to her resignation, the REC was said to have taken ill in the middle of the collation and announcement of the results from some of the affected LGAs. This was given as the official reason by INEC for the delay in releasing the results of the remaining LGAs.

In the light of the issues raised in the resignation letter and contrary to the initial official explanation offered by INEC as to why further announcement of the results was suspended, it is now quite glaring that certain unrepentant politicians, driven by desperation and greed, were poised to subvert the will of the people of Ekiti at all costs.

It was reported that Mrs. Adebayo was being pressurized to accept and announce results that were cooked up outside the designated collation centers in the affected five LGAs. The results, if they had been accepted, would have given an unassailable lead to one of the contending parties.

It was in the bid to free herself from the mounting pressure and threats, that the REC reportedly feigned ill and used that as an alibi to sneak out of the tension soaked Ekiti. The situation is such that the candidates of both parties are now laying claim to victory in the elections. While the AC has called on INEC to declare Dr. Fayemi the winner, having satisfied the mandatory electoral spread in two-thirds of the LGAs in the State, the outstanding votes in the two wards in Oye Ekiti, notwithstanding; the PDP on the other hand had organized a victory rally in Ado Ekiti to celebrate its supposed victory in the same election.

One does not need to be a soothsayer to observe that the unfolding developments in Ekiti portend serious danger to the political health of our nation. All men of goodwill must intervene to resolve the logjam before it snowballs into a major national crisis.

In deed, President Yar'Adua must break his silence on this matter and play the role expected of him as a statesman. The President must not show indifference, thinking, perhaps, that Ekiti problem is a localized one. No!

Any student of our history would recall that the chain of events that led to the 1966 national crisis also started from unresolved election disputes in that same part of Nigeria. The attendant killings, arson and unprecedented violence gave rise to the declaration of state of emergency in the old Western Region. From that emergency, the rest, as it is said, is history.

It must also be recalled that the widespread killings and destructions that attended the disputed 1983 gubernatorial elections in the old Ondo State which comprised the present Ekiti then, played a major role in the untimely collapse of the Second Republic.

The Government of the day should not allow this crisis to get out of hand. The right thing should be done, and quickly too. Since the Electoral Act empowers only the REC that conducted an election to announce the results, Mrs. Adebayo should be guaranteed adequate security to complete what she started. She must not be under any threats whatsoever. A new date should be quickly fixed for the elections in the two wards in Oye and conducted in the full glare of local and international observers amid "water tight" security.

As at press time, it was reassuring to learn that Mrs. Adebayo has resurfaced and given a firm pledge to conclude the elections in Ekiti. Although in response to reporters' questions in Abuja last Wednesday, she admitted authoring the resignation letter, but she was silent on whether she had withdrawn the letter or not.

Whatever may be the case, it is heartwarming to note that she has expressed her determination to complete the process she started. This, in my view, would save the nation a possible constitutional crisis with ominous implications to national security.

Mrs. Adebayo should be courageous enough to announce the legitimate winner based on the legitimate votes cast in the five LGAs where the announcement of results was abruptly suspended.

There should be no question of canceling the entire exercise and starting afresh. No! That option will be counterproductive. The temptation may be there to declare a state of emergency. But that also is not a viable option.

The only way forward is for the Government to provide the enabling environment that would allow Mrs. Adebayo to complete her assignment without fear or favor. This is the only reasonable path to toe in the circumstance.

_____

ThisDay, May 5, 2009

Chapter 23

Nigerian Economy and CBN At 50

The apex regulatory banking institution in the country, Central Bank of Nigeria (CBN) has been in the news in the last couple of days for a joyful reason. The bank has every reason to be in a festive mood, having clocked 50 golden years since its establishment.

The fact that the CBN had attained such a milestone in spite of all odds really calls for celebration and festivities. It must be quickly admitted that 50 years in the life of any organization is very remarkable, particularly when such an entity has continued to play a pivotal and central role in the economic life of a nation, like the Central Bank of Nigeria.

As the apex bank in the country, the CBN is saddled with the critical responsibility of managing the economy, regulating the banking sector and also husbanding the nation's foreign reserves. In keeping with its mandate as a regulator, the CBN also formulates policies and guidelines which help to regulate banking sector to ensure that banks operate within certain minimum standards.

The CBN has come a long way, given its trajectory as a forerunner to Nigeria's independence. It is commendable to note that notwithstanding many constraints and obstacles which the CBN has had to contend with in the discharge of its primary responsibilities to the nation, it has continued to weather the storms.

In some parts of the world including Africa, some economies had been run aground either because of their vulnerability to crises occasioned by the forces of globalization or much more importantly the absence of imaginative and result-oriented leadership with enough intellectual resource endowment to steer their respective national economies out of gloom and doom.

On the African continent, the immediate instances of failed economies that come to mind are particularly Zimbabwe and Uganda under the mediocre government of the fawning and self appointed Field Marshal Idi Amin Dada.

Indeed, under Idi Amin, the Ugandan economy collapsed to the extent that the national currency was described as being worse than a toilet paper. That country's Central Bank was completely emasculated to the extent that it could not come up with any marshal plan to rescue the comatose economy.

Today as all patriots join hands with the CBN family to toast its successes and resilience over the years particularly in the last five years, the Ugandan scenario of the 70s is being played out in Zimbabwe where stagflation had reduced the national currency into some thing worse than a toilet paper. A loaf of bread in Zimbabwe currently costs over a million Zimbabwe pounds. This pitiable situation underscores the helplessness of the economic situation in that country.

Many other countries in Africa at one time or the other have been unfortunate to pass through such routes. There was the case of Ghana in the pre-Rawlings era and Benin Republic under the military jackboot of Matthew Kerekou. The collapse of the economies of these two neighboring countries during those eras had its consequences in Nigeria as our country was besieged by economic refugees who were escaping from the pangs of hunger and hardships.

In spite of some social and political turbulence Nigeria has had to go through in the forty nine years of its existence, the managers of the country's apex bank have done relatively well to steer the economy out of deep crisis.

At no other time in the history of Nigeria than in the last five years that Professor Charles Chukwuma Soludo had been on the saddle as the Governor that the CBN has excelled beyond imaginations. The hallmark of the CBN's achievements under his cerebral leadership was the banking consolidation which he pioneered and saw to its logical and successful conclusion.

The banking consolidation policy which Soludo pursued with single minded energy and uncommon zeal was truly a revolution that has today strengthened the banking industry and launched the nation on the irreversible path of growth and development.

Given the stability which the consolidation has brought to the once troubled banking sector and the resultant expansion in the economy, the

CBN has every justification to roll out the drums, cymbals and trumpets to celebrate fifty years of fruitful existence.

Prior to the introduction of the consolidation policy, the banking sector in Nigeria was virtually on the verge of collapse. Most of the over 100 banks that existed then were mainly family shops which specialized in "round tripping" and money laundering.

Sooner than later the bubble bust, as several of the banks started going under. The attendant stress led to a situation where most depositors lost their deposits and were left broken hearted. Many people never recovered from the shocks.

Under Soludo's magic wand, the situation has changed for the better. Today, we have 25 vibrant banks that are doing well at home and making steady inroads into Africa, Europe, America and other parts of the globe.

Although there were initial hiccups like job losses but today the banking sector has witnessed phenomenal growth with attendant employment opportunities. The situation is such that the sector, within the last three years, has become one of the largest employers of labour in the country.

The CBN has really done well. It must, however, not rest on its oars. It should continue to take it's regulatory and oversight functions in the banking sector very seriously so that we don't have a situation where we may have to return to the infamy of the past.

Outside the banking consolidation, the CBN under Soludo has continued to make its impact felt within the West African sub-region and the continent. It has been playing a leading role towards the economic integration of the sub-region in line with the aspirations of the founding fathers of ECOWAS.

In a related development, the CBN through deft moves and suave diplomacy has been able to secure for Nigeria the hosting rights for the headquarters of the proposed African Central Bank. This is no mean achievement, for which the leadership of the CBN deserves all the accolades.

Speaking at the International Conference to mark the 50th anniversary of the CBN in Abuja, Soludo said the Memorandum of Understanding which has just been signed by the African Union Commission will materialize into African Central Bank.

His words: "The very key one is regionalism. There will be common currency and regional central bank in Africa and around the world.

Nigeria just signed an MOU with the African Union Commission granting Nigeria the hosting right for the African Central Bank."

There is no doubt that when Soludo leaves the CBN, he would be leaving behind a legacy of achievements. His shoes would be too big for the ramp of ethnic bigots who are currently engaged in an unrelenting campaign to get rid of him from the CBN.

ThisDay, May 12, 2009

Chapter 24

Remembering Sam Onunaka Mbakwe

On Thursday, 23rd April, 2009, at the Aso Hall of the sedate and serene International Conference Center, Abuja, many Nigerians, in their numbers, from all walks of life gathered to pay homage to the memory of Chief Sam Mbakwe, PhD, the first Executive civilian Governor of old Imo State, whose high standards of performance in office have remained till date the benchmark for measuring service delivery in public office in the South East of Nigeria.

The occasion was the 2nd Sam Mbakwe Memorial Lecture and public presentation of his authorized biography, "Weeping for the Sunrise", authored by Tobs Agbaegbu, an eminent journalist with the Newswatch magazine. In attendance were very high profile personalities from both the private and public sectors. The traditional institutions and academia were also not left out.

From the robust attendance and the arrangements put in place, the organizers were obviously meticulous and methodical in the conception and execution of the project. It couldn't have been anything less, given the accomplishments of Sam Mbakwe as a charismatic leader, statesman and patriot who was held in very high esteem by Ndigbo and in deed all Nigerians.

A roll call of who is who on the occasion included but not limited to the following: Amb Raph Uwechue, the President General of Ohaneze Ndigbo; Dr. Sam Egwu, Honorable Minister of Education who represented President Yar`Adua; Governor Isa Yuguda of Bauchi State; Owelle Rochas Okorocha; Alhaji Isyaku Ibrahim; Prof. Maurice Iwu; Chief Ben Obi, former Vice Presidential candidate of Action Congress; Hon. Emeka Ihedioha, Chief Whip of the House of Representatives; Senators Chris Anyanwu and Annie Okonkwo; Dr. Ihechukwu Madubuike, former Minister of Health who also served as Commissioner for Finance under Mbakwe; Dr Eddie Iroh, former Director General of Federal Radio Corporation of Nigeria (FRCN); Eze Cletus Ilomuanya,

Chairman, South East Council of Traditional Rulers and Eze Ibe Nwosu, the Ezeigbo of Abuja.

From the academia came Prof. Fred Onyeoziri, Political Adviser to the PDP National Chairman, Prince Vincent Ogbulafor, who also doubled as the book reviewer and Ambassador Joseph Ayalogu who delivered the 2nd Mbakwe Memorial Lecture. There were other prominent dignitaries too numerous to mention for lack of space.

One striking observation on the occasion, regrettably, was the conspicuous and disturbing absence of all the Governors of the South East, particularly those of Imo, Abia and Ebonyi which were part of the old Imo which Mbakwe governed. Also embarrassing was the absence of his colleague Governor then, Chief Jim Nwobodo, who presided over the affairs of the old Anambra State.

Similarly, no explanation could be given for the absence of former Governors of the Igbo-controlled States, some of whom were known to have interacted closely with Mbakwe when he was alive. Also missing in action were prominent political actors from the zone who had been privileged at one time or the other to hold high political offices. They include the likes of former Vice President Ekwueme, Chief Ken Nnamani, Chief Adolphus Wabara and Chief Anyim Pius Anyim, all of them, former Senate Presidents.

I would have also loved to see on the occasion a personality like Ikemba Nnewi, Chief Chukwuemeka Odumegwu Ojukwu, a very close ally of Mbakwe both of whom with Ekwueme provided a robust leadership for the Igbo delegates to the 1994/95 National Constitutional Conference in Abuja. In addition, Mbakwe served under Ojukwu in Biafra as the Administrator of Okigwe Province.

It is equally disgusting to note that none of the members of the so-called Progressives to which Mbakwe belonged in the 2nd Republic made an appearance on the occasion. The Solomon Lars, Abubakar Rimis , and Balarabe Musas just to mention but a few were no where to be found within the precincts of the International Conference Center. This is not comradeship enough!

The worst culprit, however, was Chief Ikedi Ohakim, the current Governor of Mbakwe`s home State of Imo who was supposed to be the Chief Host on the occasion. No excuse for his absence would be tenable, the low level delegation he sent, notwithstanding. Even the delegation led by the Commissioner for Agriculture, Chief Longers Anyanwu, made no commitment in support of the Mbakwe initiative. This is really a pity.

Mbakwe was a Nigerian patriot but an excellent Igbo man with excellent credentials. In matters that concerned the welfare interests of Ndigbo, he never wavered. Prior to his emergence as a Governor in the Second Republic, he had already made a name for himself as a crusader for justice, equity and fair play. He stuck out his neck to fight against the illegal confiscation of Igbo property in Rivers State, which the victorious Federal authorities in the Civil War, in collusion with the new local overlords in Port Harcourt, termed and confiscated as abandoned property.

During his governorship in the Second Republic, even though he found himself in opposition to the ruling National Party of Nigeria (NPN), he constructively engaged the Shagari administration to the extent that he was able to attract many federal projects to Imo State. When it was ideal for him to cajole, he cajoled. When it was convenient for him to humor the powers that be, he humored them tremendously. When it was necessary for him to weep, he wept.

Hence, those in opposition derisively called him the weeping governor. But he had many federal projects to show for his "weeping". Some of the projects included the Federal University of Technology, Owerri (FUTO), federal intervention in the Ndiegoro flood disaster in Aba, the release of the abandoned property in Port Harcourt and payment of compensation on those that had been alienated and approval for the construction of Imo Airport in Owerri.

In all ramifications, Mbakwe was an outstanding political leader who stood by his people. I recall with nostalgia during my student days at the University of Nigeria, Nsukka, when Mbakwe, at the instance of the Political Science Department came to the campus to deliver a public lecture titled "The Challenges of a Governor in A War Affected State". It was vintage Mbakwe that catalogued the entire infrastructure in Imo that was destroyed by the federal troops.

In the lecture which was laced with humor and wisecracks, Mbakwe gave graphic details of the decapitated infrastructure and their locations. He also reminisced on his role as a combatant during the war. He kept the students spellbound as he regaled his audience with his war exploits and the various sectors in which he fought to prevent the total annihilation of Ndigbo by the federal forces.

He repeatedly called on the NPN-controlled Federal Government to declare the Igbo areas devastated by the war, a disaster zone so that the region could attract special funding for the reconstruction of crippled infrastructure.

It still beats my imagination that the memory of such an outstanding patriot who served with distinction should be treated by his own people with such contempt. My heart bleeds that just only five years after the passage of this icon, our people have turned their back on him and the values he stood for. Igbos should rethink. A society that does not honor or appreciates the contributions of its heroes, for me, has not gotten its values right.

A situation in which we are fighting for a space in Nigeria, commonsense demands that we get our priorities right and put our house in order. If the memory of a great statesman like Mbakwe would be so callously treated by the people he had stood by all through his career, we may be sending the wrong signals that fighting for the public good is not an ennobling virtue.

After the exit of Dr. Michael Iheonukara Okpara (Premier, Eastern Nigeria 1959-66), the trail blazer who pioneered the infrastructural revolution in the East, arguably no other leader in Igboland can rank with Mbakwe in terms of concrete achievements.

It is instructive and ironic that the only Governor present on the occasion was Isa Yuguda from far away Bauchi State, Northern Nigeria. Those who call themselves our leaders in the South East should search their conscience. Sam Onunaka Mbakwe`s memory deserves a better treatment. I congratulate Tobs Agbaegbu, through whose efforts the memory of Mbakwe is still being kept alive.

ThisDay, May 19, 2009

Chapter 25

Yar`Adua and the Media

Successive chain of events in the last two years of the Yar`Adua administration in which the Government has had to wield the big stick against the media over what may be regarded as limited acts of inadvertent infractions portrays President Yar`Adua and his Government as being intolerant of dissent. We are worried at the way and manner this Government reacts each time the media manifests any excesses, no matter how minor, in the discharge of its constitutional responsibilities to the society.

If the Government does not moderate itself, we foresee a creeping descent on the part of the Yar`Adua administration into a full blown civilian dictatorship. Yet, we are supposed to be savouring the blessings of democracy, among which are fundamental freedoms including the freedom of the press!

One may not be totally surprised at the unfolding turn of events, given the undisguised determination of the ruling party, Peoples Democratic Party (PDP) to bring the entire country under its complete control and domination. We have seen this in the opportunistic defection of some opposition governors to the PDP.

Through acts of subterfuge some of the governors elected on the platform of opposition parties have been lured to cross carpet to the ruling party. Those who have not jumped ship yet are said to be under tremendous pressure to do so.

Even the manipulations that took place in the re-run election in Ekiti which saw the PDP taking over the State against the expressed will of the people is all in line with the resolve of the party cabal to turn Nigeria into one party dictatorship.

Only recently, it was reported in the news that Adaba 88.9 FM, a private radio station located in Akure, Ondo State capital, had been closed down on the "orders from above". A combined force of security operatives, acting on instructions from higher authorities, was reported to have effected the closure of the broadcasting outfit.

It was gathered that the National Broadcasting Commission (NBC) closed down the station for its alleged failure to pay a N500, 000 fine imposed on it by the Commission for running foul of the broadcasting code.

The NBC had alleged that during the coverage of the April 25, 2009 governorship re-run election in Ekiti State the station had broadcast materials "that were capable of inciting members of the public to violence and consequently leading to breakdown of law and order".

The inciting material was said to be an interview with some leaders of the Action Congress (AC), one of the two leading contending parties in the governorship re-run. It was learnt, however, that the imposition of the fine did not follow due process because the organization was never queried before it was fined. We will come back to this.

The latest incident in Akure is not an isolated case. It followed what has become a consistent pattern of media clamp down by this administration at the slightest excuse.

Some media outfits in the country had, before the Akure incident, tasted the bitter side of the Yar`Adua administration; a situation that hinted at the movement of the administration into a dictatorial direction in its relationship with the media.

Earlier in the life of this government, the Publisher of Abuja Inquirer, a publication based in the FCT, Mr. Dan Akpovwa, was arrested and hounded into the detention cells of the State Security Services (SSS) because he published a material which in the opinion of the authorities was likely to cause a breach of public peace. It took the intervention of many well meaning Nigerians for him to be left off the hook.

On the 17th October, 2008, the popular Channels TV in Lagos was shut down and it's broadcasting license withdrawn because it aired wrong information on the President. The Station had, based on an agency report, alleged that President Yar`Adua was planning to resign on health grounds. Shortly after airing the news, the station realized it was false for which it repeatedly tendered unreserved apologies. But that did not save it from the wrath of the Government.

The offending staff were arrested and hauled into detention. It also took the intervention of some eminent Nigerians and severe criticisms in the press for the Government to back off.

Some months later, the Abuja based Leadership Newspaper was to receive its own dose of repression in the hands of security agents for publishing a story on Yar`Adua`s alleged ill-health that contained some factual errors. For several days, security agents laid siege on the newspaper, taking away some of its editors and also carting away materials including computers.

In spite of the prompt apologies carried by the newspaper, the Government refused to bulge. President Yar`Adua made good his threat to sue the newspaper and its editors to court in his personal capacity. The matter, as at today, is still running at a magistrate court in Abuja.

The repressive attitude towards the media at the Federal level would seem to have been carried over to the States. Not quite long ago, the agents of Akwa Ibom and Bayelsa State Governments, in different but similar incidents, in commando style, seized some journalists from their newsrooms in Abuja and spirited them away to their States where they were made to stand trial for publishing materials that offended the Governors.

It would seem that the governors were encouraged by the bad examples set at the center to engage in such despicable and condemnable acts. On the orders of Governor Godswill Akpabio, an editor with Abuja based newspaper, Fresh Facts, was captured in Abuja and taken into captivity in faraway Uyo, Akwa Ibom State capital for exposing some alleged shady business deals of the youthful Governor.

In the case involving Governor Timipre Sylva, security goons, acting on his authority, came all the way from Yenegoa to apprehend an Abuja correspondent of a Lagos based newspaper for writing an offensive article on him.

These lawless acts stand condemnable before God and man. It is even inconceivable that such brazen acts of infringement on the fundamental rights of the said journalists should be taking place under the watch of an administration that makes a fetish out of its commitment to the rule of law.

It is not on record that either the Yar`Adua Government or the ruling party deplored the illegal actions of these two governors who were elected on the platform of the PDP. In any case, it would have been strange if the Government had done otherwise since it was the one that set the dangerous example in the first place.

With the increasing clamp down on the media, the Yar`Adua administration is now showing its real color away from its pretentious paternalistic posturing at inception. What we have on hand today is an incipient civilian dictatorship that is totally intolerant of dissent. This is a dangerous development which must be resisted as history has proven elsewhere that civilian dictatorship can be worse than military dictatorship.

We have seen it in Arap Moi's Kenya, Robert Mugabe's Zimbabwe, Yaya Jammeh's Gambia, Omar Bongo's Gabon, and Nguema's Equatorial Guinea just to mention but a few.

The panicky measure in closing down a media station under a democratic dispensation is unjustifiable and unacceptable. Such an uncivilized behaviour belongs to the past. The resort to the withdrawal of licenses of broadcasting houses or arrest of newspaper reporters at the slightest provocation is an act of intimidation that should stop forthwith.

We are in a democracy. This means that in any action Government takes against its perceived or real enemies, it must follow due process. The Nigerian Press Council and National Broadcasting Commission are there to exercise their mandate in accordance with the enabling laws. They should always strive to resist external political pressures in the discharge of their responsibilities.

The Akure incident which clearly bears the imprimatur of a powerful political cabal is a worrisome development that should not be allowed repetition elsewhere in the country. More than any other groups or institutions, the press fought for this democracy we have today. The media, therefore, must be allowed unfettered freedom to discharge its responsibilities as guaranteed by Section 22 of the Constitution of the Federal Republic of Nigeria. Enough provisions exist in our laws on how to deal with issues of slander, libel, defamation, sedition and the like.

The Government must resist the idea of going outside the laws of the land to deal with individuals and institutions that dare to challenge its excesses or cross its path in any way. This democracy is still very fragile. We must refrain from acts that are capable of heating up the system.

ThisDay, May 26, 2009

Chapter 26

Needed: Legislative Impact

As Nigeria celebrates ten years of uninterrupted and sustained democratic governance, a remarkable feat in its political annals, there is the need for an appraisal of the role of the Legislature in the preservation of our renascent democracy. This is more so considering the fact that the parliament had always been at the receiving end each time the Military intervened in the political process.

But for the periodic incursions by the Military into the political arena, the Legislature as a pre-eminent governmental institution would have been institutionalised in Nigeria. The parliament, world over, is the engine room of participatory democracy or representative governance. It is gratifying to note that in the last ten years, parliamentary practice has begun to take roots in our country.

Given the strategic and significant role which the legislature plays in any organised political society, the institution has come to symbolise the sovereignty of the people. It is, therefore, unthinkable that any democratic political order at all will ever exist without the prominent presence of the legislature.

In the case of Nigeria, from independence when we practised the parliamentary system of governance through the 2nd Republic to the present era, in which we have adopted the presidential model, the legislature has always taken its pride of place in the Constitution.

Under the 1979 and 1999 Constitutions, the legislative powers of the Federation which are the powers to make laws for the peace, order and good governance of Nigeria are vested in the Legislature as symbolised by the National Assembly.

Specifically, section 4(5) of the 1999 constitution stipulates as follows:

"The legislative powers of the Federal Republic of Nigeria shall be vested in a National Assembly for the Federation which shall consist of a Senate and a House of Representatives"

It went further in subsection 2 to state inter alia:

"The National Assembly shall have power to make laws for the peace, order and good government of the Federation or any part thereof

112

with respect to any matter included in the Exclusive legislative list set out in Part I of the Second Schedule to this Constitution."

In that schedule is listed several items to which only the National Assembly can legislate upon to the exclusion of any other legislative bodies at the regional, state or local government levels. And those issues like defence, currency, mineral resources, foreign affairs, aviation, and revenue allocation amongst many others are quite critical to the survival of the country as a sovereign political entity.

With such enormous powers which the Constitution vests on the Legislature, the institution is placed in a vantage position to make a positive difference in the lives of the people if it chooses to play its role constructively.

Section 4 of the 1999 Constitution, as noted earlier, recognizes the need for peace, order and good government in relation to Nigeria as a nation just as it also recognizes the need for peace, order and good government in relation to each separate State of the Federation, hence it confers such extensive powers on the National Assembly to enact laws to achieve that objective.

It is worthy to note that the National Assembly, through the instrumentality of legislation, has been able to play a stabilizing role in the polity especially in the last ten years in which the Nation has had the good fortune of operating a civil democratic order uninterruptedly.

Within the last decade, the legislature has made many meaningful interventions in the polity which have helped to strengthen and deepen our democratic experience.

At the inception of the Fourth Republic in 1999, when the then President Olusegun Obasanjo arbitrarily increased the pump price of petroleum products, the country faced serious threats from the organised labour which almost shut down the economy.

Our renascent and fragile democracy faced its first real acid test in the new political dispensation as the organised labour led by the then President of Nigeria Labour Congress (NLC), Comrade Adams Oshiomole mobilized and sensitized Nigerians for a show down with the Government.

The National Assembly, in the discharge of its duties as mandated by Section 4 of the Constitution, waded into the matter and constructively engaged the Labour. That strategic intervention by the National Assembly saved the day.

The National Assembly through its leadership was able to get the presidency to back down and reverse itself on the price hike, citing insufficient consultation as the primary reason for the misunderstanding with Labour. The action of the National Assembly buoyed public confidence as the people rightly began to see the legislature as the real defender of their interests. Even the partial deregulation in the petroleum downstream sector which the government achieved in 2004 could not have been possible without the intervention of the National Assembly which insisted on Labour being carried along. It is not out of place, therefore, to suggest that the relative industrial peace we have had in this country since the return to democratic rule in 1999 is due primarily to the continued patriotic interventions of the National Assembly in the polity.

In times of national crisis, the National Assembly has never been indifferent. It has continued to engage all the relevant stakeholders of the Nigeria Project in meaningful dialogue to ensure that the country remains peaceful and united.

One of such moments of crises which the National Assembly successfully resolved was the face-off between former Governor Chinwoke Mbadinuju of Anambra State and his House of Assembly shortly after their inauguration in 1999. Even though the majority of the members of the House of Assembly and the Governor belonged to the same party, PDP, the misunderstanding involving the two parties, did not stop the House from threatening the Governor with impeachment.

Many eminent Nigerians including the clergy stepped in to resolve the matter, but to no avail. It was the intervention of the House of Representatives led by its Speaker, Hon Salisu Buhari that saved the situation and ensured that peace returned to the state. Earlier in one of its plenary sessions, the House of Representatives had passed a resolution threatening to take over the proceedings of the Anambra State House of Assembly and legislate for the state in line with constitutional provisions if the crises which had polarised the state Assembly into two factions persisted.

Speaker Salisu Buhari led a delegation of House members from Abuja to Anambra state, and through constructive dialogue, a peace formula acceptable to the squabbling parties was worked out, thus bringing the crises to an end.

And recently in a similar crisis in Ogun state, the House of Representatives under the leadership of Hon. Dimeji Bankole also passed a resolution to take over the conduct of proceedings in the Ogun State

House of Assembly if the face-off between Governor Gbenga Daniel and his Assembly members continued to threaten the peace of the state.

The House of Representatives further directed the police authorities in Abuja and Ogun state to provide the enabling environment for the House of Assembly to hold its sittings without any encumbrances from the State Government. Prior to the adoption of that resolution by the House of Representatives, the House of Assembly could not sit because of the prevailing climate of insecurity around the Assembly complex.

But with the intervention of the House of Representatives, the House of Assembly has resumed business.

So, in the instant cases of Anambra and Ogun state, we have seen a pro-active legislature that is ever willing to intercede on the side of justice and equity.

Other areas where the National Assembly has been able to make the desired impact on the society include the effective exercise of its power of Appropriations and oversight.

The single most important power of the Legislature is that of appropriations. Under the laws of the land, no revenue accruing to the Federation Account can be expended without the authorization of the National Assembly. It is against this background that the yearly Federal Budget is presented before the National Assembly for consideration and passage into law.

The situation thus provides the Federal Lawmakers the opportunity to influence the provision and funding of projects that impact positively on the lives of the people. It can, therefore, be safely concluded that the Legislature is the vehicle through which the impoverished masses in our society receive the dividends of democratic governance. But it is a different ball game whether this onerous responsibility is being faithfully discharged or not.

Nevertheless, in the last two years, the National Assembly has consistently provided in the Federal Budget what it called Millennium Development Goal (MDG) projects, aimed at poverty reduction and wealth creation among the populace. In the 2009 Federal Budget, the National Assembly appropriated the sum of N60 billion for the MDG projects, spread across the various Federal constituencies in the country. This amount was shared equally among the constituent six geo-political zones in Nigeria.

In addition to its power of appropriations, the National Assembly is also empowered by the constitution to exercise oversight powers over Ministries, Departments and Agencies (MDAs) of government that receive their funding from the Federation Account. The National Assembly receives and approves their financial estimates and also monitors their utilization in compliance with the law.

The oversight function of the National Assembly is one such very powerful constitutional instrument through which it checks and balances the excesses of the Executive. By this way, the National Assembly is able to check wastes and control leakages in the system.

Through the discharge of its oversight responsibilities, the National Assembly is expected to ensure that the dividends of democracy are delivered directly to the door steps of the people. This is notwithstanding the fact that in several instances, the oversight powers have been employed as an instrument of blackmail on the Executive by some greedy and corrupt members of the National Assembly.

In spite some flashes of brilliance on the part of the Legislature, the truth is that the story of the National Assembly since 1999, sadly has been that of financial scandals, scams, extortions, graft, certificate forgeries and other sundry acts of malfeasance.

The National Assembly as the repository of the power of the people in a democracy can do better. As the nation marches forward in its democratic consolidation, the peoples` representatives should endeavour to remain on the path of reason and sanity and refrain from unethical conducts which have tended to lower their esteem before the electorate.

As our democracy takes deeper roots over time, the Legislature is expected to continue to employ the instrument of legislations to better the lot of the common man.

ThisDay, June 23, 2009

Chapter 27

The Presidential Amnesty for Militants

President Umar Musa Yar'Adua, recently raised hope on the possible and imminent resolution of the Niger Delta crisis when he expressed the readiness and commitment of his administration to embrace the militants who were willing to drop their arms in exchange for amnesty being extended to them. The Presidential proclamation was in reaction to the reported move by a section of the militant leaders to lay down their arms and halt further escalation of hostilities in the crisis-ridden Niger Delta region.

In what appeared to be a surprise gesture, one of the unrepentant and notorious militia leaders, Mr. Ateke Tom, had offered to accept the Presidential amnesty and discontinue the armed rebellion in the Niger Delta once the details of the amnesty were made known. He, however, gave some conditions.

He demanded that the amnesty offer must include the disbandment of the military Joint Task Force (JTF), the government security outfit deployed to counter the insurgency in the Niger Delta, and the opening of the water ways which had remained blockaded following the recent military expedition ordered by the Defence authorities.

President Yar'Adua, it would seem, was obviously thrilled by the unexpected gesture of Tom Ateke, a militant hardliner who had severally engaged the men of JTF in shooting wars with resultant loss of uncountable lives and property. It is instructive to note that Ateke is one of the dangerous militant leaders on the wanted lists of both the JTF and Rivers State Government.

In a rare display of statesmanship, Yar'Adua welcomed the decision of Ateke and promised to personally receive him and other of his compatriots if they would make good their intentions to lay down their arms. He noted as follows:

"I am highly delighted by this news that one of the militant leaders is prepared to accept the granting of amnesty by government. In fact, I would hope that all militant leaders will do the same.

"We are not fighting; we are all Nigerians and what we are trying to do is to guarantee peace and security in the Niger Delta just like in any other part of Nigeria so that people can live, work, carry on their normal duties without fear within the region so that the region and the State can realize the great potentials for attracting foreign direct investments and boosting economic activities…I will personally make public all the conditions, procedures and mechanisms for the amnesty. The amnesty center that will be established, the procedures for granting the amnesty, documentation, camping, training, rehabilitation, getting jobs; for those who require education, sending them to school, all the terms will be made public.

"I will welcome any leader, in fact, I might make bold to say that it will be a great pleasure for me to personally accept the first militant leader who takes advantage of this amnesty to encourage others to do so, so that they can have confidence that we are sincere and honest in granting of this amnesty".

We have gone this length in quoting Mr. President to be able to capture and properly situate his mindset on the lingering crisis in the Niger Delta that had posed serious security and economic challenges to the nation. The remarks clearly indicate a strong desire and commitment of this administration to conclusively resolve the crisis.

Reading carefully the lips of the President, it appears obvious that he has shown some good faith. This demonstrable display of Presidential good faith and goodwill is highly commendable as it will go a long way in building confidence in the system; a necessary precondition for securing the trust of the militants who might be unsure and apprehensive on the true fate that awaits them should they accept the amnesty.

The Niger Delta crisis has been a long drawn one which started a few years ago as a legitimate agitation by the neglected people of the oil rich region for resource control and political empowerment. The struggle, however, took a dangerous dimension when criminal gangs, masquerading as freedom fighters, hijacked the process. Their nefarious activities have blurred the initial noble objectives of the struggle, brought incalculable disaster to the people of the region and economy of the nation while posing a potent threat to the sovereignty of Nigeria.

As at press time, the government has kick started the process for granting the amnesty. The President has held a very high level security meeting with Vice President Goodluck Jonathan, Governors of the Niger Delta States, top Defence Chiefs and Chairman of the Amnesty and

Disarmament Committee, Brig. Gen. Godwin Abbe (rtd) in attendance to discuss and work out the modalities for the amnesty. A few other measures had since been taken by Government in furtherance of President Yar`Adua`s desire to secure an enabling environment for the implementation of the amnesty and disarmament.

The Chairman of the Amnesty Committee, Brig. Gen. Abbe and Inspector General of Police, Mr. Mike Okiro, a few days ago undertook an exploratory visit to Port Harcourt, Rivers State where they met and discussed with representatives of the various militia groups operating in the Niger Delta on the amnesty package. The fears and concerns of the militants were reportedly allayed by the Federal Government delegation which also gave assurances on the sincerity of Government. Following the success recorded at the meeting, some of the militant leaders were reported to have offered to surrender the arms in their posesion well ahead of the formal take off of the amnesty.

The Council of State, the highest national advisory body consisting of former Heads of States, Senate President, Speaker of the House of Representatives and serving Governors, was as at press time, being expected to make its inputs into the amnesty package in line with the President's determination to consult broadly and widely on the matter.

It is being expected that after the meeting of the Council of State, Government would make public the entire package, specifying the procedures and the timelines for implementation of the amnesty. Available information suggests that President Yar`Adua was ready to go the extra mile to ensure that comprehensive peace is achieved in the troubled region.

Part of the deal, it was gathered, is a proposal to grant unconditional pardon for the leader of the Movement for the Emancipation of the Niger Delta (MEND), Henry Okah who is currently facing treason charges at a Federal High Court in Jos, and other militant leaders like Ateke Tom and Tompolo who was declared wanted by JTF in the wake of the search and rescue operations in Gbaramatu Kingdom in Delta State. It is apposite to note that one of the persistent demands of MEND and other fighting groups in the Niger Delta and on which they predicated their condition for cessation of hostilities was the unconditional release of Okah from prison.

From every indication, President Yar`Adua has exhibited a very high sense of statesmanship and magnanimity in the way and manner he has handled the Niger Delta crisis so far. He has extended enough carrot to the militants. This is the time for the militants to reciprocate the good gestures by dropping their arms and taking full advantage of the amnesty so that they can meaningfully re-integrate themselves back to the civil society.

No useful purpose would be served by the continued intransigence of the militants and their backers. The region has seen enough of bloodshed, misery and wanton destructions. This is the time to open up a new chapter in the story of the Niger Delta.

The strategies for addressing the developmental challenges of the region are already well documented. The Government must, as a matter of urgency, revisit the recommendations of the Ledum Mittee Presidential Technical Committee on Niger Delta Development and commence their implementation without further delay.

We should not lose sight of the fact that the inhuman condition and squalor of the area, in spite of the fact that the bulk of the nation's wealth is derived from there, are at the heart of the ongoing war of destructions in the region. Government, as part of the total package to end the crisis, must demonstrate concrete commitment towards the accelerated development of the region.

We know that there is in existence the Niger Delta Development Commission (NDDC), an interventionist agency put in place by the Obasanjo administration to address the Niger Delta question. The Commission is making efforts in tackling the developmental challenges in the region. But given its configuration, it is not in the best position to transform the region. The creation of the Niger Delta Ministry by the Yar'Adua administration is also a welcome development to the extent that it shall be the potent vehicle for delivering infrastructural development to the region.

But above all what the Government must do as a matter of urgency is to move in multinational construction giants into the region with a mandate to transform the area like Abuja which was developed from the scratch with oil resources. This should be followed with a program aimed at the massive employment of the idle youths, most of who were recruited as foot soldiers by the militia leaders. In deed, what is required is a sort of Marshal Plan, with timelines for the speedy and orderly development of the region. The people of Niger Delta do not deserve anything less.

Such a programmed approach to the development of the region will go a long way in healing the wounds in the area which had festered for decades and engendering lasting peace and harmony.

The useful lesson in the Niger Delta saga is that we do not have to wait until a genuine grievance of any section of Nigeria snowballs out of control before we start seeking remedies. Government should therefore build on the current peaceful efforts in the Niger Delta by engaging other genuinely aggrieved groups in the country. In this regard, Ralph Uwazurike and his MASSOB should be engaged in a dialogue with a view to addressing their grievances.

I don't think that the group is campaigning for the dismemberment of the Nigerian Federation. On the contrary, I think they are trying to draw attention to the structural marginalization of Ndigbo since after the unfortunate civil war by successive federal authorities. Their pacifist approach is evident in their non recourse to violence.

Providence has brought all the various ethnic groups in Nigeria together as one nation. By pooling together our collective strengths and endowments, we will make Nigeria a better place for all. We must therefore support President Yar`Adua in his present effort to provide an alternative path to national development through the Seven-Point Agenda.

ThisDay, June 30, 2009

Chapter 28

Ogbulafor and the PDP Elders' Committee

Given the unending intra-party conflicts, majority of which is self-inflicted, that have continued to dog the ruling Peoples Democratic Party (PDP) and its penchant to appropriate to itself leading members of the existing opposition parties in the country, it was generally feared before now that the party may witness an implosion. It was further speculated that its predilection towards crises upon crises may result in an act of self immolation.

It was not surprising, therefore, when a former National Chairman of the Party, Chief Audu Ogbe, overwhelmed by the wars of attrition within the party fold, described the PDP as a rally; a contraption of sort, consisting of many political strange bed fellows. Many political observers were of the opinion that the inherent contradictions within the system would generate enough conflicting realities that would result into the ultimate dislocation of the PDP.

In spite of these predictions of doom and calamity, the ruling PDP undoubtedly has continued to weather the storm. Given so many measures which the party has taken in recent times to reposition and re-launch itself on the path of sanity, development and progress, it must be acknowledged that the leadership of Prince Vincent Eze Ogbulafor has given a new lease of life and sense of direction to the party, reputed as the largest in Africa.

When Ogbulafor emerged early last year as the consensus Chairman of the Party, after heated and vigorous electioneering campaigns in which Chief Anyim Pius Anyim, former Senate President and Dr. Sam Egwu, former Governor of Ebonyi State, were seen as the frontrunners, not many political pundits gave the Umuahia prince any chance of making any difference in the affairs of the party.

His emergence upset a lot of calculations within the party and shocked so many political observers who never for once looked in his direction. There is no doubt that his ascendancy in the party is an act of Providence.

Ogbulafor, to the surprise of his critics, has continued to confound and astound Nigerians with the stellar performance he has shown so far in the office. From some of the actions he has taken, he has been able to prove that he has the vision and the political capacity to turn the fortunes of the party around.

Some of us who are his kinsmen are quite proud of the dynamic and pragmatic leadership which he has clearly demonstrated in running the affairs of the largest party in Africa. Some of the actions he has taken have been courageous and politically correct.

His decision, upon assumption of office, to pursue the vigorous implementation of the recommendations of the Dr. Alex Ekwueme Reconciliation Committee, showed Ogbulafor as a leader that is independent-minded and endowed with innate capacity to withstand political pressures. After Dr. Ekwueme had submitted the report of his Committee to the party, then under the leadership of Dr. Ahmadu Ali, the exponent of garrison politics, there were spirited efforts by some top party shots that were not disposed to some of the key recommendations contained in the report to kill it.

It will be recalled that one of those recommendations was the rejection of the illegal amendment to the PDP Constitution that allowed former President Olusegun Obasanjo to become the life Chairman of the Board of Trustees (BOT) of the party. That amendment which was procured through subterfuge by Obasanjo and his henchmen when he was still calling the shots from Aso Rock also transferred most of the powers of the National Chairman of the party and vested same in the BOT chair.

The amendment clearly detracted from the visions of the founding fathers of PDP who conceived the BOT as the moral authority of the party which would exist to ensure that the party does not deviate from its core principles and ethos. That Committee also recommended that those who were forced out of the party on the account of the exclusionist policies of the Obasanjo-Ali era must be recalled and reconciled with the party which they helped in founding.

That infamous amendment has since been reversed under the superintendence of Prince Ogbulafor. To his credit most of the founding fathers who left the party on principle or were forced to leave have returned to the fold.

The resolve of Ogbulafor and members of his National Working Committee to pursue the implementation of the Ekwueme Committee

Report to the letter, in spite of pressures from very powerful figures in the party, shows a stubborn insistence on principles, a rare commodity before now in the party.

This brings us to the decision of Prince Ogbulafor to set up an Elders' Committee, charged with the responsibility of resolving conflicts where they exist in the various State chapters of the party. The 14-member Committee which has Senator Ike Nwachukwu as the Chairman was last week inaugurated by Ogbulafor at the party's National Headquaters, Abuja.

A careful look at the composition of the Committee shows that they are men and women of substance with sufficient clout to achieve lasting reconciliation and unity in the States where the party suffers from fragmentation and fractiousness. They include the following: Professor Jerry Gana, former BOT Secretary; Governor Danjuma Goje of Gombe State; Alhaji Dahiru Mangal and Ignatius Ajuru.

Others are Alhaji Shuaib Oyedokun, former Deputy National Chairman of the party, Governor Gabriel Suswam of Benue State; Chief James Ibori, former Governor of Delta State; Senator Anyim Ude, Chairman, Senate Committee on Aviation; Hon. Dave Salako, Chairman, House Committee on Communications; Chief Ebenezer Babatope, a former Minister of Transport under the Abacha regime; Mrs. Herberta Okonofua and Hajia Zainab Maina, former President, National Council of Women Societies (NCWS), with Dr. Musa Babayo as Secretary.

Speaking at the inauguration, Ogbulafor noted the importance of the Committee to the party and President Yar'Adua, and urged the members to work very hard to ensure that the party achieved unity within its fold as it would be dangerous for it to go into the 2011 General Elections as a divided body. The Chairman of the Committee, Ike Nwachukwu, in his response, identified unbridled ego and arrogance on the part of some leaders who place their self interests above that of the party as one of the factors responsible for the crises that exist within the party. Above all, he pledged the resolve of the Committee to realize its mandate.

The work of the Committee is, by no means, going to be easy as a good number of the State chapters of the party are embroiled in serious crises, with some assuming intractable status. The States that will greatly task the mental faculties of the Committee include Anambra, Oyo, Plateau, Borno, Lagos, Akwa Ibom, Kano and Edo.

Of all these, Anambra will prove a very serious nut to crack, given the deepening cleavages in the party arising from conflicting claims on the leadership and structures of the party in the State by two equally formidable factions led separately by Uche Emodi and Ivy Obi-Okoye.

Previous efforts to resolve the crisis failed to yield any dividends. One of such efforts was the Jim Nwobodo Action Committee and the Jerry Gana Peace and Reconciliation Committee variously instituted by Ogbulafor to bring enduring peace to Anambra PDP. All the efforts came to naught as none of the warring groups was willing to shift grounds.

Without pre-empting the Ike Nwachukwu Committee, the only viable option for peace to return to the party in Anambra is the dissolution of the feuding groups and constitution of a broad based Caretaker Committee which must reflect all the contending interests in the State. Any other solution short of this is a sure recipe for electoral disaster in the State.

A similar formula may be applied in other States facing intractable leadership crises. This is about the only way the party may be able to forge unity before the next elections.

Prince Ogbulafor, by taking this initiative, has proven himself as a man with high sense of clairvoyance and having a keen eye on history. From the way he is going, posterity will judge him fairly.

ThisDay, July 7, 2009

Chapter 29

Taming the Upsurge in Kidnapping

The country is undoubtedly under siege by kidnappers. The impunity and audacity with which they carry out their work is, indeed, very worrisome. It would appear as if the North and Kaduna in particular, are the preferred destinations of kidnapers. I was born in this great cosmopolitan city; so I should know what the situation used to be in its glorious days.

The only negative side to this city prior to the deadly incursions of kidnappings is the periodic eruptions of ethno-religious crises that have come to define social existence in the area. Even at that, the series of the politically motivated religious crises were a later day phenomena which were unknown to the city until in the 1980s.

But lately, this beautiful city that is regarded as the melting pot of diverse cultures has come under siege by kidnappers, armed robbers and other criminal elements. To say that the situation has reached a frightening dimension is nothing but stating the obvious fact.

What started as a localized and isolated problem in the Niger Delta region has steadily grown in intensity and beyond the borders of the oil-rich region and South East geo-political zone, the two areas where the crime had become endemic, to other parts of Nigeria that were initially assumed to be immune to the kidnapping syndrome.

The first recorded case of high profile kidnapping in the North, involving a visiting Rotarian on an exchange programme, Mrs. Anne Mulligan, a Canadian, took place in Kaduna a few months ago. It was a most embarrassing moment for the country, given the diplomatic dimension to it.

To the credit of the State Security Service in Kaduna State, the abducted Canadian was freed from captivity whilst some of the perpetrators of the crime were nabbed in a painstaking and well-coordinated security operation in which the operatives were able to showcase a very high level of professionalism.

With the successful bursting of the kidnapping ring, it was erroneously thought that the city of Kaduna would become a no-go area for these agents of Lucifer. On the contrary, the incidents of kidnapping would seem to have become the order of the day in this once serene and cosmopolitan centre. Even Kano, the commercial nerve center of the North and Zaria, the intellectual hotbed of the North, located in the north of Kaduna have also not been spared the menace.

Only recently the Secretary to the State Government (SSG), Mr. Waje Yayok was kidnapped by unknown gun men and taken to an unknown destination, which later turned out to be Warri in Delta State. The kidnappers were reported to have placed a ransom of N40 million on his head shortly after his abduction.

Although the gang reportedly agreed to N15 million as the least amount in their negotiations with the authorities, the SSG, unfortunately, was held incommunicado, with anxiety and tension mounting among the family members over the health of their bread winner.

The initial reactions by the Police and Kaduna State Government to the incident when the news broke in the press were very unhelpful and disappointing to say the least. The State Commissioner of Police, Alhaji Tambari Mohammed, who was intimated with the development shortly after it had occurred, reportedly refused to confirm the abduction, saying that the SSG, in spite of the report of kidnapping by the family, would not be declared missing until after 48 hours. This is unimpressive. No matter whichever law the Police was quoting to justify its sluggish response to the abduction of such a high level government functionary, the situation was an emergency which required a swift response from the Police and other relevant security agencies.

The worst culprit was the Special Adviser to the State Governor on Media and Public Affairs, Alhaji Umar Sani whose reactions on behalf of the Government were both reckless and unprofessional. He first denied the abduction story, saying that the SSG was on official assignment to the southern part of the State and would get in touch with the Government to allay the growing fears over his whereabouts.

His words: "While it is true that the SSG was on official assignment to the southern part of Kaduna, we are yet to get in contact with him over his supposed location. We believe he will get in contact with us soon…The security agencies have the details of the place, the nature of the assignment and all his contact details to enable them trace his whereabouts and douse the tension created by such rumours".

He further noted that he did not believe the N40 million demand until the kidnappers got in touch with the State Government, adding that the family members of the SSG were "raising dust unnecessarily". The facts that have since emerged clearly indicated that the SSG, who had since be released, was abducted in Kaduna metropolis on the night he went out to distribute invitation cards for the forthcoming wedding ceremony of his daughter. This contradicted the position of the Special Adviser.

While the riddle surrounding the abduction of the SSG was yet to be unraveled, gun men again struck in Zaria, kidnapping a wealthy businessman, Alhaji Bala Bello, from his residence. He was released a few days later after the family had met the financial demands of the kidnappers.

Besides these highbrow cases, there were other incidents in Kaduna, Kano, Zaria and other parts of the North that had gone largely unreported. There was a case of an abducted woman whose husband was thought to be rich. She was reportedly taken to Abuja from Kaduna and dumped there, when the kidnappers realized that the husband was a poor civil servant.

And just last week too, many incidents of kidnappings were reported in Benin City, Edo State and parts of Abia, Anambra and Rivers States. In the instant case of Benin City, a former Chairman of Nigerian Bar Association (NBA), Mr. Solomon Odiase and the aged parents of the ex-Chairman of Ovia North-East LGA, Mr. Faustine Ovienroba were kidnapped at separate incidents. It is very worrisome, that in our own country, in our own villages and homes, we no longer feel safe. It is a tragedy that must be quickly addressed by concerned authorities at all levels.

The essence of government any where in the world is to protect lives and property. It is stipulated clearly in Section 14(b) of the 1999 Constitution of the Federal Republic of Nigeria that "the security and welfare of the people shall be the primary purpose of government". The government of President Yar`Adua, therefore, owes it as a constitutional responsibility to protect Nigerians and other foreigners resident in the country from the continued menace of kidnappers.

Now that the problem is no longer a localized one, the President should declare a state of emergency in the area of security and roll out all the necessary arsenals required in apprehending the dangerous trends.

The urgency of the situation on hand is such that calls for an international summit on terrorism by the Federal Government with a view to sharing information and ideas with countries that have gone through this type of experience and dealt successfully with it.

In the interim, the Federal and State governments must come up with measures in which serious sanctions must be applied against any village head, traditional ruler, Divisional Police Officer (DPO) and Council Chairman in whose domain kidnappings occur.

As a remedial measure also, the government at all levels must assist the Police by ensuring that they are properly equipped and motivated to rise to the occasion. Recently, the Inspector General of Police, Ogbonnaya Onovo, disclosed that the Police was in the process of acquiring portable electronic devices that intelligently gather and rapidly intercept phone calls from kidnappers. It was gathered that the device has the capability of tracking within minutes, the very spot from where suspicious telephone calls are made. The facility is said to be an Israeli technology.

The government should not delay any further in making sure that the Nigerian Police acquires this device in large numbers and deploy same immediately. This, perhaps, may be the solution to the menace of kidnapping. The country has been scandalised enough. Yar`Adua must act now, before it gets too late.

ThisDay, October 13, 2009

Chapter 30

Fasttracking the Amnesty Deal

The Umar Musa Yar`Adua administration, as a matter of fact has not measured well in public estimation as a result of what is widely acknowledged as its intrepid and half-hearted approach to governance. Such an unfancied style has ensured that the administration moves at a snail speed. It is therefore hardly surprising that some critics have dubbed the Yar`Adua administration a sleeping government.

The supporters of the government, however, give a different interpretation to this negative branding. For them, President Yar`Adua is being cautious and careful not to repeat the mistakes of the past administrations. According to them, he takes his time to think through and weigh policy options before arriving at conclusive decisions. Such an approach implies that the President has to do a lot of planning and cross-checking of facts.

The President admitted this much when, at a press interview he granted a section of the Nigerian media to mark his first anniversary in office, he said that he had used the preceding one year to plan and formulate policies and that the coming years would witness action.

He further re-echoed this in his 48th Independence broadcast to the nation on 1st October, 2008 when he said: "We are resolved as an administration, not to resort to quick fix methods and short cuts in approaching fundamental problems which require methodical and sustainable solutions. The review of key sectors of our national economy, which we have embarked upon so far, points to the wisdom of this approach."

Two and half years on the saddle the jury is yet to be out on whether the President has kept faith with his promise. Although the experience with the public is that of rising expectations and declining performance, the administration cannot be out rightly dismissed for non-performance.

The administration has to its credit a few remarkable achievements that compel acknowledgement. There is relative stability in the relationship between the Executive and the Legislature, a vast improvement on the adversarial relationship that existed between his immediate predecessor and the National Assembly.

Under Yar'Adua's watch, Nigeria has been elected to join the club of "big boys" at the United Nations as a non-permanent member of the Security Council. Although Nigeria had been similarly elected into that position on three previous occasions in the past, the implication of this current election is that our country, under the leadership of Yar'Adua is still a force to reckon with in the international arena, our domestic problems notwithstanding. No matter whatever critics may say to the contrary, the election of Nigeria into the Security Council of the United Nations, is a remarkable development.

The greatest achievement of the Yara'Adua administration to date is the amnesty deal which has resulted in the cessation of hostilities in the volatile Niger Delta region and the gradual return of peace and normalcy. This is no mean achievement. It is surprising President Yar'Adua has not received commensurate accolades in the media for this significant feat. It is an achievement that deserves national and international celebration.

The President has shown the world that we are capable of resolving our domestic problems, no matter how intractable they may prove to be.

Using dialogue and diplomacy, President Yar'Adua has been able to get the heavily armed militant groups in the region to surrender their weapons of mass destruction and embrace peace without declaring war in the region.

Past leaders before him tried to use the force of arms to suppress the agitations in the Niger Delta but to no avail. Yar'Adua's approach of constructive dialogue and peaceful engagement which has yielded positive dividends is in deed a potent strategy which marks him out as a man driven by an inner wisdom and sound judgment.

The real challenge of ensuring peace in the Niger Delta region on a sustainable basis, however, lies in the actions the President will have to take in the aftermath of the amnesty deal.

So far, the President has shown enough commitment in driving the amnesty process to a successful conclusion. The recent direct meetings he had with the former militant leaders in the Presidential Villa, Abuja, to my mind, is a good confidence building measure which will go a long way in fostering a climate of mutual understanding for meaningful development to take place.

Given the sincerity of purpose which the President has demonstrated in the pursuit of the amnesty, the militants and other stakeholders in the region are no longer in doubt as to the commitment of Yar'Adua to ensure that justice is done to the people of the region.

The President must, therefore, endeavour to see that the next phase of the amnesty deal which has to do with the re-integration and rehabilitation of the repentant militants proceeds immediately without any encumbrances. This is a very critical phase in the entire amnesty deal. The way and manner the matter is handled will determine to a great extent whether the peace that has been won is durable or that of the grave yard.

History, however, beckons on Yar'Adua to push the amnesty programme beyond irreversible limits. Now that the militants and other violent agitators in the region have laid down their arms in response to the amnesty offer, it is incumbent on the Yar'Adua administration to commence without further delay the massive social and economic reconstruction, rehabilitation and transformation of the region for the benefits of the people in the area.

All the recommendations of the previous panels that looked into the problems of the Niger Delta should be re-visited, particularly the Ledum Mitte's panel, and implemented in a holistic and methodical manner. This will go a long way in assuaging the feelings of the people of the area who for many years have remained marginalized and deprived by the nation which gets the bulk of its wealth from the region.

While the government is proceeding with the re-integration and rehabilitation programme, reputable construction giants should be immediately commissioned and handed over the Niger Delta Master Plan as articulated by the NDDC to commence the development of infrastructure in all the communities in the region. The standard of infrastructure that is in Abuja is attainable in the Niger Delta, the complexity of the terrain notwithstanding.

It is in deed reassuring to note that the President has set aside the sum of $950 million, which is the Federal Government's share of the $2 billion stimulus package released into the economy for the kick-off of post amnesty public works in the region. It is gathered that this is a "down payment" or first instalment in Yar'Adua's overall post-amnesty package to accelerate development in the region after many years of youth restiveness.

Also in line with the expectations of the people of the Niger Delta, the President has approved that 10 percent of equities must be reserved for communities in which oil exploration and exploitation activities are taking place. This is already incorporated into the Petroleum Industry Bill that is currently receiving attention by the National Assembly.

If all these efforts are properly coordinated and backed with the requisite political will, the Niger Delta will become an oasis of peace and development. And there would be no basis for further violent agitations in the region.

_____

ThisDay, October 27, 2009

Chapter 31

The Fall of Olabode George

The unexpected happened last week in Lagos as soccer-loving Nigerians were engrossed with the on-going U-17 FIFA Football World Tournament in the country. When the news came, it was unbelievable. Lo and behold, the reality has dawned on every one in the land. The conviction and sentencing of Chief Olabode George, the powerful and loquacious PDP chieftain to 28 years imprisonment by an Ikeja High Court presided over by Justice Olubunmi Oyewole came like a thunderbolt from the blues.

This rare news immediately reminded one of the heart-rending lamentations of David following the death of Jonathan in the hands of the Philistines led by Goliath: "How are the mighty fallen! Tell it not in Gath, publish it not in the streets of Ashkelon; lest the daughters of the Philistines rejoice, lest the daughters of the uncircumcised triumph... And the weapons of war perished."

The current travails of George had its genesis in the libel suit he instituted against The News magazine, based in Lagos, which had exposed his alleged malfeasance at Nigeria Ports Authority (NPA) where he held sway as Board Chairman between 2001 and 2003. The magazine's report was anchored on the indictment of George by the EFCC which investigated his activities in NPA.

The libel suit prompted the EFCC to revisit the matter which many Nigerians thought had been swept under the carpet. George and five others were accused and subsequently arraigned on a 68-count charge bordering on N84 billion fraud at the NPA.

In the judgment that lasted over three hours, Justice Olubunmi Oyewole sentenced George and the other five co-accused for abuse of office and disobedience of lawful order. Thus marked the journey of infamy into Kirikiri Maximum Prison for George! How are the mighty fallen!

Given the rarity of such an occurrence in this clime and the far-reaching implications which this landmark judicial development holds for the country, the story will not only be told in Gath, it has already been published beyond the streets of Ashkelon. And therefore, let the weapons of war perish!

The responses and reactions by various organized groups in the country have been very instructive. The judgment is hailed widely as being courageous, bold and forthright. It is no wonder that the Economic and Financial Crimes Commission (EFCC) is receiving kudos for securing the conviction of this man who, within the eight-year reign of the immediate past Obasanjo administration, was an untouchable.

A civil society group, Socio-Economic Rights and Accountability Project (SERAP) described the judgment as "an important development in the fight against political corruption and impunity of perpetrators in the country" while the Afenifere Renewal Group (ARG), a foremost Yoruba socio-political organization hailed the verdict as "a bold judicial pronouncement".

The Conference of Nigerian Political Parties (CNPP), an umbrella organization for opposition political parties in Nigeria gave thumps up to the judiciary, saying that the judgment has rejuvenated the comatose war on corruption. A statement endorsed by Osita Okechukwu, the spokesman of the group, noted: "It is our considered view that the judgment served the cause of justice and most importantly, the anti-graft war, which is almost dead".

A Lagos lawyer and human rights activist, Festus Keyamo who was the EFCC prosecutor commended the EFCC for the diligent prosecution of the case. His words: "This is the first full trial conducted in respect of a public officer as regards charges bordering on corruption since the establishment of the EFCC".

Like William Shakespeare in Julius Caesar, it could be said of Olabode George that "he doth bestrides the world like a colossus, so that we petty men can walk under his huge legs and find for ourselves dishonourable graves". At the height of his power, which has now become transient, George, with the backing of former President Obasanjo, bestrode the political landscape, particularly, the South West of Nigeria like a tin god.

Within his party, he brooked no opposition. Those who dared challenged him, have bitter stories to tell. He was said to have stepped on so many toes as he worked his way to becoming the pre-eminent political czar in the South West PDP. Those who tasted the bitter side of the man were many. We can ask Senator Adeseye Ogunlewe, former Minister of

Works; Anthony Adefuye, a Third Republic Senator who once nursed the ambition of governing Lagos State and Senator Musliu Obanikoro, former governorship candidate of the PDP in Lagos State and current Nigeria's High Commissioner to Ghana.

It is against this background that the media celebration of the imprisonment of Bode George should be appreciated. He carried on as if he was bigger than the State and above the law. I remember clearly when upon arrival from a holiday abroad sometime ago, he boasted to reporters at the Murtala Muhammed Airport, Ikeja who hinted him that the EFCC was looking for him, that "nobody can arrest me".

This, at once, was a clear demonstration of unbridled arrogance and impunity for which George was known. He thought he was still living in a fool's paradise. He didn't know that the times have changed with the change of batons at the Aso Rock Villa.

Under Yar'Adua and his rule of law dispensation, present and past public officers must be held accountable for their actions and inactions.

With the conviction and imprisonment of George, a major victory has been achieved with the war against corruption and impunity in high places. The judiciary has again demonstrated fearlessness, courage and forthrightness.

There is thus no more hiding places for today's and tomorrow's tin gods whose only relevance is that they exercise ascribed power. Today's power brokers have a lesson to pick from the travails of George. There will always be a day of reckoning. It may be soon; it may be later. But surely there is no running away from justice.

Like President Barrak Obama said when he visited neighbouring Ghana a few months ago, "the challenge of democracy in Africa lies in building strong institutions instead of strong men". With the conviction and imprisonment of a high profile politician like George, this country must begin to strengthen all its democratic institutions so as to ensure that the rule of law rather than the rule of the thumbs prevails at all times.

ThisDay, November 3, 2009

Chapter 32

The Changing Face of Kaduna

In a recent article where I expressed concern and revulsion at the growing menace of kidnappings and abductions in Kaduna, I, in passing, noted that my sentimental attachment to this cosmopolitan city is rooted in the fact that it is my place of birth. As a child growing up in the city before the unfortunate Nigeria-Biafra war, Kaduna was great in all its ramifications. It was a meeting point of various heterogonous groups, coming from different corners of the country.

There was deep and great bonding amongst these diverse groups; and they co-existed peacefully. People were going about their normal businesses and practicing their faiths without let or hindrance. Kaduna was in deed the real center of Nigerian unity. Till date, I still cherish my childhood memories of this wonderful city.

It is therefore only natural that one would always show some concern when there is any development in the city, negative or positive.

Nevertheless, I am not ready to give up on my optimism about the promise which this city still holds as a melting pot of diverse Nigerian cultures. This is why, at any given opportunity, one would not shy away from engaging in any social discourse on the continued challenges and prospects of this great city that was once famous for its wild crocodiles.

I visited Kaduna a few days ago, a little more than two years after my last trip to the area on the campaign train of a National Chairmanship aspirant of the PDP in which I was privileged to serve as Publicity Director. The face and story of the city that I met a few days ago are totally different from what they were two years ago.

I must confess right away that the Kaduna that I saw recently is a city that is fast diminishing in infrastructure and social profile. Some critics are wont to disagree with me, but, in keeping with democratic norms, I am entitled to my opinion.

In spite of the professed commitment of the current administration in the State led by Governor Namadi Sambo to reposition the State and its capital city for the better, Kaduna has become a shadow of its old bubbling self. The decadence can be felt all over the place as one moved from one part of the city to another.

There is no place where the decay is more pronounced than the popular Ahmadu Bello Way. The road presents its own different and difficult challenges as it is perpetually congested, thereby effectively imposing serious constraints on the free movement of people. Also lamentable is the fact that most of the big businesses that had their corporate offices along the Ahmadu Bello Way have either closed shops or relocated elsewhere.

The few that still maintain their presence in the city, it would appear, only provide skeletal services. The affected organizations include GB Ollivant; Kingsway; UTC Stores; Chellarams; United Nigeria Textile Limited (UNTL) amongst many others. Some major public buildings on the Ahmadu Bello are in deed in an advanced state of decay. Not forgetting the Durbar Hotel on Waff Road. This once imposing edifice was built the same time with the Durbar Hotel in Festac, Lagos which has transformed into Festac '77 Hotel. The two hotels were built and commissioned in 1977 to accommodate thousands of the Blacks in the Diaspora who thronged the country for the 2nd World Black Festival of Arts and Culture, otherwise known as FESTAC '77.

While the Festac Hotel in Lagos is still functional, its counterpart, Durbar Hotel in Kaduna is a complete wreck. The once majestic edifice that dictated the social pace in the city, today lies prostrate and fully stripped. It was gathered that a former Head of State appropriated the property to himself. But whatever the situation is concerning the ownership of the hotel today, the Kaduna State Government has a responsibility to take a quick decision in the environmental and security interest of the people of the State.

Most of the roads in the metropolis are in terrible state of disrepair. The popular Nnamdi Azikiwe bye-pass that links the city to Zaria and Kano is in very bad shape. So also is the network of intra city roads that connects the major highways such as Ahmadu Bello Way, Constitution Road, Junction Road, Independence Road, Waff Road, Rabah Road and Golf Course Road. All these roads without any exception are in very dilapidated state.

The beautifully constructed and decorated roundabouts on the major streets of Kaduna which were the hallmarks of the defunct military administration of Sarki Muktar are being poorly maintained to the extent that some of them now serve as a place of rendezvous for street urchins.

A few of the roundabouts which, by their original alluring design and set-up, are major tourist attractions, received some renovations on account of the fact that Kaduna is a host center for the on-going world youth tournament in the country.

But most of these roundabouts including the very one in front of the Ahmadu Bello Stadium are in various stages of degradation. These monuments, like other landmark infrastructure that mark Kaduna out from other cities in the country are not supposed to be left so carelessly in the lurch. A little effort by the concerned authorities would have made a great difference.

In spite of the increasing tempo in the deterioration of general infrastructure in the State, the greatest problem facing Kaduna however lies in the unseen bifurcation of the city into two mutually exclusive enclaves controlled separately by Christians and Moslems, each of them seeking to maintain a firm grip on the levers of political power at all cost. The series of tragedies and sectarian crises that had been the lot of the city in the recent past have helped to turn Kaduna into a divided city like Jerusalem and Beirut in the Middle East.

In the balkanized city, majority of the Muslim residents are domiciled in the Northern part while the bulk of the Christians including the indigenous tribes from the Southern part of the State and those referred to as stranger elements, mainly from the Southern tribes in the country reside in the southern half of Kaduna. It is the River Kaduna that physically separates the two enclaves.

My enquiries revealed that this unfortunate development was the outcome of various sectarian and ethnic clashes that had continued to define social relations in the city particularly in the aftermath of the horrendous Sharia killings in the year 2000. From my interactions with the people, it is obvious that fear and uncertainty still rule the city.

It was noticed that once it was getting late in the day, residents scampered towards their own side of the divide where they feel more secured. This is notwithstanding the fact that so many military institutions are located in the city and State.

The social demarcation of the city, even if inadvertent, has exposed the hatred and hypocrisy in the character of men. It beats my imagination that a once flourishing city has been so terribly diminished by those seeking to expand their territory of domination.

As a stakeholder in the Kaduna project, I wish to use this medium to appeal to all other stakeholders including the government of the day to come together in peace and concord and re-launch Kaduna back on the path of greatness. It is unacceptable to have Kaduna balkanized into Muslim and Christian enclaves. Kaduna must be retrieved from the grips of empire builders.

ThisDay, November 17, 2009

Chapter 33

Senate and the South-East Erosion

One of the major fall-outs of the recent annual retreat of the Senate staged in the serene and beautiful coal city of Enugu was the resolve of the upper legislative chamber to intervene in the horrendous environmental problems posed by erosion menace in the South East of Nigeria.

This, to me and other well meaning Nigerians, especially the teeming population in the South East who live daily at the mercy of dangerous gully erosions, is a very welcome development.

For several decades since after the civil war, the people of the South East have been shouting to whoever cared to listen that the area was gradually being eaten up by erosion. Several representations had been made to successive administrations at the Centre for their decisive intervention but to little or no avail.

To date, I stand to be contradicted, the only Federal administration that made tangible efforts to address the problem was that headed by Alhaji Shehu Shagari (1979-1983). President Shagari is on record to have visited the major erosion sites in then Imo and Anambra States controlled by the opposition Nigerian Peoples Party.

The sites he visited included Amucha in Imo and Nanka in Anambra. Touched by the magnitude of the havoc and disaster to human lives and settlements in those areas, Shagari wept profusely and there and then resolved to bring in the federal might to mitigate the problem. And he did.

By the time he returned to State House, Ribadu Road, Lagos, which was then the seat of power, concrete measures, through the award of contracts, were taken to address the problems.

Following the military coup that led to the overthrow of the Shagari administration in December 1983, the erosion control projects initiated by that government were stalled. The consequence of the criminal neglect by succeeding administrations is the monumental environmental disaster

141

which presently stares the entire geographical landscape of the five South Eastern States in the face without any exceptions.

Since after Shagari, no Head of State, dead or living, has personally undertaken an official trip to see for himself how erosion menace has forced fellow Nigerians in that part of the country to live in precarious situations.

It is against this background that one appreciates the concern expressed by the Senate-in-Retreat to give the erosion threats in the South East the national attention it deserves. It does not matter, whether the Senate was just pandering to the emotions of the people of the South East or not.

The notable point, however, is that the Distinguished Senators of the Federal Republic of Nigeria have actually and physically visited some of these erosion sites and seen first hand the tragedies which gully erosion poses to a significant population of Nigeria.

The team of Senators led by the Senate President, David Mark, to Imo State visited some of the most devastating sites including Njaba and the same Amucha erosion sites which Shagari similarly visited about 25 years ago. In Imo alone, the Senators were informed that the documented erosion sites are about 460.

In Anambra, the active erosion sites are more than a thousand. The Nanka-Oko-Ekwulobia sites can melt the most hardened of hearts. In this axis alone, many lives have been lost and several homes including ancestral places of worship swept away by frightening and creeping erosions.

In my home State of Abia, virtually every community is affected in one way or the other. The worst affected areas include Umuahia, Ikwuano, Ohafia, Isuikwuato, Abiriba, Igbere, Nkporo and parts of Arochuku. It is the same story in Enugu and Ebonyi States.

The control of these erosion sites is beyond the individual governments in the South East. It will require huge financial resource outlay to put the menace in total check. And it is only the Federal Government that has gotten the financial muscle to address the problem on a permanent basis. Any intervention on an ad-hoc basis cannot endure.

What is required is a Marshal Plan to tackle the problem frontally and holistically. To implement the plan, the Federal Government must seriously consider the setting up of a South East Erosion Control Commission (SEECC) with direct funding from the Federation Account.

Now that the Senators have gone to the East and seen for themselves the devastations that erosions have wrought on the various communities in the area, they are, presumably, now in a better position to give these proposed measures the desired push.

The ball is now in the court of the lawmakers from the South East to take up this challenge. There is no doubt that they will get good support from their colleagues from other geo-political zones who now appreciate that the danger of gully and sheet erosion is real.

And like the Deputy Senate President, Ike Ekweremadu stated at the Enugu Retreat, "if nothing urgent was done to address the development, the zone (South East) might be highly vulnerable to higher environmental degradation".

The Senate deserves commendation for taking the Retreat to East, and going beyond holding their deliberations there and moving to the affected erosion sites to see things for themselves. This is how it should be.

By this action, the Senate has proven to be an activist parliament. It is not just enough to sit in Abuja and pretend to be legislating for the good governance of the Federation without being acquainted with the problems of the people that elected you into power. There is wisdom in going beyond oversight duties in the Ministries and Parastatals and engaging the electorates in their natural habitat and knowing their problems.

It is only through such initiatives that our lawmakers will be in a better position to make laws that have direct and positive bearing to the lives of the people they represent.

ThisDay,November 24, 2009

Chapter 34

Media and National Security

The choice of my topic today, I must confess at the outset, is provoked by the presentation made by the Director General of the State Security Service (SSS), Afarkriya A. Gadzama at a recent national workshop organized by the Nigerian Press Council to appraise the conduct and performance of the Nigerian media in ensuring the enthronement of good governance.

The Executive Secretary of the Press Council, Mudashiru Bayo Atoyebi, in his welcome address, had set the tone of the deliberations by properly locating the context that accounts for the tension and adversity in the relationships between the media and security agencies in the country.

His words: "Those in governance must perceive Journalism as partners in advancing our common humanity. When journalism correlates its surveillance of the environment for our attention, those in government ought to be responsive…..While we seek information to publish as news, they (security agents) seek information to keep as intelligence".

The questions were then posed. In this circumstance where the two institutions are doing the same thing (information gathering) but from different professional perspectives, are the media and security agencies necessarily adversaries or partners? If they are partners, why then is the media always held in distrust by the security agencies?

These questions were squarely addressed by the Director General of the SSS in his paper which was ably delivered and defended by his representative, Marilyn Ogah, the spokesperson of the Security Service.

He stridently acknowledged the noble and robust role of the media in the political emancipation of Nigeria from colonial domination and its evolution as a nation-state. He further paid tribute to the media for complementing security agencies in promoting national stability and also aligning with the people against unjust and inequitable policies.

He noted: "…the unbiased and fearless work of the media ensured that the country's democracy and political progress was not undermined by parochial interests. In many occasions, desperate political and economic maneuverings were nullified following a wave of intense media activity carried out on behalf of the people".

Although he did not give any instances of the maneuverings, but the June 12 annulment by Babangida and the transmutation agenda of Abacha were classical examples of such desperate maneuverings which greatly threatened the security and unity of the country. The media as he rightly pointed out played outstanding roles in frustrating the devilish agenda.

This was where the accolades ended. Thereafter, the Director General came out smoking against the media, accusing it of being dominated by 'unpatriotic interest groups'.

From the weighty charges he levied against the media and its practitioners, it is very glaring that the Security and Intelligence Services still hold the media in deep suspicion and contempt. And for them, if it were possible to run the government without the 'irritating presence' of the media, they will go for it.

Or how else can one situate the following conclusions made by the DG: "The press has strongly emerged as a medium for advocacy yet that platform has been dominated by unpatriotic interest groups whose positions are devoid of any considerations for peace, stability and development. Rather, their primary allegiance is owed to any one who can afford them. Instead of the media remaining a platform for the people's needs to be projected, it is increasingly offering podiums for those who are ready to disparage economic, political and other form of opponents".

Then the bombshell: "In our general appraisals of the country's security profile, we have come to realize that one of the most potent threats against the country is the COLLAPSE OF THE MEDIA (emphasis mine). That collapse occurs when the form and direction of news is totally determined by pecuniary interests guided by those who wish to actualize selfish goals".

Let me quickly acknowledge that the media, like any other institution has its own share of the good, the bad and the ugly. The media in Nigeria has never laid any claim to infallibility. Therefore, there are bound to be some misfits in the profession. But it will be very dangerous for the entirety of the Nigerian media to be so demonized and denigrated by our own Security agencies for the actions of a few bad eggs within.

Adequate provisions exist in our Constitution and statute books to deal with any acts of infractions or malfeasance on the part of journalists or other professionals for that matter. In situations where it is evident that a journalist has overreached himself in the discharge of his duties, the law is there to take its course.

We cannot make separate punitive laws for the media simply because certain powerful persons in government are not comfortable with the watch dog role of the media.

The security agencies must begin to appreciate the media as major stakeholders in the Nigeria project and wean themselves of this mentality that the media is an agent of subversion and destabilization. Such an unjust labeling can neither promote development nor stability. We must do away with this notion that the media is populated by unpatriotic elements.

The point that must be quickly noted is that those in the security service of the nation are Nigerians like those practicing journalism. The earlier the security agents appreciate that Nigerian media professionals are not coming from the moon but from the various communities that make up the nation, the better for the orderly development of our country.

The Nigerian journalist is not an enemy and therefore should not be treated as one. The unhealthy relationship that exists between the media and the security agents has always derived from the perception of the average journalist as an enemy of the State.

The media and security people need each other to move the country forward since by their different callings they engage in information gathering. The two can share information and intelligence if need be, but the security agents must come to terms with the fact that for any journalist, the confidentiality of news or information source is sacrosanct. This is important to note because most times security agents would want to know the source of a media report. This has always been a major source of friction. However, we are bound by professional ethics to protect the source of our information whether it is obtained confidentially or not.

I believe there is hope for an improved and better relationship between the media and the security agencies. By even coming out from their cocoon to engage the media in a dialogue, the SSS under Gadzama has shown the direction to go. This is a positive development which will go a long way in enhancing national security.

Constant interactive exchanges like the one organized by the Press Council must be encouraged. By so doing, all grey areas that cause mistrust and distrust will be mutually addressed in the best interest of our nation.

ThisDay, December 8, 2009

Chapter 35

Still on 'Changing Face of Kaduna'

Exactly four weeks ago on this page I wrote on what I titled 'The Changing Face of Kaduna'. The motivation for the said piece came from my observations on physical and social developments in the city slightly more than two years after my last visit to the area.

I did not in the wildest of any imagination expect that the article written in good faith would attract the kind of vile vituperations as expressed in a response by one John Danfulani who claimed to be a Senior Special Assistant to the Executive Governor of Kaduna State.

I would not have bothered to waste my precious time to respond to him. The media being a market place for robust intellectual exchanges, views and opinions, no matter how truculent and divergent, are welcomed.

It is in keeping with such time-honoured intellectual tradition that I welcome the reaction of Mr. Danfulani to my piece. It is shocking, however, to note that some one who is supposedly a high-ranking official of Kaduna State Government would descend so low as to engaging in name name-calling and hurling personal abuses instead of competently addressing the issues raised for the benefit of his readers.

I am compelled to respond by the overriding public need to state the facts as they are and leaving readers to make their deductions.

Danfulani in a manner that suggested unseriousness, tried to make an issue out of the allusion to Kaduna as my birthplace. In his opening paragraph he noted: "Emeka Nwosu claimed that Kaduna was a place where his umbilical cord was buried many decades ago". This type of derogatory language, to say the least, is not what is expected of a government functionary wearing the garb of 'Senior Special Assistant to Governor'. By resorting to such banality, he only succeeded in cheapening the position he occupies and the office he speaks for.

He went further in subsequent paragraphs to query my motives and also accused me of harboring erroneous and biased opinion against the State Government. Even though he could not prove any of these, he still went ahead to charge me for engaging in a blackmail. I do not know the

148

background of Danfulani, but it is scandalous to brand people names when they share contrary opinions. A better and well rounded image maker in his position would have taken up all the issues in contention and counter them with facts, superior argument and sound logic. He would not resort to the use of intemperate and foul language because no argument can be won by resorting to such underhand tactics.

Whether I was born in Kaduna or not, I have the right as a free citizen of Nigeria to comment on the social condition of our country or any part thereof. As a journalist, this responsibility even becomes more compelling by virtue of the express provisions of Section 22 of the Constitution of the Federal Republic of Nigeria. If Danfulani does not know, this Section empowers the media to hold those in government accountable to the people.

The least any media professional can do under the circumstance is to point to those in authorities observed lapses and ineptitude in governance. And it is for them to take corrective measures in the overall best interest of the masses.

But people like Danfulani who are supposed to mirror the true feelings of the society to the powers that be, who most often are separated from reality, always fail to do so for very selfish and parochial reasons. The impression that is constantly given to 'His Excellency' is that he is doing very well and that the people are solidly behind him. This is where the journey to dictatorship and perdition begins.

Now, what are the issues that I raised which rankled the 'Senior Special Assistant' to the point of throwing caution to the wind?

The first point I noted in the 'provocative' piece is that the Kaduna that I saw on my recent trip was fast diminishing in infrastructure and social profile. And I went further to buttress the point with undeniable facts on the ground. And much as he tried in his abusive response, Danfulani could not disprove the factuality of my observations. Instead he resorted to buck passing and obfuscation tactics to confuse the reading public.

For instance, he admitted that the Nnamdi Azikiwe bye-pass, a major link road to Zaria and Kano, was in bad shape but tried to tutor me that it is a federal responsibility. Fine! But this vital road link serves primarily the people and residents of Kaduna. What stops the Kaduna State Government from fixing the road in the interest of the people that elected it into office and later seek refund from the concerned federal authorities?

149

Must the State Government wait endlessly for Abuja to the detriment of its populace?

Some State Governments, faced with similar circumstances, have acted proactively to save the lives of their people without waiting for the Center. The cases of Lagos and Abia States are quite instructive. Lagos under Fashola has rehabilitated several federal roads including the strategic Ikorodu highway.

Governor Theodore Orji of Abia similarly rehabilitated and dualized the Ossah-Umuahia federal road, the main gateway to the State capital. Some other State Governors are known to have done similar things. Why must Kaduna State Government wait for Aso Rock before it can fix that very important road?

I talked about the high profile companies including multinationals on the popular Ahmadu Bello Way and elsewhere that have closed shops. Danfulani's response is that the closures did not take place under Governor Namadi Sambo. And I did not say so either. But even at that, what efforts are being made by the State Government to attract back those companies and new ones to the State? Danfulani did not address that.

Now on the issue of the derelict Durbar Hotel, he agreed with me that in its present state, it poses serious environmental and security threats. He said that the State Government was restrained from taking action because of conflicting claims of ownership and multiple litigations on the property.

I quote him: "On the issue of Durbar hotel, the Ministry of Environment has waded into the matter two years ago but encountered hurdles due to multiplicity of litigations or claims of ownership". This reason, in my opinion, is not sufficient to dissuade any imaginative government from taking action. The Governor is protected under the Land Use Act to acquire any property in public interest and pay adequate compensation. Why has the Government not invoked this Act if it really believes that the Durbar Hotel, in its present state, constitutes an environmental and security threat to the people of the State? Must it wait for a calamity to occur before the matter is addressed?

I further observed that there is an unseen social bifurcation of Kaduna into two mutually exclusive enclaves controlled separately by Christians and Moslems. I lamented this sad development and likened Kaduna to Jerusalem and Beirut in the Middle East where such sectarian divisions exist. For me, the situation was unacceptable. In spite of accusing me of habouring a hidden agenda, he still tacitly acknowledged the division, but concluded that there was nothing wrong with that.

His words: "Beirut and Jerusalem are not the only divided city (sic) in the world. Sharp division existed in all the major world cities like Paris, Washington, London, Moscow, Texas, California, etc. This pattern of settlement is also in all the major cities of Nigeria like Lagos, Shagamu, Ibadan, Enugu, Port Harcourt, Kano, etc. People clustered around with people they share similar norms, mores and culture".

What Danfulani is telling the whole world is that the Sambo administration is supportive of, or at most indifferent to, this unhealthy social development in Kaduna. What kind of embarrassing defence is this? This cannot be the best way to defend a government! It says much about the intellectual depth of some of the people who are saddled with sensitive portfolios in public service.

Like I noted in my earlier piece, "the social demarcation of the city, even if inadvertent, has exposed the hatred and hypocrisy in the character of men". The Kaduna State Government should face the issues that have been identified and deal with them squarely. The buck-passing and shadow chasing should stop.

It is unhelpful to continue to demonize and denigrate people who have legitimate reasons to hold contrary views from our own. We in the media are conscious of our constitutional responsibility as the watch dog of the society. No amount of intimidation and name calling will deter us from this onerous duty. After all Socrates said, "an unexamined life is not worth living".

We shall continue to beam the searchlight on every aspect of the social life of the nation with a view to promoting probity and accountability in public affairs. We do not care whose ox is gored.

ThisDay, December 15, 2009

Chapter 36

Mismanaging the Affairs of State

It is exactly four weeks and four days today that President Umar Musa Yar`Adua was flown to the Kingdom of Saudi Arabia on a medical emergency. His departure was reportedly abrupt and sudden. On the very day he was taken out of the country, the President was said to have complained of severe chest pain after returning from the Friday Juma`at service at the National Mosque, Abuja. A statement that was later issued by the Presidency disclosed that the President who was admitted at the King Faisal Specialist Hospital and Research Center, Jeddah was diagnosed with acute pericarditis, an inflammation of the membrane around the heart.

Ever since, no one can say with certainty what exactly is the true health situation of the President. All that we have been getting from several news sources are conflicting reports on his health condition. At a point when the President was said to have left the intensive care unit of the hospital and was recuperating at a private ward, other reports indicated that his doctors were contemplating the option of transferring him to either the United States or Germany where it is believed that he may receive a better attention.

As at press time, the Nigeria`s Ambassador to Saudi Arabia, Alhaji Abdullahi Aminchi who appears to be the only one apart from the immediate Yar`Adua family members, that has access to the hospital ward of the President, was quoted in an agency report as saying that President Yar`Adua would be discharged from the hospital last week. He hinted that the President might stay behind in Saudi Arabia for a while to properly recuperate before returning to his duty post in Nigeria. Aminchi`s words: 'Since his arrival in the Kingdom, he has been feeling better by the day…the doctors will decide when he can leave. Now they said he should rest in the hospital and they have not given a date for when he can leave'.

In this past one month, the nation has been united in prayers for Mr. President. It has been prayers galore all over the country in Churches, Mosques, private homes and offices. The common thread that runs through in all the prayers is the speedy recovery of the President.

Nevertheless, the sudden exit of the President from the political scene without any arrangement on the ground for Vice President Goodluck Jonathan to act in his place in line with constitutional provisions has heightened tension and uncertainty in the land. We now have a situation on our hand in which no one appears to be in control of the ship of state.

The Vice President is reported to have declined taking certain decisions that require Presidential consent since he was not invested with any authority to act for the President. The consequence is that the country today is almost grounded. Nothing seems to be happening.

The drift is apparent. In deed, the ship of state appears rudderless. The Vice President has reportedly declined the convening of the Council of State which is supposed to meet to vet and endorse this year's list of nominees for national honours awards. Some of the International Oil Companies (IOCs) operating in the country, particularly Shell and Chevron, which mining and exploration licenses have expired are said to be in a quandary as their mining leases cannot be renewed because of the absence of the President.

Again, the National Assembly is in the process of passing the Petroleum Industry Bill, a critical legislation that would open up the oil sector and ensure the equity participation of the oil producing communities in Nigeria. It is a single bill that contains all the legal requirements that will apply to the entire petroleum industry in Nigeria. If this bill is passed tomorrow, it cannot become law because the assent of the President is required. And the Vice President cannot give such assent in the present circumstance.

The 2010 Federal Budget is at the moment under consideration by the two chambers of the National Assembly just as the 2009 Supplementary Appropriations are due to be passed. When the National Assembly is through with both bills, their fate will still hang in the balance if the President does not recover quickly and return to resume duties. Another area that is of concern to the nation and in deed the international community is the amnesty program in the Niger Delta.

The Presidential amnesty deal initiated by President Yar'Adua has helped to ensure the return of relative peace to the embattled region. The continued absence of the President whose personal involvement worked the magic in the area may threaten the gains already achieved.

Again there are several critical decisions affecting good governance which only the President can take. Ministerial memos which of necessity require the approval of the President will continue to pile up until the President is back to his seat. The implication is that projects and critical infrastructure that are meant for the good of the populace will remain on the drawing board. But how did we get to this sorry pass? The President, in his current situation, deserves our empathy and prayers.

This is where the sentiments end. The matters of state are far too important to be drowned in mere sentiments and emotions. A vacuum is never expected to occur even for a moment because at any point in time someone must be held accountable for the enormous responsibilities of the state.

And many public commentators that have commented on the current situation in the country have questioned why President Yar'Adua could not hand over to Vice President Jonathan in line with constitutional provisions. The relevant sections of the Constitution which include Sections 144, 145 and 146 ought to have been applied in dealing with the tricky situation in which the nation has found itself. The Government is not the personal property of anybody, interest group or ethnic nationality. The essence of the Constitution is to ensure that the society is governed in accordance with the law. And as Thomas Hobbes, a social contract philosopher put it; a society without laws is like 'a state of nature in which life becomes short, nasty and brutish'.

By an act of commission or omission, the country today in its rudderless form is being ridiculed in the international community. The country should do the right thing by following the provisions of our Constitution. The President cannot be away for more than a month now and no one is seen to be clearly in charge. This is not a good development.

If the President cannot return soon to his office, I don`t think it is late for the provisions of Section 145 of the Constitution to be invoked so that the current vacuum that exists at the highest level of national leadership can be squarely addressed. When the President is fully recovered, he will return to his desk to continue to discharge the mandate given to him by the electorate. For now, sentiments must be set aside.

The truth of the matter is that the President, at the moment, is not in a position to pilot the ship of state. Those who are inflaming passions and heating up the polity because a possible change of the status quo will alter their selfish calculations should stop. The survival of Nigeria as one harmonious political entity is far more important than our personal ambitions and primordial aspirations. It is my prayer that the President will recover soon and return to his duty desk. But in the interim, let the rules apply.

ThisDay, December 22, 2009

Chapter 37

Widening Boundaries of Social Frustrations

It is not an overstatement to note that the country is today in a state of anomie. No part of this nation is spared the social hardship that is currently the lot of the people occasioned by crippling and debilitating fuel shortages. Whether it is Lagos in the South West, Kaduna in the North West or Enugu in the South East, the sad stories of motorists queuing on end at filling stations and travelers getting stranded at motor parks are the same.

The extreme confusions, disorderliness and chaos at various filling stations across the country bear a clear testimony to a looming danger in the land if no urgent and concerted efforts are made by the concerned authorities to squarely address the brewing social crisis. Nigerians are facing real hard times. There are growing and all pervading frustrations, agonies and anger every where.

What is demanded of the Federal Government is to find an urgent and lasting solution instead of the current buck-passing and trading of excuses by the Minister of Information and Communications, Professor Dora Akunyili. Rising from the Federal Executive Council meeting in Abuja last Wednesday, the Minister was shown on national television where she was putting the blame for the biting fuel scarcity nationwide on the door steps of oil marketers whom she accused of hoarding and manipulations of their pumping machines.

In what appears to be a calculated strategy to distance government from the problem, she poured invectives on the oil marketers, calling them wicked and heartless. She even noted that the Petroleum Minister had gone round the filling stations in Abuja and environs to see things for himself and that he reported to the Federal Executive Council that the current energy crisis had more to do with hoarding and profiteering.

This explanation beggars the issue. The Minister should stop pooling wool over the eyes of the public. The government should accept responsibility for the current state of normlessness in the land. It is glaring that there is a failure of leadership. And those State officials that have failed to deliver on their respective mandates should simply admit their ineptitude and failure and honorably quit the scene instead of engaging in shadow chasing.

In the last ten years of our return to democratic governance, none of the four refineries in the country, either by acts of commission or omission, has functioned efficiently. They have in deed been deliberately made to remain comatose and unworkable so that the few cartels of mindless business men who are favoured with contracts for the importation of petroleum products into the country would continue to hold the people to ransom.

The paradox of the people of Nigeria living in miseries and excruciating poverty in a country that is so generously endowed by God is no longer acceptable. We know that corruption in high places has been the bane of the nation. Resources that are meant to provide social infrastructure always end up in the secret bank accounts of the ruling political elite and their collaborators in the civil bureaucracy.

This is why our roads have remained in a state of total disrepair, the hospitals without essential drugs and educational institutions in advanced state of decay in spite of the yearly ritual of budgetary appropriations by the National Assembly. High level corruption also accounts for the desperate situation that exists at the filling stations.

Instead of addressing the real underlying issues, the Information Minister was busy telling us that hoarders are responsible. Nigerians are tired of meaningless rationalizations for government's ineptitude and inactions. What they want is to drive freely into any filling station and buy fuel effortlessly.

But this is not the situation. I just returned last Wednesday from a trip to Umuahia and Enugu in the South East. The energy crisis has assumed alarming proportions.

The NNPC Mega Stations in Umuahia and Enugu were totally besieged with confusion renting the air. The few private filling stations that have petroleum products were also not spared the prevalent confusion and chaos.

The situation in Abuja is even far worse than the Umuahia and Enugu scenario. Social and economic activities in the Federal Capital Territory had been crippled on account of the prevailing fuel scarcity. The queues are endless and in some instances formless, stretching several kilometers and taking up large chunks of the major highways. Similar frustrating situations exist in Lagos, Kaduna and other major cities in the country.

In spite of the reasons offered by the Information and Communications Minister, incontrovertible evidence to the contrary suggested that the Nigerian National Petroleum Corporation (NNPC) had low stock of petroleum products which could hardly meet national demands. Nigerians are sick and tired of lame excuses from those who should know better. Motorists are facing agonizing ordeals at petrol stations.

The unrelenting scarcity which started from the last Sallah period has predictably spilled over into the Yuletide and is seriously threatening to make a mess of this season of goodwill as the travel plans of many Nigerians this period have become greatly impeded.

Government ought to have known that during this time of the year, profiteering is always the order of the day by some faceless mafia groups within the oil and gas sector. This should have necessitated a proactive approach by the authorities; flooding the market with petroleum products and putting the oil marketers on strict surveillance.

The current state of affairs in the country in which petroleum products have suddenly become terribly scarce and beyond the reach of vast majority of Nigerians does not give cause to cheer. It has security implications. The government must quickly address this problem to avoid any possible social backlash.

The social boundaries of frustrations appear to be widening by the day. A few days ago, some repentant Itshekiri militants in Warri embarked on a warning demonstration to protest their continued neglect by the Federal authorities. They threatened to unleash mayhem in Warri and its environs unless the FG released their post amnesty funds.

Some weeks back, former militants in the Port Harcourt axis, out of anger and frustrations over their delayed allowances broke loose from their camps and invaded the University of Port Harcourt where they visited terror on the students, maiming innocent people and raping female students in the process.

But for the timely intervention of Governor Chibuike Amaechi and security agents in the State, no one would have predicted the outcome of the planned reprisal actions by the aggrieved students.

The government should be able to gauge the feelings of Nigerians and respond appropriately. There is no doubt that the continued absence of President Yar`Adua from his duty post has further compounded the bad situation. Those whose lot it is to exercise power on his behalf must act proactively and with dispatch to stem the impending crisis.

_____

ThisDay, January 5, 2010

Chapter 38

Nigeria, Not Terrorists Haven

The failed attempt by a suspected Nigerian terrorist, Umar Farouk AbdulMutallab, to blow up a passenger jetliner belonging to Delta airline in Detroit, United States on Christmas day and the sudden demise of Nigeria`s former First Lady, Dr. (Mrs.) Maryam Babangida, were two significant occurrences that rounded up developments in Nigeria in 2009, arguably, a very unimpressive year for our country.

A lot have been said and written about these two unrelated events with the action of the suspected Nigerian suicide bomber attracting global condemnation and unprecedented but justifiably undue media attention on the country. The failed terrorist plot has continued to provoke world-wide outrage and indignation.

My only worry is the disrepute and infamy which this singular act of senselessness has brought to our country, currently on a mission to re-brand its not-too-impressive image within the international scene. For good measure, all the international reports on the event have continued to hammer on the Nigerian nationality of the suspected plane bomber.

The reality on ground today is that by the very action of Umar Farouk AbdulMutallab, Nigeria has been blacklisted by the United States and placed on the global terrorist watch list.

There is no gainsaying the fact that real hard times await Nigerian travelers to other parts of the world. There may be no easy passage for them at foreign airports as they will be required to make themselves available for more stringent and rigorous searches.

The Vice President, Dr. Goodluck Jonathan, who commented on the incident at a recent Church service in Abuja held to usher in the New Year, clearly appreciated the problems that lie ahead. In his words:

> "This (the failed bombing mission) will bring unnecessary harassment and scrutiny to other Nigerians who want to travel outside the country. We trust in God.

He will not disappoint us and he will see us through. I therefore urge every
Nigerian to change in the way we do things and show enough commitments to
the nation."

The decision of the United States government to blacklist Nigeria, in
the light of the failed bombing plot, has confirmed the fears of the Vice
President and other concerned Nigerians who predicted such punitive
consequences. As at press time, Nigeria has been grouped together with
Saudi Arabia, Yemen, Algeria, Afghanistan, Iraq, Lebanon, Libya,
Pakistan and Somalia on the ignominious list of "countries of interest".
This means that our country, unfortunately, has been classified along with
these other countries as potential terrorist havens.

The implications of our being blacklisted according to Agency reports
include tougher and rigorous scanning, longer waiting period at foreign
airports, racial profiling, stiffer visa requirements, restrictions on use of
electronic gadgets (laptops, iPods, VCD, DVD players etc.) on board and
restrictions on in-flight movement one hour to landing.

The most dangerous fallout of the failed bombing plot, however, is
the branding of innocent and law-abiding Nigerians as potential terrorists.
This is a sad reality we may have to live with for a very long time to
come.

The unfortunate turn of events for Nigeria, some commentators have
argued, may have derived partly from the current leadership vacuum
accentuated by the disturbing and prolonged absence of President Umar
Musa Yar`Adua from his duty post. Yar`Adua has been away to Saudi
Arabia for close to two months where he is undergoing a treatment for
pericarditis, an inflammation of the membrane around the heart.

The belief is that if President Yar`Adua were to be around, he would
possibly have engaged his American counterpart and probably Nigeria
may have escaped the blacklisting. It is against this background that I
subscribe to the views ascribed to Hon. Abike Dabiri-Erewa, the
Chairperson of the House Committee on the Nigerian Diaspora.

She said: "In fact, we do not in anyway deserve this categorization
and I think this is part of failure of leadership because since this
happened, we do not have a President speaking with the US President
Barack Obama and this is one of the consequences of President Umar
Musa Yar`Adua not handing over properly before he travelled for
treatment abroad".

In spite of the evident failure of leadership in the country, it is important to note that some relevant authorities in Nigeria including the security agencies have responded positively to the development by proving clearly with facts that the youthful Farouk AbdulMutallab acted on his own without any connivance with any body or organization in Nigeria. In deed, irrefutable facts provided by government showed that the suspect who commenced his mission to the United States from Accra in Ghana spent only 30 minutes within Nigeria before boarding his flight to Amsterdam in Holland enroute Detroit.

All well meaning Nigerians worldwide must continue to condemn the action of Umar Farouk AbdulMutallab which has brought this country to the current sorry pass.

We appeal to the American government to treat this matter on its merit and do away with the temptation to brand every Nigerian on account of this singular incident.Nigerians are hardworking and law-abiding. Although there have been frequent and recurrent cases of politically instigated sectarian crises in the northern parts of the country, Nigeria is not known to habour any Al-Qaeda cells.

The suspected Nigerian bomber, from emerging facts, is said to have trained in Yemen and not anywhere in or near Nigeria. It is therefore unfair to brand Nigeria as a terrorist country.

The second major event that occurred in Nigeria as the year 2009 came to an end was the sudden death of Maryam Babangida who had rightly been described as the most glamorous First Lady ever in the history of our country.

That development took the country unawares even though some online publications had in November carried rumors of her death.The remains of the First Lady were buried according to Islamic rites in the early hours of Wednesday, 30th December. She had deservedly been receiving accolades from across the entire socio-political spectrum of Nigeria on account of her solid achievements and the grace which she brought to bear on that office.

I join thousands of other Nigerians to pay tribute to the memory of this great Amazon who played a stabilizing role in the government of General Ibrahim Babangida.

Her Better Life for Rural Women Program which sought to uplift and empower Nigerian women was the highpoint of her accomplishments in office. She did it with style and elegance as she brought smiles to many homes of the less privileged women in the society.

I wish her soul eternal repose and the bereaved husband, General Babangida and the family the fortitude to bear the irreparable loss.

ThisDay, January 12, 2010

Chapter 39

Restoring Confidence in Abia Security

A bia State, in the Igbo heartland, which prides itself as God`s Own State was, for a greater part of last year, in the news for the wrong reasons. The State recorded several cases of violent crimes including kidnappings, bank robberies, car snatchings and armed banditry.

No one, no matter the status and station in life was spared the terror that was visited on the once peaceful State by the agents of darkness operating in the area. Not even the Governor and Chief Security Officer of the State, Chief Theodore Ahamefula Orji was immune from such attacks.

At the height of the criminal siege on the State, the convoy of the Governor was ambushed at the Ugwunagbo axis of the State on the Aba-Port Harcourt Expressway and ferociously attacked by gun men who would seem to be on a suicide mission.

The Governor barely escaped death by the whiskers. Eye witness accounts of the incident indicated that it was a miraculous escape by the Governor.

Within the period, it was as if the State was under an invasion. It was reasonably suspected that most of the armed militants that were flushed out of the neighboring Rivers and Bayelsa States by the Joint Task Force in the Niger Delta region relocated to Abia.

The two major cities of Umuahia and Aba, within the period under review were held by the jugular by kidnappers and armed robbers who evidently appeared to be on the loose.

Given the regularity of such deadly occurrences, many citizens of the State resident in other parts of the country and Diaspora could no longer feel safe to return home even as their relations in Abia warned them not to do so for their own security.

This was the precarious state of security in the State until Governor T. A. Orji decided to confront the problem head-on. It would seem to have dawned on the Governor at this point that the dogged efforts he was making to reposition the State were being overshadowed by the unrelenting reports of violent crimes emanating almost on a daily basis from the State. He read the Riot Act to all the criminal groups operating in the State to turn a new leaf or quit Abia.

The alternative was to face the consequences of their nefarious actions as the Government would not fold its hands and allow a few unscrupulous elements and their sponsors to continue to wreck havoc on the people of the State.

Most political observers watched with keen interest as the Governor began to unfold what was clearly a well-articulated security blue-print to contain the gangsters that had constituted a menace to the good people of Abia State. Firstly, he made a strategic appointment in the person of a retired military top shot as his Security Adviser.

This was followed by the equipping of the Police formations in the State with hundreds of Hilux trucks and state-of-the-art communication gadgets. The Joint Military-Police Task Force in the State was re-invigorated and re-enforced.

The Governor held series of consultative meetings with several stakeholders in the State including traditional rulers who were given marching orders to fish out the criminals who use their various domains as operational bases or face deposition.

Governor T. A. Orji also announced an incentive of N1 million for any person in the State who could provide information that would lead to the apprehension of kidnappers and other criminals operating in the State.

The Governor also presented an Executive Bill to the Abia State House of Assembly which made kidnapping and hostage taking in any form a capital offence. The law was speedily passed by the House.

Acting on security reports which showed a direct correlation between the operations of commercial motor cyclists otherwise known as "okada riders" and rising crime rate in the State, the okada operators were completely banned from operating in Aba and Umuahia, the two main cities in the State. This had an immediate impact as the cases of kidnappings, armed robberies and other violent crimes became drastically reduced.

The State Government, it was reliably gathered, also deployed other covert security strategies including stepping up and enhancing the intelligence gathering capacity of the various security forces serving in the State.

The end result of all these efforts has been the return of peace and normalcy to the once troubled State. The strategies of the Governor started yielding results many months before the Yuletide.

On a trip to Umuahia, the Abia State capital sometime in August last year, I saw several of the slain bodies of suspected kidnappers and armed robbers that were dumped at a shallow and freshly dug up grave close to the mortuary located within the premises of the Queen Elizabeth Specialist Hospital in the town. Residents of the city were trooping to the place in their numbers to catch a glimpse.

Although fears were being expressed that some innocent persons might be among the victims, the overwhelming verdict of a cross-section of people I spoke with on the occasion noted that since the heat was turned on the criminals in the State, the citizens now enjoy a respite as people could go about their normal businesses without fear of any danger lurking in the corner.

The Governor has since made good his threat to depose any traditional ruler known to be harboring kidnappers or armed robbers in his domain.

Two traditional rulers in the Ngwa axis of the State have since been de-robed for their alleged involvement in providing cover to criminals. It is expected that this would serve as a deterrent to other traditional rulers whose conduct may not be blameless.

It is instructive to note that throughout the Christmas season and the New Year there was no recorded incident of kidnapping, bank robbery or any other form of heinous crimes that used to be the norm in the past. Those who accepted the assurances of the Governor and returned home had a blissful time.

People moved freely across the State without any incidents. In deed, I was personally thrilled that night life had returned to the capital city of Umuahia. All the various communities in the State celebrated without any untoward developments.

All these were made possible by the decisive and proactive measures adopted by the Ochendo administration to ensure that the people of Abia State celebrated in an atmosphere that was devoid of fear and molestation.

The governor deserves commendation for this uncommon achievement. The truth is that no meaningful development can ever take place in a chaotic and insecure environment. It is hoped that the prevailing climate of peace and security in the State will be sustained in the months and years to come.

ThisDay, January 19, 2010

Chapter 40

Anambra: Who Takes the Crown?

In the next two weeks, the people of Anambra State in the South East of Nigeria will go to the polls to elect a governor that would superintend over the affairs of the State for the next four years. Being the only gubernatorial election to be held in the country this year ahead of the 2011 General Elections, the Anambra polls is significant in the sense that it marks the beginning of staggered elections in Nigeria.

The oddness in Anambra standing alone in this election had its genesis in the Supreme Court ruling in 2006 which nullified the election of Dr. Chris Nwabueze Ngige of the Peoples Democratic Party (PDP) and declared Mr. Peter Obi of the All Peoples Grand Alliance (APGA) as the rightful winner of the 2003 governorship election in the State.

In 2007, Mr. Obi approached the Supreme Court again to determine when his 4-year tenure, as guaranteed by the Constitution would end since Ngige had already utilized almost three of those four years before the nullification of his election by the same Supreme Court.

The Supreme Court ruled in favor of Obi by clearly stating that Obi`s tenure commenced from the day he was sworn into office. It was this ruling that altered the electoral calendar of Nigeria and thus setting into motion for the first time the culture of staggered polls in the country.

In the run-up to the current Anambra election, more than 24 candidates, standing on the platform of various political parties, are challenging the incumbent Governor Peter Obi for the biggest political prize in the State.

As at press time, about seven candidates have clearly demonstrated very serious clout and commitment to win the election. They include Peter Obi (APGA), Dr. Chris Ngige (Action Congress), Prof. Chukwuma Soludo (PDP), Dr. Andy Uba (Labour Party), Hon. Nicholas Ukachukwu (Hope Democratic Party), Hon. (Mrs.) Uche Ekwunife (Peoples Progressive Alliance) and the last but not the least, Chief Ralphs Okey Nwosu (African Democratic Congress).

The seven candidates have been criss-crossing the nooks and crannies of the State, campaigning vigorously to earn the peoples` mandate.

Although the language of campaign in some instances had been intemperate and incendiary, however, no ugly incidents had been registered so far. It has also been observed that most of the candidates have shown enough desperation which portends a looming danger if the situation remains unchecked.

As the February 6 election date draws closer, indications on the ground clearly suggest that the race may be a four-cornered contest between the incumbent, Obi, Ngige, Soludo and Uba with Ukachukwu likely to spring some surprises.

Given the high stakes involved in this election and the desperation of some of the candidates to win at all cost, there are strong indications that the precarious security situation in the State may spiral out of hand if the conduct of the election is not free and fair, credible and transparent.

A critical assessment of the profiles of the contending candidates clearly shows that the people of Anambra would have a tough choice to make. The leading gubernatorial contenders, without any exceptions, are pre-eminently qualified to govern the State, going by their pedigree and antecedents.

Until the recent implosion in the PDP which led to the dumping of the party by some of its leading lights like Andy Uba, Ukachukwu and Ekwunife, the Anambra governorship race was thought by political analysts as a straight fight between Obi, Ngige and Soludo. This is no longer the situation on ground.

With the last minute entry of Uba into the race, the entire political configurations and permutations have been drastically altered with those earlier tipped as frontrunners now having their hopes hanging in the balance.

One of the candidates whose aspiration may take a nosedive as a result of this development is Soludo. Some political pundits had earlier tipped him to be having a slight edge given his brilliant academic credentials and newness in the politics of the State and perhaps his performance in office as the immediate past Governor of Nigeria's Central Bank.

The undemocratic manner through which Soludo emerged as the flag bearer of the PDP created bad blood and finally culminated in the mass withdrawal from the party of those that make things happen in the State. Those who did not leave the party, like Senator Annie Okonkwo, are believed to be indifferent to the aspiration of Soludo.

This lack of support base for Soludo also manifested in the fundraising dinner organized in his honour in Abuja. Most of the key political players in Anambra PDP were absent. At the end, only a paltry sum of about N300 million was realized on the occasion. Soludo is definitely up for an uphill task. His case is not even helped by the fact that he has no political structure of his own or political experience to fall back on. No wonder the support of former Vice President Ekwueme has been enlisted to help salvage his aspiration.

Before now, the only known political antecedent of Soludo was his role as a member of the Ekwueme Youth Vanguard in the Second Republic during his student`s days in the University of Nigeria, Nsukka.

Soludo and Andy Uba are from Aguata Local Government Area. A close reading of the unfolding political situation shows that while Uba has all it takes to win the election, he may not necessarily be running to win. Political analysts are of the opinion that Uba may have decided to run in order to spoil the fun for the PDP for not re-drafting him after he had run and won the 2003 election on its platform.

Therefore, coming from Aguata like Soludo, the calculation is that he may take the bulk of the votes from the Old Aguata Union or at worst split them with Soludo. This may now pose a setback to Soludo who may not find it easy to garner enough votes in the Agulu strongholds of Obi, Nnewi fortress of Ukachukwu or the Idemili base of Ngige.

Incidentally, the Old Aguata Union comprises three populous LGAs namely Aguata, Orumba North and Orumba South. If the rug is pulled off Soludo`s feet in his home base, then the journey to Government House, Awka would have become uncertain and precarious.

It is further speculated that Uba may decide to enter into a political trade off with Obi as he (Uba) would like to maintain some strategic relevance preparatory for a role in a post-Obi era in the State. He (Uba) is not likely to go in the direction of Ngige for reasons that are not far-fetched.

Obi, on his part is working very hard to retain the seat notwithstanding the opposition of the rapacious and selfish political elite of the State to his second term aspiration. His achievements in the last four years which had seen his administration simultaneously developing all parts of the State at the same time and in many spheres of human endeavor are working out in his favor.

Also the passionate and emotive involvement of Ikemba Nnewi, Dim Chukwuemeka Odumegwu Ojukwu, the symbol of Igbo aspiration and resilience, on the side of Obi is not only a major counter poise to Ekwueme, but a strong signal of support that cannot be ignored. Whether any body likes it or not, Ojukwu still remains the issue in Igbo politics. No amount of propaganda can diminish his towering status in the life of the Igbo nation.

Ngige on his own part is a great political force who enjoys a cult-like following in the State. His solid achievements within the three years he illegally occupied the Government House, Awka in spite of stiff and choking opposition from blood thirsty god fathers, have become the benchmark for measuring good governance.

He has the vision, charisma and the courage to move the State to the next level. The problem he faces, however, is the relative newness of his political platform, Action Congress, in the State and funding. For his popularity to be translated into electoral victory, a massive political enlightenment is required to make AC a household name like APGA and PDP in the State.

Nicholas Ukachukwu faces a similar problem in the newness of his platform, Hope Democratic Party (HDP) even though he is not new in the politics of the State. He contested for the same position in 2007 on the platform of All Nigerian Peoples Party (ANPP) when he was denied nomination in the PDP.

He has the resources to fight to the end. This former Member of the House of Representatives for Abuja Municipal and Bwari Federal Constituency is a well known political fighter but is said to lack adequate educational exposure. In a sophisticated State like Anambra, this may be a minus.

Ekwunife, a serving Member of the House of Representatives, representing Anaocha, Dunukofia and Njikoka Federal Constituency appears to be the rave of the moment. As the only woman in the male dominated race, she has been conducting her campaigns with candour and in style. She is certainly a major revelation of the on-going politicking in Anambra State.

She has a bright political prospect. However, the current race cannot be won on the basis of gender sentiments.

As for Okey Nwosu, the Ikolo Awka, he is a dogged and principled politician who has all the ideas to leapfrog Anambra to the next level. Since clinching the nomination of ADC, he has been moving around the communities in the State to solicit for support.

His predicament is the choice of platform and funding. He will do well in the election if it is free and fair.

On balance, the candidates to watch out for in this tension-gripping race are Obi, Soludo and Ngige. The outcome of the election on February 6 will tell.

ThisDay, January 26, 2010

Chapter 41

Security Challenges in the Anambra Governorship Election

The Anambra governorship election in which the incumbent Governor, Peter Obi is mainly pitched against Dr. Chris Ngige, Prof. Chukwuma Soludo, and Dr. Andy Uba, is attracting both national and global attention because it is the first to be held in any State in the country before the 2011 General Elections. It is also being seen as a litmus test on the capacity and readiness of the Independent Electoral Commission (INEC) to give the country a credible, transparent, free and fair election next year.

The election can only be a success story if all the institutions and human actors involved in it's conduct discharge their various responsibilities diligently and without fear or favor.

The real challenge in Anambra is for INEC to ensure there is a level playing ground for all the candidates and parties participating in the election. The electoral umpire must not only guarantee a seamless poll, but it must also be seen to have done so without let or hindrance.

This is where the important issue of security comes in. There is a limit to what INEC can do if the political environment is characterized by insecurity, violence and lawlessness.

And if the alarm on insecurity raised by the Inspector General of Police, Mr. Ogbonna Onovo, recently concerning the Anmbra poll is anything to go by, then there is a looming danger if no concrete step is taken by the relevant authorities to address the problem.

At a meeting with the governorship candidates and party leaders at the Force Headquarters in Abuja recently, Onovo compelled them to sign an undertaking to be of good behavior based on revelations that many of them were planning to cause trouble during the election.

He noted: 'We have intelligence information that some aspirants are acquiring police uniforms to be distributed to thugs and drivers' unions. We also heard that some of you are planning to use vigilante services made up of retired armed robbers, ex-convicts, okada riders, taxi and bus drivers as well as market associations and a certain confraternity at Oraifite to rig the election'.

These allegations, grave as they are, smack of desperation and inordinate ambition which the INEC Chairman has correctly identified as being the underlying factor behind electoral malfeasance in our country.

At a recent Public Lecture organized by the Champion Newspapers in Lagos, Professor Iwu had observed: 'The problems that have dogged Nigeria`s elections over the years have remained more or less, constant. There is virtually nothing recent or new about them. These are problems steeped in personal indiscipline and inordinate ambition'.

No matter how well-intentioned INEC may be in the discharge of its statutory mandate, if our desperate politicians and their overzealous supporters do not moderate their foul political behavior, free and fair elections may continue to elude the country.

The Professor Maurice Iwu-led INEC, however, has a huge responsibility to prove critics and cynics wrong that it will get it right in this election, notwithstanding the evil shenanigans of our undisciplined political class.

The Electoral Commission was heavily criticized in the manner it conducted the 2007 General Elections which many Nigerians and observer groups believed to be characterized by irregularities. It is therefore not surprising that in the run up to the Saturday election, INEC has through rigorous preparations left no one in doubt that it was determined to give the people of Anambra State a good election.

The Commission has held series of meetings with all the stakeholders including the candidates, leadership of the Political Parties in the State and security agencies with a view to updating them with the preparations it was making to ensure that the polls are free from irregularities.

In addition, INEC has also set up an Election Observation Board, composed of very credible and independent-minded Nigerians to monitor and observe the preparations for and the actual conduct of the election.

But all these efforts will come to naught if the prevailing political atmosphere is not conducive and satisfactory. It is, therefore, against this background that the grave allegations made by the Inspector General of Police must be thoroughly investigated and those found culpable, speedily brought to book.

It is disturbing that some evil-minded politicians would go to the extent of amassing weapons, training thugs and procuring military and police uniforms for the use of the hoodlums on the Election Day with a view to causing mayhem.

Given the revelations of the IGP on the damning plot by some desperate politicians to subvert the election, the Police in particular and other security agencies involved in the conduct of the poll must brace up for security challenges that lie ahead.

They have the responsibility to ensure that the election is not marred in any form by acts of thugerry and violence. Based on the intelligence at the disposal of the IGP which indicated an organized plot by some desperate politicians to disturb the peace of the State by engaging the services of criminal gangs and militant groups, the time has become auspicious for security agents to act with dispatch.

It is gratifying to note that over 27,000 policemen have been drafted to ensure security during the election. With such an impressive number, the Police must do everything in its power to ensure that all the polling stations in the State are properly secured and voters protected from any undue influences.

The electorate in Anambra must do their own bit too to ensure that the election is conducted in an atmosphere that is devoid of acrimony, rancor and disorderliness. They should conduct themselves in a decorous manner and refuse to play into the hands of mischief makers who may be planning to cause confusion if the trends of the voting do not favor their candidates. There must be collective vigilance on the part of all stakeholders in the State after all it is said that 'eternal vigilance is the price of liberty'.

Every hand must be on the deck to ensure that the Anambra election, like the one recently conducted in Fugar, Edo State, will be successful.

ThisDay, February 2, 2010

Chapter 42

The Recurrent Bloodletting on the Plateau

When will Plateau State be in the news for the right reasons? When will the orgy of killings stop in this part of Nigeria? Has Jos become accepted as Nigeria's version of the once notorious killing fields of Uganda's Luwero Triangle? Has human life become so cheap that it is worth nothing anymore on this Plateau that prides itself as the home of hospitality and tourism? When will this recurring human wastage and carnage on the Plateau become a thing of the past?

My heart bleeds for this nation. Or contraption called Nigeria? Why have some senseless people always made it a point of duty to kill innocent citizens and shatter the peace of the nation in the name of religion?

Within the last ten years, the city of Jos in particular and other parts of Plateau State have recorded several ethno-religious clashes resulting in huge loss of precious lives and property. This is not discounting the bloody clashes that took place in 1994 and 1997.

In September 2001, over 1000 people perished in the rioting that broke out in the State. The crisis erupted again in 2004 with Moslems and Christians taking up arms against one another. In that clash, over 700 lives were lost.

The State erupted into yet another bloody conflagration in November 2008, just barely a year ago, in which several lives and property worth billions of naira were lost to the mayhem. Among the helpless victims were innocent youth corpers serving in the State who were butchered to death. Over 500 innocent souls who were caught in the unending crisis were dispatched to the great beyond.

And today, the Plateau has gone up in flames with the attendant huge loss of lives and property even when the traumatized residents of the State were yet to fully recover from the terror visited on them barely a year ago.

The government at either the federal or state level always responded with the setting up of investigative panels of enquiry with proclamations to get to the root of the crises. In deed at the height of the 2004 crisis, a state of emergency was declared on the State.

Following the declaration of emergency, a Sole Administrator in the person of the former Chief of Army Staff, General Chris Ali was appointed for the troubled State. The civilian Governor of the State, Chief Joshua Dariye and his administration were sacked by the Obasanjo-led Federal Government. The emergency period lasted for six months.

From the recurrent crises, it would appear that no useful lessons had been learnt from past experiences. The latest orgy of violence in which more than 500 souls are reported to have been killed for no justifiable reasons is not only disturbing but questions our pretence to being a united country with a common destiny.

The vicious and hate killings in Jos which take on the coloration of ethnicity and religion cannot be rationalized on any grounds. If we love ourselves and share a common destiny as a nation in spite of our diversities, a section of our society cannot wake up any day and begin to levy a war of extermination on sectarian, religious or political considerations.

The gory pictures of deaths and destructions coming from the various theatres of the conflict in Jos appall our sense of being and also diminish our common humanity. It is unbelievable that such level of destructions and waste could be visited on Nigerians by their fellow citizens in a peace time.

Media reports have shown massive destruction to human lives and property, notwithstanding the presence of soldiers who, on the orders of the Federal Government, have taken over the security of the State. The unprecedented level of destructions, coming even at a time the dust raised by the November 2008 blood bath was yet to settle, defy logic and common sense.

Even though the security agents are doing their level best to contain the situation, the crisis unfortunately escalated to some communities in the hinterlands. A Western news agency, AFP of France, reported that over 150 people were killed and their bodies dumped in shallow wells and pit latrines in what was ostensibly a reprisal action in a village known as Kuru Karama outside the State capital.

With the death tolls mounting, over 18,000 people who narrowly escaped the fighting, according to the Red Cross, are currently seeking refuge in military and police barracks, churches and mosques scattered in different parts of Jos metropolis. It is really disturbing that Nigerians are being turned into refugees in their own country, not on account of any natural disaster or invasion by any external power, but on account of unprovoked aggressions by agent provocateurs in their midst.

The current bloodletting on the Plateau is one too many. It stands condemned before God and man. In this crisis, no one has been spared on the grounds of his ethnicity, religion or political affiliations. Both indigenes and so-called settlers have not been spared. Among the dead are Christians, Moslems and animists.

The sad irony of the situation in Plateau is that every body knows where the problem is coming from, but the authorities at both State and Federal levels appear to lack the requisite political will and determination to deal decisively with it.

The current conflagration was said to have been sparked off by a dispute over an alleged land encroachment by a Moslem who was reportedly rebuilding his house which was burnt down in the 2008 sectarian crisis. He was said to have been challenged by a Christian neighbor on whose plot he allegedly encroached. What a flimsy excuse for the unwarranted carnage and destructions that followed!

The truth is that Jos has become a tinder box, always waiting to explode at the least provocation. The reasons, as many previous public inquiries had shown, are firmly rooted in the competing struggle for land ownership and political control by the Hausa Fulani who are considered as settlers by the Beroms, Anagutas, Afizeres and other tribes indigenous to Plateau.

As at last count, there are over a dozen reports from previous Judicial Commissions of Inquiry on the recurrent sectarian crises on the Plateau with far-reaching recommendations on how to keep and maintain lasting peace in the area. The last of such reports was that of the Justice Bola Ajibola panel which was put together by the State Government to investigate the 2008 mayhem. Even as the Plateau State Government was dragging its feet on the implementation of the recommendations contained in that report, the Major General Emmanuel Abisoye panel set up by the Federal Government on the same 2008 crisis was still sitting in Jos before the present bloodbath erupted.

At the same time action was yet to be taken on the report of the Bayero Nafada-led Ad-Hoc Committee of the House of Representatives that also investigated the 2008 Jos conflicts more than one year after it was tabled on the floor of the House.

Now, the Federal Government has vowed to bring the culprits and organizers of the current mayhem to book as a way to check future occurrences. But nobody is taking the Government seriously because such previous avowals have never been matched with actions.

The culture of impunity which has ensured that none of the culprits in the previous crises had been appropriately punished would seem to have continuously provided the impetus for the serial killings on the Plateau. I believe that with the current disturbances, the time has finally come for a decisive decision to be taken to put this recurrent tragedy on the Plateau to a final stop.

The sponsors of the crises must be fished out and dealt with according to the laws of the land. The culprits are well known. Just like Vice President Goodluck Jonathan said, nobody should hide under the cover of group action to evade justice. Those who engineered and participated in the killings must be identified and made to be answerable for their individual actions no matter how highly placed. This is the only way we may begin to bring sanity into the troubled State.

Government must show determination to address the Plateau problem on a permanent basis. The first step will be to dust up the existing reports of previous judicial panels and take conclusive decisions on them with a view to putting a permanent stop to the recurrent orgies of violence.

Since land ownership and clamor for political control are at the heart of the Jos problem, the Federal and State Governments should look at the possibility of granting self autonomy to the settler communities within the areas they are domiciled in Jos without endangering the power and right of the indigenous people of Plateau to determining the political destiny of their State.

The Constitution of the Federal Republic of Nigeria is quite clear on the issues of citizenship and indigene ship. Until the Constitution is amended, the applicable provisions on who is an indigene and citizen cannot be compromised in favor of any group in Plateau. The killings on the Plateau must stop.

ThisDay, February 9, 2010

Chapter 43

Prolonged Absence of Yara`dua

The polity has become increasingly overheated following the prolonged absence of President Umaru Musa Yar`Adua from office and his refusal to hand over the reins of power to his deputy, Dr. Goodluck Jonathan in accordance with constitutional provisions. In the next few days, the President would have been away for three months, leaving a very dangerous vacuum at the seat of power.

He left the country precisely on the 23rd of November, 2009 for Saudi Arabia on a medical emergency to attend to a life-threatening heart condition. For this length of time, no Nigerian except perhaps members of his immediate family has been able to see or speak with the President.

Until it became evident that the President is seriously incapacitated to continue in office, notwithstanding the efforts of the members of his inner caucus to give the wrong impression that all is well, Nigerians have been fed with a cocktail of lies, misinformation and disinformation on the true health condition of Mr. President by various high ranking government officials.

It is apparent from the unfolding events that those government officials including Ministers who had been claiming that they had been in regular touch with Mr. President and that he would soon be back, are shameless and blatant liars who do not deserve to be in governance in any capacity whatsoever.

It is also becoming increasingly evident that the 2009 Supplementary Appropriation Bill purported to have been signed by Yar`Adua, may have been a ruse, after all. It is feared that the said Presidential assent may have been procured under questionable circumstances.

The issue that arouses the suspicions of Nigerians is the fact that no body including high ranking government officials have been able to meet with or fellowship with the President. The iron curtain that has been erected around him by his wife, Hajia Turai, ensures that the medical condition of the President is shrouded in absolute secrecy.

The situation is so bad that the top ranking government officials, who ordinarily ought to know the true state of affairs, would seem to be in the dark as to the possibility of the President returning soon to his seat. Nothing else dramatizes this point more than the recent expositions by the Secretary to the Government of the Federation, Alhaji Yayale Ahmed and ForeignMinister, Chief Ojo Maduekwe.

When he appeared before the Senators at an Executive session in the Senate chamber, Yayale Ahmed reportedly told the lawmakers that he had not been able to see or hear from the President since he left the country hurriedly in November 2009.

Again, at a public affairs programme of the British Broadcasting Corporation (BBC), Maduekwe similarly admitted that he had not seen his principal since he left for Saudi Arabia for medication. Meanwhile, the Federal Cabinet to which these top government functionaries belong adopted a resolution in which they gave the President a clean bill of health, noting that he was fit to continue in office as the President.

This laughable decision has however brought the Cabinet into public ridicule and odium. It has shown the characters we have in the Federal Executive Council as an unprincipled and opportunistic bunch that is driven by pecuniary considerations.

Even the last minute change of gear by the Information and Communications Minister, Professor Dora Akunyili, cannot be considered to be truly altruistic. The Minister, before now had been part of the conspiracy by the Executive Council of the Federation to deceive the nation on the true health condition of the President.

Akunyili's volte face which has caused a crack in the Federal cabinet can only be seen for what it is: a fake heroism and fraudulent attempt to acquire cheap popularity. The discerning public cannot be hoodwinked by this spurious antic of the Minster.

If the cabinet has committed any acts of indiscretion by feeding the nation with lies on the health status of the President, Akunyili is guilty of that collective action. No amount of playing to the gallery now will exonerate her from that collective guilt.

It is against this background that I express disappointment at the stance of the governors of the South East on the Yar'Adua saga which is clearly at variance with the mood of Ndigbo and the nation. At a recent meeting in Enugu, the governors pledged support for the President, arguing that he was not under obligation to transmit any communication to the National Assembly for Vice President Jonathan to act for him. For them, the President can continue to run the country from his sick bed in Saudi Arabia as long as it is necessary.

No one knows the premise on which the governors took the decision. But one thing is clear; they are not known to have had any access to Yar'Adua on his hospital bed or even his medical records in the Saudi Kingdom.

In a situation where eminent and non-partisan statesmen like Alhaji Shehu Shagari, Gen. Yakubu Gowon, Dr. Alex Ekwueme, Chief Ernest Shonekan and several others including the Senate of the Federal Republic of Nigeria have called for transfer of power to Jonathan in line with constitutional provisions, it is difficult to fathom out the motivations of these governors. Their ill-advised position is unpopular and may be injurious to the political interests of the South East zone in the long run.

The unpopular position of the governors has attracted condemnation from well meaning groups and individuals. For instance, the South East chapter of the Save Nigeria Group, the Prof. Wole Soyinka-led coalition of civil society groups calling for constitutional transfer of power to Jonathan, said of the South East governors: "For the avoidance of doubt, we dissociate completely the patriotic and progressive people of the South East from the shameful statement credited to the governors of the region condemning calls for President Yar'Adua to transfer power to Vice President Goodluck Jonathan."

It is however heart-warming to note that Ohaneze Ndigbo, the umbrella socio-political organization of the Igbo nation, has stated the correct position of the Igbo people in Nigeria which contradicts the views of the governors.

According to Ohaneze: "Ndigbo are not satisfied and totally disagree with the current situation in which the President is seriously ill and receiving treatment abroad for over two months, and the Vice President is not bestowed with the status of Acting President. Ndigbo consider it inappropriate and unhelpful on the side of the President for not transmitting his long absence to the National Assembly and making provision for the Vice President to assume full responsibility as Acting President. We urge Mr. President to immediately rectify this unacceptable situation. Ndigbo stand by the Constitution of the Federal Republic of Nigeria." This represents the true feelings of Ndigbo.

What this clearly shows is that the governors acted on their own and without due consultations with the people they purport to represent. In future, our governors and other elected officials at various levels must learn to imbibe the democratic culture of gauging the true feelings of their people on any contentious national issues before taking a stance on their behalf. This is to stave off contradictions and avoidable national embarrassment.

ThisDay, January 16, 2010

Chapter 44

Yar`Adua and the Web of Intrigues

T he political milieu had suddenly come alive following the historic February 9, 2010 resolution of the National Assembly empowering Dr. Goodluck Jonathan as the Acting President of the Federal Republic of Nigeria. Prior to that development, the country had been precariously perching on a cliff hanger, occasioned by the prolonged absence of President Umar Musa Yar`Adua from the country.

The ailing President left the country abruptly and unceremoniously on 23rd November, 2009 for the Kingdom of Saudi Arabia on a medical emergency without handing over the reins of power to his deputy, Dr. Jonathan. For three months that the President was away, the country was rudderless and tottered dangerously on the brink.

Several efforts that were made by many groups and individuals to ascertain the true health condition of the President were effectively rebuffed by a cabal surrounding him. The delegations from the House of Representatives, Governors` Forum and the ruling Peoples Democratic Party met a brick wall in the Saudi Kingdom.

Worried by the deepening leadership vacuum at the apex of power in the country and looming danger which it portended for the unity and corporate existence of Nigeria, a national consensus was reached to transfer power to Dr. Jonathan pending the full recovery of Yar`Adua from his sickness.

The cabal consisting of Turai Yar`Adua, the ambitious wife of the President; Michael Andooaka, the former Minister of Justice and Attorney General of the Federation; Sayyadi Abba Ruma, the arrogant Minister of Agriculture and Water Resources; and Dr. Yakubu Tanimu Kurfi, the Economic Adviser to the President worked tirelessly and pulled all kinds of stunts to ensure that the national drift continued as they were not ready to accept the reality of a Jonathan Presidency.

Part of the compromise that was reached by pro-Jonathan forces and the Yar`Adua loyalists in the Villa was to send a delegation of the Executive Council of the Federation to visit Yar`Adua in Saudi Arabia and express the appreciation of the people of Nigeria to the Saudi monarch for the hospitality of the Kingdom to the ailing Nigerian leader.

That decision was seen in many informed political circles as the beginning of the end of the ineffectual Yar`Adua`s Presidency.

One thing was, however, clear. Whether the delegation saw him or not, the state of the health of the President which many foreign intelligence sources believe was very grave meant that the Council would activate Section 144 of the Constitution and declare the President incapacitated.

After some initial delays arising from issues in diplomatic protocols, the six-man delegation of the EXCOF, comprising the Minister of Foreign Affairs, Chief Ojo Maduekwe; Minister of Health, Prof. Babatunde Oshotimehin; Minister of Petroleum Resources, Dr. Rilwan Lukman; Minister of Agriculture and Water Resources, Dr. Sayyadi Abba Ruma; Minister of Justice and Attorney General of the Federation, Chief Adetokunbo Kayode and the Secretary to the Government of the Federation (SGF), Alhaji Yayale Ahmed left the shores of this country on Monday, 22nd February, 2010 on a fact finding mission to Saudi Arabia.

Unknown to the team and the rest of the country, the cabal was determined to frustrate any moves geared towards unraveling the true health condition of the President. In what amounted to a well executed coup d'état, the cabal moved a step ahead of the visiting EXCOF delegation and immediately commenced the evacuation of the President from Saudi Arabia.

As the delegation was arriving the Saudi Kingdom on Tuesday night, the cabal swiftly moved the President same night out of Jeddah to Nigeria, thus denying the six-man team the opportunity of meeting with the President.

The ailing President returned in a mysterious and dramatic circumstance in the ungodly hours of Wednesday, 24th February, 2010. As reported in the news, the President arrived in an air ambulance in the pitch of darkness. The staff of the Federal Aviation Authority of Nigeria (FAAN) and other Airport personnel on legitimate duty that night was reportedly chased out of the airport.

The entire Presidential route from the Aso Rock Villa to the Nnamdi Azikiwe International Airport was policed and cordoned off by military men fully armed to the teeth purportedly acting on the orders of the Commander, Brigade of Guards without the knowledge of the Acting

185

President, who by virtue of that position had become the Head of State and Commander-in-Chief of the Armed Forces of the Federation.

It reportedly took up to one hour to move the occupant of the air ambulance, presumably the ailing President, to a waiting land ambulance for an onward journey to the Villa. Daring news men, despite the thick veil of secrecy weaved around the returnee President, were on hand to puncture that web of secrecy notwithstanding the obvious threats to their lives. Thanks to the enduring commitment of journalists, Nigerians were able to see through the high stake games being played by the Yar`Adua kitchen cabinet to thwart the common will of the Nigerian people as reflected in that historic resolution of the National Assembly.

Tongues had been wagging as to what would have prompted the cabal to bring the President in such a bizarre manner into the country. The issue is that if the President had recovered or was recuperating as we had been made to understand by the President`s spin doctors including Alhaji Abdullahi Aminchi, Nigeria`s Ambassador to Saudi Arabia, why would the leader of the most powerful country in Africa be brought into the country in such an embarrassing circumstance?

The truth of the matter is that the cabal wrongly thought that by ferrying the President into the country, notwithstanding his physical and mental health, they would have been able to take the wind out of the sail of the acting Presidency of Jonathan. It was a big miscalculation.

No serious person would take the purported return of the President to the country for anything. The country has since moved on. The acting Presidency of Jonathan is a product of national consensus. For the baton of power to move back to Yar`Adua, he must transmit a letter to the National Assembly intimating it that he had returned back and was physically and mentally fit to resume on his seat. And the President must come out to address Nigerians on national television for the people to believe that he is physically fit to regain his seat. Anything short of that cannot work. There would be no room for a Presidency by proxy.

It is certainly clear that the intention of the cabal by smuggling the President back to the country even when he was yet to recover is to undermine Jonathan and whittle down his powers. This is a serious miscalculation. Until the National Assembly reverses itself based on incontrovertible evidence that the President is now hale and hearty, Jonathan remains in charge.

No amount of intimidation and subterfuge can change the situation on ground. Jonathan must however move fast to assert himself. He must immediately order investigations into the circumstances surrounding the deployment of troops in and around Abuja without his knowledge. Those found culpable in this treasonable act must be appropriately sanctioned to serve as a deterrent to any future occurrence.

He must also move fast to rejig the Cabinet with a view to dislodging disloyal Ministers from the Executive Council of the Federation. We have had enough of the web of intrigues woven by the cabal around Yar`Adua. We cannot continue this way. This country must move on to realize her manifest destiny.

_____

ThisDay, March 9, 2010

Chapter 45

Rediscovering the University of Nigeria, Nsukka

M y recent trip to the University of Nigeria, Nsukka (UNN), the great citadel of learning located within the ambience of a conclave of seven rolling hills was a good home coming of a sort, being the second time I was visiting the institution 26 years after graduation.

The previous trip was in 1996 during the funeral ceremonies of the founder of the University, the late Dr. Nnamdi Azikiwe, the Owelle of Onitsha and Great Zik of Africa. On that occasion, I was detailed by the Daily Times in my capacity as the Political Editor to cover the momentous event.

By that singular responsibility, I followed the funeral train from Lagos through Abuja and Nsukka to the Inosi Onira Retreat, Onitsha, the final resting place of the great African Nationalist.

By coincidence, my recent trip to Nsukka was as a result of another funeral involving the mother of Dr. Emeka Enejere, a renowned Political Operator, who incidentally was my lecturer in the Department of Political Science.

I took advantage of the funeral which was happening at Ibagwa Aka, on the outskirts of the University town, to undertake a first hand visit to my great alma mater.

To say the least, the picture that greeted me was not cheering enough. It is true that some major strides had been made over time to reposition the University infrastructure wise, the present state in which I found this great citadel of learning leaves much to be desired.

It would appear that after the exit of Professor Frank Ndili as the Vice Chancellor in 1985, whose tenure could be likened to the golden era in the history of the institution, the UNN has found itself in a state of arrested development. Except perhaps for some modest achievements that were reportedly recorded by the immediate past Vice Chancellor, Professor Chinedu Nebo, the degradation and degeneration in existing infrastructure remain very appalling.

Nevertheless, I can report that some key structures that were initiated by Ndili which defied succeeding administrations had been conclusively completed. My investigations revealed that the feat was recorded by Nebo. They include the Nnamdi Azikiwe Library, reputed as the largest in Africa, South of the Sahara; the Arts Theatre; Faculty Building for the Social Sciences etc.

Other areas where impressive achievements had been recorded are the sporting facilities on the campus. They include the famous Akanu Ibiam Sports Stadium, the Olympic size swimming pool and several training pitches etc.

Beyond these, it was observed that some serious decay had eaten deep into the University. It is sad and regrettable to note that 40 years after the Civil War, the vast landscape of the University is still dotted with abandoned structures including those that were destroyed during the Nigeria-Biafra War.

There is no reason on earth why structures that were conceived to enhance learning and research should still be allowed to remain in their derelict form 43 years after the end of the war, unless they are being preserved for succeeding generations as the physical evidence of the defeat of Ndigbo by the victorious Federal forces.

It saddens the heart to see the majestic Library Building within the Ziks Flats Hostels, Onuiyi Haven donated by the Great Zik of Africa along with the flats to the University still standing as a carcass more than 43 years after it was looted and destroyed by the invading federal troops.

We want to know from the University authorities why this is the case. For Christ sake, why can`t that building be restored to its original status? Is there any legal instrument that imposed any restrictions on the restoration and rehabilitation of the structures destroyed in the University as a result of the unfortunate Civil War?

The popular Princess Alexandria Auditorium, which was the centre of intellectual activism in the University before the war, suffered a similar fate. For ages, the roof of the building blown off during the war could not be replaced. It remained in that condition for a very long time.

We the alumni of this great citadel of learning that was conceived to restore the dignity of man cannot shy away from asking the necessary questions. Unless there is a legal instrument somewhere that ties the hands of the succeeding Governing Councils of the institution, the University authorities owe the UNN alumni movement and in deed

Nigerians an explanation on why some of the infrastructure on campus have remained decadent. I also wish to report that the entire Ziks Flats which at the moment house female students are in a state of disrepair. Until not long ago, the Ziks Flats were the abode of fresh male undergraduates coming into the University for the first time. That place, from what I saw, is no longer fit for human habitation.

The inhabiting students need to be evacuated from the area to make room for total reconstruction and rehabilitation. Even, the several hostels that dot the campus are in vey bad shape. Those that cry for urgent attention are Akpabio Hall, Isa Kaita, Okeke, Okpara, Balewa and Mary Slessor.

I also observed with disgust that the Students' Union Building and the adjoining Multi Purpose Block initiated in 1982 are still standing at the heart of the campus as abandoned projects. For those that graduated from the University several decades ago, they would be surprised to see that temporary wooden structures otherwise known as prefab buildings are still very much pronounced. For instance, the Medical Center still operates from makeshift structures in the name of prefab buildings. This certainly is not dignifying.

The current Governing Council of the University must initiate moves to apprehend the prevailing decay on campus. Excuses for non-performance will be unacceptable. To the glory of God, an alumnus of the University, Dr. Sam Egwu, is the Federal Minister of Education. Admittedly, he holds a national position of trust; he also has a moral responsibility to his alma mater which is a federal institution.

As an institution crippled by the war, I am not away that the University has benefited from any Marshal Plan by the Federal Government to upgrade its facilities. A case can be made for the setting up of a Special Fund for the purpose of mitigating the lingering effects of the war damages. Dr. Egwu, as a 'Great Lion', has a big role to play in this respect. It is my prayer that God will give him the enabling grace to do so.

ThisDay, March 16, 2010

Chapter 46

Jos: Triumph of Impunity

The most recent in the serial tragedies that had befallen the city of Jos, Plateau State boggles the mind. It is unimaginable that a group of Nigerians under any guise or justification could visit such level of horror on their fellow human beings.

On the night of Saturday 6th March, 2010, the innocent inhabitants of the sleepy villages of Dogo Nahawa, Zot and Rassat in Jos South and Barkin Ladi Local Government Areas went to bed after a hard day`s hustle for survival.

They must have offered their sincere supplications to God, hoping that the next day would bring brighter prospects, oblivious of an impending tragedy.

They were to be rudely woken up by the shattering sounds of guns and bombs in the wee hours of Sunday by an invading army of Hausa-Fulani herdsmen allegedly on a revenge mission.

What followed was unspeakable massacre of defenceless men, women and children in cold blood. The images of women and children including toddlers with severed heads and butchered bodies as published in the media can melt the most hardened of hearts.

The rampaging invaders were reported to have encircled the villages, blocking all the entry and exit routes and moving from house to house slaughtering their hapless and unsuspecting victims in a most atrocious manner.

The murderous herdsmen operated unchallenged for three hours. By the time they were through, over 500 innocent souls had been summarily dispatched to the world beyond.

The whole world woke up the following day only to behold the gory sights of headless and mutilated bodies of mostly women and children. The reactions from across the globe, in condemnation of the atrocity, had been swift and poignant. The killings have been qualified as a genocide and crime against humanity.

Those who perpetrated this heinous crime and their sponsors must be arraigned before the International Criminal Court as was done in the Rwanda genocide. We can no longer continue with such acts of impunity.

This is one crime too many. All those directly or remotely involved in the current genocide on the Plateau must be speedily brought to book.

To imagine that such an organized crime against humanity could take place unhindered and undetected in a State that is under a military-imposed curfew is beyond any reasonable contemplation, not with the Plateau brimming with all manner of security personnel especially in the aftermath of the January killings in Jos.

This is certainly a clear case of failure of the Nigerian State in its primary responsibility to protect life and property. It is also the failure of intelligence on the part of our security forces particularly the Army which had taken over internal security in Plateau following the January killings.

The Federal Government must therefore bear full responsibility for what has happened. Heads must roll. The government must start with the security agencies that let the country down either through complicity or inaction on their part.

A special investigation should be instituted to ascertain who played what role especially in the light of conflicting claims by the military commander in Jos, Major General Saleh Maina and Governor of Plateau State, Commodore Jonah Jang (Rtd).

An angry and distraught Jang had put the blame for the disaster on the door steps of the General Officer Commanding (GOC) the 3rd Amoured Division, Jos, Maj. Gen. Saleh Maina whom he accused of not acting on the distress calls and messages to his telephone.

Jang, at a press briefing at the Presidential Villa, Abuja, pointedly stated that he called the GOC to alert him on the information he received from the villagers that fateful Saturday evening on the invasion of the area by strangers with dangerous weapons.

He said that the GOC promised to take action. Jang noted that when the actual killings started the GOC had switched off his phones as subsequent calls made to him did not go through.

Jang's words: "I received reports at about 9pm that some movement of people with arms was seen around those villages and I reported to the GOC and he told me he was going to move some troops there, and because it is near where I live, I even saw a tank pass through my house and I thought it was going to towards the area.

"Three hours or so later, I was woken by a call that they have started burning the villages and people were being hacked to death and I started trying to locate the GOC but I couldn't get him on the telephone. It could have been avoided if they acted on my report."

Other high ranking officials of Plateau State Government, including the Commissioner for Information and Communications, Hon. Gregory Yenlong also admitted reaching the military commander via text messages when they could not access him on his lines.

General Maina had since responded to all the accusations; denying that neither Jang nor any other official of Plateau State Government talked to him or text any message to his phones. He claimed that the alert messages he received came from his military colleagues and unidentified members of the public.

Between Maina and Jang, it is not difficult to discern who is saying the truth. Now, even if Jang did not reach the GOC, which is unlikely, how come the GOC did not act on the several text messages which he admittedly received from other sources?

His argument that the messages deliberately misled the Army on the exact locations of the mayhem flies in the face. It is untenable and totally unacceptable.

I am of the conviction that the GOC has a case to answer. The Army and other security agencies are sustained by the tax payers' money to protect life and property and also safeguard the sovereignty of the nation. The inability of the military to act in the face of such grave danger to the lives of innocent villagers is worrisome.

The military must insulate itself from the ethno-religious politics of the civil society and remain the symbol of national unity and cohesion for which it had been known all along.

Like General Domkat Bali said in a recent interview on the current massacre, the day the Army begins to show bias in favour any particular religion or ethnic group, that will mark the beginning of the end of the country.

The government must therefore get to the root of this genocide. The full weight of the law must be applied against any person or persons convicted of participating in any manner in the mass slaughter.

The time to act is now. Strong signals must be sent that the era of impunity is over. Any person that engages in any act of rascality and atrocity must be answerable for his or her actions.

Nobody should be allowed to escape justice under the guise of group actions.

The Acting President, Dr. Goodluck Jonathan, must firmly demonstrate to Nigerians that under his watch, the country would not allow any acts of impunity to go unpunished. The place to start is this unwarranted massacre on the Plateau.

ThisDay, March 23, 2010

Chapter 47

Battle for the Soul of INEC

L ast week, the Senate began the consideration of the recommendations of the Senator Ike Ekweremadu-led Committee on the Review of the 1999 Constitution ahead of the 2011 General Elections. Although the 44-Member Committee in its wisdom rejected the popular view that the power to appoint the Chairman and members of the Independent National Electoral Commission (INEC) be vested in the National Judicial Council (NJC), a critical recommendation of the Justice Mohammed Uwais Committee on Electoral Reforms, it however adopted some key proposals which if fully endorsed by the Senate and the House of Representatives would go a long way in guaranteeing the independence of the electoral body and strengthening its institutional capacity to effectively discharge its constitutional mandate.

As at press time, however, the good news is that the Senate, sitting in plenary, has endorsed all the recommendations made by the Committee, with minor adjustments in some instances.

One of such proposals is the placement of INEC on first line charge of the Consolidated Revenue Fund of the Federation. This means that the funds appropriated for the Commission by the National Assembly shall be paid directly into its accounts without recourse to the Executive. The general belief is that such a constitutionally guaranteed financial autonomy would give the Commission the needed leverage to assert itself and rebuff any attempt aimed at compromising its capacity to act independently.

It was also widely reported in the media last week that the House Committee on the Review of the 1999 Constitution which rose from a retreat in Makurdi, Benue State recently, like its Senate counterpart, similarly dropped the Uwais recommendation that rather than the President, the NJC should appoint the Chairman and members of INEC.

The Uwais Committee, composed of eminent Nigerians, had in its well-reasoned arguments, submitted that the only way to truly guarantee the independence of the electoral body was to locate the power to appoint its Chairman and members outside the Presidency. This was to avoid a situation where the man that calls the piper dictates the tune. This recommendation, alongside other progressive proposals by the Uwais Committee, has been widely hailed by majority of Nigerians as a major antidote to acts of malfeasance that characterize the conduct of elections in the country. It is for this singular reason that many people including the civil society and opposition are insisting on the retention of the recommendation of the Uwais Committee on the composition of INEC.

But curiously, there exist some interest groups whose conception of electoral reforms is the removal of the current leadership of INEC. In this category are a section of the opposition, some civil society groups and a section of the media.

The Nigeria Labour Congress (NLC) lately has joined the mushrooming groups to crusade for the removal of the Chairman of INEC, Professor Maurice Iwu. Ordinarily, in a democracy like ours, there should be nothing wrong with these agitations. It is consistent with the constitutional rights of the people to freedom of expression.

But the worry now is the partisan colouration which these agitations are dangerously assuming. It is true that under Professor Iwu, one of the worst elections took place in Nigeria. I, for one was a victim of the electoral heist of 2007 in my quest to represent the people of Umuahia Federal Constituency, Abia State in the House of Representatives for which I cried foul.

A dispassionate analysis of the situation has shown that the problem of having a free and fair election in Nigeria goes beyond the cosmetic demand for the removal of the leadership of the electoral body. The problems are systemic and institutional. For the nation to achieve transparent and credible elections, these problems must be frontally tackled. Otherwise, no matter the individual that is put in charge of INEC, including an angel, the issue of credible elections may continue to elude us. And this is where the laudable recommendations of the Uwais Committee come in.

If the independence in the composition of INEC is guaranteed, its financial autonomy firmly secured, and an Electoral Offences Commission exists to rein in election riggers, then the nation would have been on its way to fixing permanently the problems associated with our elections. If this is not done, the problems will still remain with us whether Iwu is there or not.

The truth is that no past chairman of the electoral body right from the time of Esua to date has been spared any public vilification on account of election conduct. The job is a difficult one, it must be admitted. Ovie Whiskey was condemned. Eme Awa was deprecated. Humphrey Nwosu who conducted the June 12, 1993 elections reputed to be the freest and fairest, is still a subject of ridicule in the media. Akpata and Guobadia have also not been spared. If all these gentlemen failed, then something is wrong some where. Perhaps, like Shakespeare said, the problem may not be in us but in our stars.

Against this background, therefore, the concerns of Nigerians should centre on how to evolve deep-seated reforms that should guarantee the independence and autonomy of the electoral body and insulate it from the manipulations of an overbearing Executive. If this is not achieved, we will still be confronted with flawed elections in the future.

A Presidential Candidate in the June 12 Election and currently, the Chairman of the Elders' Committee of the All Nigerian Peoples Party (ANPP), Alhaji Bashir Tofa shares the same view. He noted in an interview: "I do not believe that you can pin this problem on any particular person. I know Iwu is the head but if the environment allows these things to continue, they would continue. There had always been laws in Nigeria and there are people who are always breaking these laws. That is why I am saying that whoever it is, Nigerians as well as politicians must take it upon themselves to ensure credible elections."

And like we have seen in the recent elections conducted by INEC in Edo and Anambra States, if the environment is not fouled, a credible outcome is achieved. A critic like Governor Adams Oshiomhole had to lead a delegation of his cabinet to Abuja to commend INEC for the transparent conduct of the re-run elections in Etsako Local Government Area of Edo State.

Similarly, other known critics of INEC like the National Leader of APGA, Chief Chukwuemeka Odumegwu Ojukwu and Governor Peter Obi of Anambra State had been singing the praises of INEC and Iwu for the huge success recorded in the last gubernatorial elections in the State. Unlike the controversial Ekiti re-run elections, all the independent groups that monitored and observed the elections in Edo and Anambra States gave INEC a clean bill of health in the manner it handled the elections. What this means is that once the atmosphere is not polluted by desperate politicians and their collaborators in the system, the nation is not incapable of having free, fair, credible and transparent elections.

The way forward now is for all well meaning Nigerians to mount pressure on the National Assembly to retain and restore all the key recommendations of the Uwais Committee which are very capable of taking the country to the next level. We must appeal to members of the National Assembly on whose shoulders lies the responsibility of institutionalizing credible electoral reforms not to allow their sense of objectivity to be beclouded by considerations of political exigencies. To do so, will be a great disservice to the nation and future generations. There lies the challenge.

_____

ThisDay, March 30, 2010

Chapter 48

A Resurgent Spirit in the Senate

T he Senate of the Federal Republic of Nigeria would seem to have weaned itself of the image of a lackluster and impotent Chamber that is always bickering over the welfare and pecuniary interests of its members. Until recently, the rating of the Senate was very poor in public estimation.

The image crisis dated to the inception of the Fourth Republic in 1999 when the body became embroiled in leadership crises. The emergent Evan Enwerem leadership was accused of incompetence and playing stooge to the Presidency of Olusegun Obasanjo.

The Chuba Okadigbo leadership that took over following the impeachment of Enwerem ran into problem with President Obasanjo whose Presidency was not only meddlesome in the affairs of the National Assembly but also very overbearing.

The impeachment of Enwerem naturally brought deep cleavages in the Senate to the extent that the Senators became very suspicious of one another. Okadigbo also did not help matters with some insensitive comments ascribed to him which brought the Senate into direct collision with the civil society.

At the height of the controversy surrounding the furniture allowance, considered grossly disproportionate by the public, Okadigbo as the Senate President was reported as saying that Senators were not in Abuja to amass poverty. Such elite posturing alienated the lawmakers from the electorate that elected them into office.

The Senate was later to be rocked by certificate and contract scandals, resulting in the forced removal of the Okadigbo leadership in the Senate. The Senate did not quite recover from those self-inflicted crises until the emergence of Ken Nnamani, whose leadership gave the Senate a new lease of life and propelled the august body to a new pedestal of respectability and authority.

Not many Nigerians would forget in a hurry the high level of patriotism and statesmanship demonstrated by Senator Nnamani during the debate on Tenure Elongation otherwise known as Third Term.

Nnamani masterfully and bravely handled, to the admiration of Nigerians, what was clearly a delicate and tricky situation.

The brief period that Nnamani held the forte as the Senate President could be described as a major turning point in the history of the Senate.

After Nnamani, came David Mark. Although his emergence was not as contentious as that of his predecessors, nonetheless there was a division in the Chamber between those who backed his aspiration and those that supported his only challenger, George Akume, a former Governor of Benue State.

In the last three years that he had been on the saddle of leadership, Mark, to his credit, has done very well in holding the Senate together. But if the truth must be told, the Senate under his leadership has not really flourished unlike the experience under Nnamani.

At a time, the House of Representatives showed better promise in their approach to national issues. For instance, in the consideration of the 2008 Federal Budget, the House was more thorough than the Senate. Whereas the Senate passed the budget as presented to it by President Umar Musa Yar'Adua within a record time of two weeks, the House through a rigorous analysis of the budget was able to discover and cause to be repatriated over N300 billion of federal funds placed in hidden accounts by the Executive.

However, the Senate under Mark has not been forthcoming on major national issues, until much more recently when it would seem that it has suddenly woken up from a very deep slumber. For instance, while the controversy raged over the continued absence of President Yar'Adua from office without informing the National Assembly in compliance with Constitutional provisions, the Senate sided with the likes of Michael Aaondooaka, former Attorney General of the Federation and Minister of Justice, who told the nation that Yar'Adua could run the country from any part of the world.

The Senate failed to provide leadership at that particular moment when it mattered most. Not even the protest march to the National Assembly by the Professor Wole Soyinka-led Save Nigeria Group could arouse the Senate from its slumber. The leadership of the Senate ignored Soyinka and his group as none of them came out to address the protesters. Interestingly, it was the Speaker of the House of Representatives, Hon. Dimeji Bankole that even offered to address and pacify the protesting group.

As pressures mounted from several quarters including representations by former Heads of States and Governments, eminent group of leaders led by former Senate President, Anyim Pius Anyim and many others, the Senate could not act on the side of the Constitution. A motion tabled to discuss and ascertain the health status of the President was frustrated in the Senate Chamber.

However, the Senate has recently and suddenly changed gear and is beginning to show leadership that is expected of it. Although it acted belatedly, the invocation of the Doctrine of Necessity by the Senate which allowed the Vice President, Dr. Goodluck Jonathan, to assume the position of Acting President and Commander-in-Chief of the Armed Forces, obviously saved the nation from sliding into anarchy. The Senate under Mark deserves national commendation for doing so even though it fell short of the expectations of the vast majority of Nigerian people that wanted the relevant sections of the Constitution to be applied.

The Senate under Mark has since seized the initiative and is now providing leadership between the two co-ordinate chambers.

The resurgent spirit in the Senate also manifested in the business-like manner it handled the issue of Constitution amendment. Upon the presentation of the report of the Ike Ekweremadu Committee on the Constitution Review, the Senate in a rare display of seriousness and commitment considered the proposed amendments clause by clause and subsequently passed same without much ado. This is a major feat considering the fact that similar efforts in the past never went beyond the second reading.

At the moment the House of Reps is still playing politics with the Constitution review. The report of the Bayero Nafada-led Constitution Review Committee is yet to be considered by the House.

The Senate also showed leadership in the way and manner it handled the screening and confirmation of Ministerial nominees presented by the Acting President, Dr. Goodluck Jonathan. The dispatch with which it handled the issue shows a Senate that is in tune with the mood of the nation.

The Senate should sustain the momentum and never relapse into inertia and ineptitude. As it has now find its bearing, it is hoped that the Senate would revisit Section 144 of the Constitution in respect of the lingering absence of Yar`Adua from office and do the right thing. The ever lurking shadows of Yar`Adua within Aso Rock Villa is not a good omen for the Acting Presidency of Jonathan. The matter should be resolved by following the provisions of the Constitution.

_____

ThisDay, April 6, 2010

Chapter 49

Can the Jonathan Team Deliver?

Since the National Assembly came up on February 9 with the novel strategy termed "the doctrine of necessity" through which the reins of State power were transferred to Dr. Goodluck Jonathan as the Acting President, a measure of stability has returned to the polity. Prior to that historic decision, a dangerous void had developed at the highest level of national political leadership occasioned by the lingering absence of President Umar Musa Yar`Adua from his duty post without handing over to his deputy in compliance with Constitutional provisions.

No one was clearly in charge. The ship of State was floating rudderless on the political high sea with no captain to steer it safely ashore. A faceless cabal consisting of the most ambitious members of the kitchen cabinet of Yar`Adua was said to have seized control of State power and was illegally exercising same without the consent of the nation.

The then Vice President, Dr. Jonathan who ordinarily should have taken control in the absence of the President was completely sidelined. The cabal and their supporters not only employed all kinds of tricks in the books but also came up with some meaningless rationalizations to justify the hopeless and laughable situation in which their collective contrivance had pushed the country to.

Goaded by their obstinacy and false sense of importance, they took hostage of the ailing President and denied any form of access to him. For the more than three months Yar`Adua was hospitalized at a Saudi hospital, no one except high-ranking members of the so-called cabal had access to him. Attempts by Dr. Jonathan and other top government officials including leaders of the ruling Peoples Democratic Party (PDP) to see the President at his sick bed in Jeddah were rebuffed.

When the tide of public opinion was beginning to swing in favour of transmitting power to Jonathan so that the nation could move forward, the ailing President, in what could pass for a well hatched and executed coup d`etat, was smuggled back to Nigeria in the dead of the night and taken straight to the Presidential Villa. But that plot to stop or rewind the clock of progress turned out to be a disastrous failure. Today, against the wish of the cabal and their unpatriotic supporters, the nation is moving forward, courtesy of the doctrine of necessity.

A lot has since happened. With the support of the National Assembly, the Acting President has stepped up the tempo of governance through some thoughtful decisions he had taken since assuming the reins of power. He has reconstituted the Executive Council of the Federation (EXCOF), setting in the process, well-defined targets against which the performances of members would be measured.

A close reading of the cabinet clearly shows a bold attempt on the part of Acting President Jonathan to leave a legacy of service and achievements. He realizes that the time left is short, but within the shortness of the time, the fortunes of the nation can still be turned around. He retained some Ministers in the dissolved cabinet and deployed them appropriately. There is no doubt that the retained Ministers in their new portfolios would add good value to governance.

No matter our personal opinions to the contrary, the likes of Diezani Allison-Madueke, Dora Akunyili, Dr. Usman Shamsudeen, Odein Ajumogobia, Remi Babalola and John Odey were impressive in their last outing. With so much expectation from the nation and limited time available, these Ministers would need to double their efforts to assist Jonathan make the desired impact in the months ahead.

Acting President Jonathan has similarly brought into the cabinet some well tested technocrats and pragmatic politicians who are expected to team up with the re-appointed Ministers to advance the frontiers of good governance. In the line up are the likes of Labaran Maku, immediate past Deputy Governor of Nasarawa State now the Minister of State for Information and Communications; Segun Aganga, the former Managing Director of the London-based Goldman Sachs, the world`s most powerful investment bank, now holding the Finance portfolio; Mohammed Bello Adoke, SAN, a legal luminary who dazzled in the Senate at the confirmation hearings, now the Minister of Justice and Attorney General of the Federation (AGF); Captain Emmanuel Iheanacho who, until his appointment as the Minister of Interior was a big time player in the maritime sector; Senator Bala Mohammed, the new FCT Minister who, before now, was the Deputy Chairman, Senate Committee on Aviation and Professor Onyebuchi Chukwu, an eminent medical scholar who has just been nominated to fill Ebonyi slot in the cabinet. He hails from Afikpo in Afikpo North Local Government Area of the State.

Until his nomination to replace the immediate past Minister of Education, Dr. Sam Egwu, Professor Chukwu was the Chief Medical Director of the Ebonyi State University Teaching Hospital, Abakaliki. He is an accomplished Orthopedic and Trauma Surgeon. Professor Chukwu holds the Fellowships of West African College of Surgeons and International College of Surgeons. He is also an International Affiliate Member of the American Academy of Orthopedic Surgeons.

He is expected to bring on board the vast experience he has garnered over the years in the field of medicine as a scholar, consultant and expert both in the clinical ward and classroom to bear on his present assignment.

Since Dr. Jonathan has allocated almost all the cabinet positions with the exception of Health and Human Services, it is naturally expected that Professor Chukwu would be assigned the Health portfolio where his expertise will be of much relevance to the nation if, hopefully, he is confirmed by the Senate.

A dispassionate analysis of the Federal cabinet, shows that the Acting President has made efforts to place round pegs in round holes. It is expected that the Jonathan team would much likely deliver on their mandate.

ThisDay, April 20, 2010

Chapter 50

Police Oppression on Eastern Roads

A lot has been written and said about the intimidating presence of the men of Nigeria Police Force on all available roads in the whole of South East and parts of South South. Ideally, their presence should be able to inspire a sense of security among the road users and motorists. But this is hardly the case.

Their ubiquitous presence has been a mixed bag of unpalatable and nightmarish experiences for those who regularly ply those death traps in the name of Eastern roads. My recent trip by road from Abuja to the South Eastern States of Enugu and Abia yielded enough evidence on the misconduct of some of the policemen manning the numerous road blocks on the Eastern highways.

The impression one gets when you pass the Benue-Enugu boundary at Orokam and moves into the Igbo territory, commencing from Obolo Afor is that of a people under police occupation; a conquered enclave or if you like a vassal State. The kind of tyranny and oppression to which our people are subjected on these roads by very hostile and unfriendly mobile policemen drawn mainly from a certain section of the country makes one to begin to feel that the entire arrangement is deliberately put in place by anti-Igbo forces at the highest level of power to intimidate, harass and humiliate Ndigbo.

If this assertion is not true, how then can we explain a situation where at every pole along the entire stretches of Eastern roads particularly Nsukka-Enugu; Enugu-Umuahia-Aba-Port Harcourt; Owerri-Aba; Owerri-Elele-Port Harcourt; Owerri-Onitsha; Onitsha-Enugu is a check point manned by these hostile and unfriendly policemen?

The cheap argument that has always been made to justify such an anomalous situation is that there is rising incidents of kidnapping and armed robberies in that part of the country. The situation might appear to be endemic, but the truth of the matter is that there is no part of the country that is free from the menace of criminals in whatever guise.

Places like Abuja and some parts of the North that were previously considered relatively safer no longer enjoy such status any longer. We have seen a situation where in the month of February alone this year two violent crimes were recorded in Karu, a suburb of Abuja in which innocent Nigerians were butchered to death by axe men. Only the other day, Alhaji Abubakar Rimi, a leading politician in Nigeria died out of shock, resulting from a robbery incident in Kano.

These incidents, as unfortunate as they were, had not resulted into a situation where all the highways in Abuja and the North are littered with menacing road blocks and oppressive policemen. Why is the South East different?

Again, even with the ubiquitous presence of the mobile policemen all over the South East, kidnappings and other violent crimes have continued to occur, indicating that what is required is to beef up and enhance the intelligence gathering capacity of the security agencies and not littering the roads with policemen who are only interested in extorting money under all kinds of pretences from innocent motorists. It must be clearly stated here that those who ply the Eastern roads are under police siege and are being visited with untold hardships. Our people are suffering in silence. It is just that protest culture is lacking in the East, otherwise the people would have taken to the streets to protest the continued menace which some of these uncultured policemen pose on the roads.

I feel embittered by the level of oppression and intimidation to which innocent motorists are subjected on a daily basis on the bad and poor Eastern roads. There are better and modern ways of fighting crimes. It cannot be by mounting road blocks with metal contraptions and logs of wood at every pole with half literate and drunken policemen whose only stock in trade is to molest and extort money from road users.

I have been privileged to travel to many places outside Nigeria. We should not even go far to Europe, America or Asia to borrow a leaf from what they are doing to tackle crime. Examples from some African countries should suffice here. Today, every body is talking about the transformation that has taken place in Ghana and a few other places in Africa. Why can't we pick some ideas from there and advance our situation here?

The last time I was in Accra and its suburbs, there was no single police check point any where on their roads. The few policemen that were seen were those that were directing traffic at road junctions. Instead, what were evident were police patrols on the roads.

Similarly, in Uganda under Yoweri Museveni, the roads are regularly being monitored by motorized patrols. As you drive from the Entebbe Airport to the city center in Kampala, you only encounter policemen on patrols not road blocks. It is the same situation when you ply the Kampala-Jinja highway, enroute the source of River Nile. The issue of road blocks is no longer fashionable. Their presence has not deterred armed robberies, kidnappings or other heinous crimes. The emphasis now should be on intelligence gathering, deployment of surveillance cameras along strategic points and motorized patrols. These uncouth and hostile policemen who have been a terror to road users should be withdrawn from the highways. They have caused untold hardships to motorists.

The Inspector General of Police, Ogbonnaya Onovo must take decisive steps to address the oppression to which travelers on Eastern highways are subjected. If for any untenable reason, the police check points cannot be dismantled, then they should be reduced to the barest minimum since the East is not at war with the rest of Nigeria. Again, he should look into the composition of the policemen that man these road blocks with a view to reflecting federal character which is a constitutional requirement.

The security of the people cannot be left in the hands of hostile, uncaring and oppressive policemen who do not believe they have anything at stake in the environment in which they operate. The unbecoming behavior of these policemen who act as occupation forces is what has hastened the calls for State-controlled Police in Nigeria. Onovo should do the right thing now. I also appeal to our representatives at the National Assembly to come together on the platform of the South East caucus to make strong representations to the relevant authorities on this vexatious matter. They should be able to extract firm commitment from the Police hierarchy on the need to do away with these road blocks that have not really served any useful purpose.

Our people have suffered enough humiliation in the hands of these "invaders". They should be removed from the highways.

ThisDay, April 27, 2010

Chapter 51

Leadership Crisis in the House

T he House of Representatives has been in the news lately, though, for the wrong reasons. The newspapers were awash recently with stories on the plot by some aggrieved members of the House to remove the Speaker, Rt. Hon. Dimeji Bankole from office for reasons that are not quite discernible.

The plot as usual is assuming a familiar trend or tradition in the House which seems to bother on the politics of bread and butter. Experience has shown that each time there was a planned reshuffling of the Standing Committees of the House, some faceless groups and individual members would always spring up with allegations of wrongdoings against the leadership of the House.

It happened during the reign of Ghali Na`Abba and Aminu Masari. Those who lose out during the constitution or re-constitution of the House Committees would always forge themselves into opposition groups to plot the downfall of the leadership.

Both Na`Abba and Masari had running battles with such aggrieved groups during their time. Several impeachment plots were hatched against them but they never succeeded.

In the case of the first female Speaker of the House, Hon. Patricia Olubunmi Etteh, who was forced out of office on alleged contract inflation, the undisclosed reason had to do with the fact that some ranking and influential members of the House were denied chairmanship of 'juicy' Committees.

Is it therefore surprising that the recent plot to remove Bankole from office is coming on the heels of a planned move by the leadership of the House to reconstitute the Committees for effective and optimum performance?

The impending tinkering of the House Committees also means that lawmakers in 'juicy' committees may lose out in the power game. The anxiety and tension it has generated are quite understandable. This accounts for the growing state of uneasiness in the House at the moment.

Apart from the issue of the planned reconstitution of the membership and chairmanship of the House Committees, which some very selfish groups consider as potent threats to their interests, there are also underlying issues which have to do with permutations and calculations on the 2011 general elections.

Unverified reports associate a pressure group in the House, Nigeria First Forum (NFF) with the current plot to oust the leadership. This group and its counterpart in the Senate, National Interest Group, (NIG), led by Senator Bala Mohammed, now Minister of the Federal Capital Territory (FCT), spearheaded the campaign for the transmission of Presidential powers to Dr. Goodluck Jonathan as the Acting President pending the time ailing President Umar Musa Yar`Adua would be fit enough to return to his duty post.

It is gathered that the NFF, believed to be working for the political interest of Acting President Jonathan, wants a total cleansing of the House leadership in order to forestall any obstacle on its ultimate plan to remove President Yar`Adua from office on health grounds, yielding the coveted Presidential seat to Jonathan in a substantive capacity.

Speaker Bankole`s perceived closeness to Yar`Adua is seen by the strategists within the NFF as a major hurdle that must be overcome for the main plan of the group to sail smoothly. The loyalty of Bankole to Yar`Adua is cited as the key reason why the House resisted for a very long time the national clamour for Jonathan to take up the reins of power on account of the dangerous void that was created at the Presidency following the prolonged ill-health of Yar`Adua.

The office of the Acting President has however washed its hands of any links with the NFF or any faceless group on the brewing crisis of confidence in the House. Jonathan is said to be uninterested in the power tussle in the House as any involvement in the plot to remove the House leadership would be seen as interference in the internal affairs of the legislature.

The NFF on its part has however denied any plot to oust Bankole from office. In a statement in Abuja last week and endorsed by the Chairman, Hon. Abba Anas Adamu and Secretary, Hon. Ishaku Joshua Sharah, the NFF noted that the stories linking it with the purported impeachment plan against Bankole were 'false, and misleading but also calculated to blackmail the group which was existing to pursue laudable national objectives devoid of primordial sentiments'.

The group further said that it haboured no agenda of impeaching President Umar Musa Yar`Adua who has been sidelined for sometime now by illness but it however reassured that within the period of the indisposition of Yar`Adua, it would 'mobilize members to support the policies and actions of the Acting President, Dr. Goodluck Ebele Jonathan in the national interest, pursuant to the Constitution of the Federal Republic of Nigeria'.

The seeming retreat of the NFF from the impeachment plan against Bankole may have been informed by the unpopularity of the action and the likely uncontrollable furore it may generate within the polity.

Emerging facts however indicate that the real sponsors of the impeachment plot are from Ogun, the home State of Bankole. Former President Obasanjo and Governor Gbenga Daniel are being separately fingered in the plot. Two members of the House from Ogun State who are being positioned as possible replacements for Bankole and a former Speaker were alleged to have attended a meeting in Ogun recently where the strategies for the impeachment plot were fashioned out.

These arrow heads are to reach out to other House members from the North, South East and South South to get them to buy into the plot. The whole plan appears to be running into a hitch as majority of the members so far approached have not shown any keenness because of the likely unintended consequences which the action may produce.

It is believed that any change in the leadership of the House at this critical period when the members are set to consider and pass the Constitutional Amendments and Electoral Reforms Bills as the Senate had done over three weeks ago, may be a major setback in the determination of Acting President Jonathan to conduct a credible, free and fair election in 2011. Analysts are worried that the unfolding drama in the House may do the polity no good, particularly when we are almost at the last lap of the national journey to 2011 general elections. It is in the interest of the lawmakers to resolve whatever differences they have among themselves amicably without overheating the system.

ThisDay, May 4, 2010

Chapter 52

The Coming Implosion in the PDP

A serious tussle for power is on in the Peoples Democratic Party (PDP). The game of wits that played out recently among the various interest groups in the party over the scheduled National Executive Committee meeting in Abuja is an indication of a brewing crisis of confidence which may put the biggest political party in Africa in very serious disarray if commonsense does not prevail.

The unfolding drama which has thrown up many combatant groups with entrenched political interests has the potential of causing a major implosion within the ranks and file of the party.

What is happening in the party today has long been predicted by political analysts who have followed closely the trends of events in the party from inception in 1998. Although over time, the party has somehow managed to moderate its internal contradictions, it must be acknowledged however that the seeds of the interminable crises in the party were sown when various ideologically incompatible groups, out of convenience, came together to form the party with the sole aim of wresting power from the military.

This was why the reactionary and progressive factions of the political elite which in the First and Second Republics fought themselves to a bitter end in the struggle for political control suddenly found themselves operating under one umbrella. No single effort was made to rein in the same centrifugal forces in the party who in the past brought the country to its knees.

The abiding philosophy was to get the military faction of the ruling elite out of the way so that power could be seized for its own sake. Karl Marx in the Communist Manifesto said that "capitalism shall sow the seeds of its discord". This prophetic statement is particularly true of the PDP where both centrifugal and centripetal forces are pretending to be working together for the common good.

Any dispassionate and unbiased analysis of what is going on in the party at the moment must take into account the internal contradictions that were inherent in the PDP at formation. A closer look at the political orientation of the dramatis personae in the current imbroglio clearly shows that they are lacking in ideological compatibility, hence they are mutually suspicious of one another.

The objective for the coming together of people of different political persuasions for the purpose of retrieving power from the military may have been propelled by patriotic intentions. But good intentions are not enough to guarantee a stable and coherent political organization because a political party properly called must be a grouping of people who subscribe to common ideology and philosophy. It was not so in the case of the emergent PDP.

Unlike in the past when there was a semblance of ideological and principled politics, today our so-called political leaders are driven by inordinate desire for primitive capital accumulation. That is why politicians are changing their membership of political parties at will without caring a hoot.

Part of the underlying reasons for the crisis in the party is the hijack of its commanding heights by the elements that are considered strangers in the fold. For example, some of the leaders of the party who are today calling the shots were not original members of the party. They include the National Chairman, Prince Vincent Ogbulafor; National Secretary, Mohammed Kawu Baraje; Chief Emmanuel Iwuanyanwu, Member, Board of Trustees (BOT); Dr. Bukola Saraki, Chairman, Governors' Forum and his father, Dr. Olusola Saraki, the leader of PDP in Kwara State. They all came from the rival All Nigerian Peoples Party (ANPP).

In the case of Ogbulafor, he was the governorship candidate of the All Peoples Party (APP) in Abia State in the 1999 general elections in which he lost to Chief Orji Uzor Kalu of the PDP. But today, these former members of the opposition party are the ones dispensing patronages within the party.

This anomalous situation has brought some distortions which are at variance with the vision of the founding fathers of the party who have been sidelined or have given up in frustrations. Such founding fathers include the likes of Dr. Alex Ekwueme, Malam Adamu Ciroma, Chief Solomon Lar, Professor Jerry Gana, Prince B.B. Apugo, Chief Yomi Edu, Chief Dapo Sarumi, Alhaji Lawal Kaita, Alhaji Iro Dan Musa, Mrs. Titilayo Ajanaku, Dr. Okwesilieze Nwodo and many others.

It is against this background that the current battle of wits by some contending forces for the soul of the party must be appreciated and understood. Although there may be some hidden motives on the part of the PDP Reform Group led by former Senate President, Senator Ken Nnamani and former Speaker, House of Representatives, Hon. Aminu Bello Masari, their mission to retrieve the party from the grips of those they consider political interlopers and buccaneers and reposition it in line with the visions of the founding fathers can hardly be faulted.

According to Political Scientists, the only thing that is constant in life is change. And change in whatever form or shape is always resisted by those whose privileges may be negatively affected. But in all situations, change is inevitable. The current wind of change that is blowing in the PDP has the potential of either strengthening the party if it is well managed or causing an implosion that may spell doom to the party that wants to rule Nigeria for the next 60 years.

At the moment the party is said to have been split into four major camps, with each of the factions fighting to take control of the machinery of the party ahead of the 2011 general elections. The factions include the Reform Group said to have the sympathy of Acting President Goodluck Jonathan, the Babangida group, the Governors' forum which is backing Ogbulafor and his National Working Committee and the faction loyal to former Vice President Atiku Abubakar who has just returned to the party from the opposition Action Congress.

The suspension of Nnamani, Masari and other members of the Reform Group, the move to arraign Ogbulafor before an Abuja High Court for corruption and the plot to stop the return of Atiku to PDP are parts of the scheming and counter scheming by the various contending groups to gain the upper hand and take control of the machinery of the party. This, analysts fear may result into an implosion.

The decision to arraign Ogbulafor for an offence allegedly committed about ten years ago when he was the Minister of Economic Affairs is clearly politically motivated. Since after serving as Minister, the man has gone ahead to serve as the National Secretary of the same party. How come that he has not been prosecuted until now when some vested interests are variously scheming for the presidential ticket of the party?

For whatever reason, it is in the interest of the PDP that Prince Ogbulafor is not disgraced out of office. If the powers that be are determined that he should go in order to pave way for their political calculations, Ogbulafor should be given a soft landing.

If he is shoved out unceremoniously, such an action may trigger off a chain of reactions which no one, not even the champions of his ouster, may be able to control. It is, therefore, in the interest of the party, like

Adamu Ciroma stated recently, to abide by its own rules and constitution in arriving at any decisions. It will save the country from unintended political consequences.

ThisDay, May 11, 2010

Chapter 53

Jonathan: A Man of Destiny

Thursday, May 6, 2010 was a day of mixed feelings for the nation. The former ailing President, Alhaji Umaru Musa Yar`Adua had died the previous night and by the next morning the news, which caught many people unawares, had spread like a wild fire around the country.

Though the President had been sidelined by prolonged illness which kept him out of public orbit since November 23, 2009, the news of his death was received with sorrow and sympathy, all the same. Here was a President who had the best of intentions for his fatherland but could not unfold his full potentials because of the challenges of a heart condition that continued to weigh him down.

As Yar`Adua joined his ancestors, he will be remembered for his disarming humility, sincerity of mind, simplicity, honesty and integrity. He was a true democrat who strongly believed in the rule of law and due process.

His greatest achievement in office was the Amnesty Programme which led to the peaceful disarming of the various militant groups in the Niger Delta and a strong commitment to transform the crisis ridden Niger Delta from a zone of misery and poverty to a region of peace, prosperity and development.

In spite of the activities of a cabal that took him hostage for pecuniary considerations towards the end of his Presidency and which almost threw the country into anarchy and chaos, history will be kind to Yar`Adua for his efforts to foster the culture of probity and accountability in public life.

As the chapter on Yar`Adua`s Presidency was closing, another chapter was opening with the inauguration of Dr. Goodluck Jonathan as the substantive President of the Federal Republic of Nigeria in accordance with the provisions of the Constitution. Jonathan, I must say is really a man of destiny.

There is something in a name. Since he emerged on the political scene in 1999 as Deputy Governor in Bayelsa State under the administration of Chief Diepreye Solomon Alamieyseigha, good luck has continued to follow Dr. Jonathan. Even though he never manifested any ambition to succeed his boss, destiny however propelled him to the governorship of the State against his wish when Alamieyeseigha was removed from office through impeachment by the Bayelsa State House of Assembly mid way into his second tenure in office.

Before he was picked in 1999 to run with Alamieyeseigha, Jonathan was largely an unknown quantity, politically speaking. He was serving as an Assistant Director in the defunct Oil Minerals Producing Areas Development Commission (OMPADEC), a forerunner to the present Niger Delta Development Commission, created by the General Ibrahim Babangida regime before he was approached to take up the No.2 slot in Bayelsa State.

His acceptance of the offer to serve in that position would seem to be the divine guidance that he needed to unlock hidden fortunes which destiny had in stock for him. Destiny has since then continued to propel him forward. He served the people of Bayelsa very loyally and dutifully. Jonathan discharged his duties with a very high sense of responsibility and purposefulness. Above all he was very loyal to his then boss, DSP Alamieyeseigha who was popularly known at that time as the Governor-General of the Ijaw Nation.

When Alamieyeseigha was impeached, he hesitated to take up the governorship. In deed he was said to have gone into hiding, but with sustained pressures from the then President Obasanjo, he reluctantly accepted to serve as the governor. As at 2007 when he had completed the truncated tenure of Alamieyeseigha, he sought and won the nomination of his party, the Peoples Democratic Party (PDP) to run in his own image as the governor of Bayelsa State.

But before one could say Jack Robinson, he had been catapulted to the national political stage as the Vice Presidential running mate to Alhaji Umar Musa Yar'Adua who had just emerged as the presidential candidate of the PDP. Nobody gave him any chance because he was not in the presidential calculations. There were other major political actors from the South South geo-political zone like him who ran impressive campaigns for the Presidential ticket of the PDP who many political observers had thought would be considered for the Vice presidential ticket.

The powers that be at that period did not look in that direction. Like David in the Bible who was picked from the grazing field where he was tending his flock and made king, Jonathan was picked from the creeks of Bayelsa to become the No.2 man in Nigeria.

His emergence as the Vice Presidential candidate stunned bookmakers who were busy peddling big political names. He ran with Yar'Adua and they went ahead to win the Presidential election. He was sworn in on May 29, 2007 as the Vice President of the Federal Republic of Nigeria. The rest as they say is history.

Jonathan comes across as a humble, cheerful, calculating, dependable, self-effacing and unambitious leader who could be loyal to a fault. His humility and loyalty which some analysts consider as weakness have in deed proven to be his strength.

With his divine elevation to the Presidential seat, Dr. Goodluck Jonathan now needs more than luck to run a complex country like Nigeria. If before he operated under the shadows, now he must be his own man and stamp his feet on the ground.

Much as humility and goodness are fine political virtues, Jonathan must be ready to take tough decisions in the national interest regardless of whose ox is gored. With some decisions he made in his capacity as Acting President, there is no doubt that he is fully prepared for the challenges of the office. He must assert himself and take full control of the reins of power.

I have no doubt in my mind that he will be fair to all Nigerians irrespective of tribe, religion and geography. In the lighter mood, those of us from Abia State consider ourselves lucky with Goodluck Jonathan. Since his wife, Dame Patience Jonathan, has her roots in my community, Ohuhu in Umuahia, Abia State, our people in Abia are hopeful that his Presidency will rub off positively on them. We wish him a successful tenure in office.

ThisDay, May 18, 2010

Chapter 54

Giving Impetus to Electoral Reforms

L ast week, President Goodluck Jonathan made good his promise to unveil his nominees for the positions of Chairman, Independent National Electoral Commission (INEC), Federal Electoral Commissioners and Resident Electoral Commissioners. The list which has a former President of Academic Staff Union of Universities (ASUU) and current Vice Chancellor of Bayero University, Kano, Professor Attahiru Jega as the Chairman was unanimously endorsed by the National Council of State after a presentation by the President.

Among the Federal Commissioners are Professor Lai Olurode, a renowned Political Scientist at the University of Lagos and General Bagudu Mamman, a former Minister of the FCT, Abuja. A thorough scrutiny of the list immediately shows a painstaking effort on the part of President Jonathan to ensure that only men of integrity, principles and moral high standing in the society were assembled for the urgent and important task of giving the nation a flawless and credible election in 2011.

The composition of INEC as made public shows that President Jonathan can be taken seriously on his professed commitment to bequeath the nation electoral reforms that would usher in a new era of hope in the sanctity of the ballot. President Jonathan had at a forum in Nice, France recently assured the international community that his government was going to nominate very credible and respected Nigerians to INEC, adding that the prospective nominees were people he had never met or interacted with in his life.

With the names on the list which has now been forwarded to the Senate for confirmation, President Jonathan has proven to be a man of his words who means well for our nation. It is an incontestable fact that flawed and manipulated elections in which the people and their votes never counted had been the bane of our political process since the attainment of political independence in 1960.

There is therefore a near consensus that if we are able as a nation to get the conduct of our elections right, then the country would have been launched on an irreversible path to national greatness and economic growth. For too long, Nigerians have yearned for the power to freely choose their representatives in any election without let or hindrance. This power has always been denied them; to the extent that election results had never really reflected the will of the people. Nigerians therefore want a situation in which their votes will count in every election.

The clamor for a credible electoral system resonated across the length and breadth of Nigeria when the Justice Muhammed Uwais panel on electoral reforms traversed the country in solicitation for written and oral memoranda from members of the public. In all the public hearings that were held in the six geo-political zones of the country, the people were united in their demand for a credible and transparent electoral system that would ensure that the outcomes of elections truly reflect the will of the electorate.

It is the general consensus that once we are able to get our elections right, the 'do or die attitude' and desperation that often characterize the conduct of political contestants would be considerably minimized if not totally abated. Once a level playing field is created for all political parties and their candidates and the votes are made to count, elections will no longer be seen as a warfare which must be won through fair or foul means.

With the appointment of Professor Jega, a man widely respected for his high moral standing and impeccable integrity, there is great hope that Nigeria may eventually cross the Rubicon as it were. One interesting thing about the new appointments at the INEC is that political actors both in the ruling party and opposition are mutually agreed that the right choices have been made.

The Presidential candidate of the opposition All Nigerian Peoples Party (ANPP), Major General Muhammadu Buhari hailed the appointments, saying that the nominees merited them. Buhari who is the symbol of political opposition in Nigeria said in a recent interview "we have the CVs of all those recommended and I think they are worthy of the positions approved for them".

Governor Adams Oshiomhole of Edo State who is of the opposition Action Congress (AC) commended President Jonathan for the decisions, saying that he (Jonathan) "exercised very sound judgment, which needs to be commended". As for Jega, Oshiomhole said: "With Jega as chairman, I believe that INEC would be in safe hands and we can expect fundamental improvements in the conduct of elections".

The spokesman of the House of Representatives, Mr. Eseme Eyiboh who is of the ruling Peoples Democratic Party, described the appointment of Jega as a positive step towards entrenching credibility in the electoral process. In his words: "The appointment has brought to the fore the collective determination of all arms of government to create the desired leverage for the attainment of our national goals. With this appointment, the challenge of national integration becomes more compelling on every Nigerian now more than ever before".

The expectations on Prof. Jega are not misplaced, given his track record in the academia and public service. As ASUU leader during the military era, he left a legacy of integrity and service. Between 1988 and 1994, he led ASUU negotiating teams which extracted enhanced emoluments for university teachers and improved funding of the ivory towers.

Jega has a very rich academic pedigree which positions him properly for the tough job. He was a visiting Senior Research Fellow at the Nigerian Institute of International Affairs (NIIA), Lagos, from 1992 to 1993; a visiting Research Fellow, Department of Political Science, University of Stockholm, Sweden in 1994; Deputy Vice-Chancellor (Academic), BUK between 1995 and 1996; Director, Center for Democratic Research and Training, Mambbaya House, BUK from 2000 to 2004 and he became the Vice-Chancellor of BUK in 2004.

Aside from several public service positions he has held, it is particularly instructive to note that Prof. Jega served on the Justice Uwais panel which made far-reaching recommendations for the reformation of the nation's electoral system. He has a reputation as a no-nonsense radical scholar with leftist inclinations. There is no doubt that he possesses the intellectual capacity and the presence of mind required to succeed on the job.

Luckily, Prof. Jega is not known to have any partisan political affiliation. Being politically neutral, he is therefore expected to conduct elections that will be free from any negative influences or political manipulations. Jega must, however, learn from the pitfalls of his predecessors. He should remain firm and politically detached. The first thing he must do is to sanitize the electoral body and ensure that corrupt and politically compromised staff of the Commission is shown the way out.

He must also move fast to clean up the voters` register which at the moment cannot be relied upon for any free and fair polls. Above all, he must carry all his National Commissioners and Resident Electoral Commissioners along as a team. It is only when unity of purpose exists that the electoral body can record any meaningful achievements.

_____

ThisDay, June 15, 2010

Chapter 55

Making the Second Niger Bridge A Reality

The unending controversies and long drawn political intrigues associated with the construction of a proposed second bridge over River Niger at Onitsha have continued to defy reason and logic until recently. Given what may pass as a national conspiracy against the project by successive Federal administrations in the country, debates or discussions on the subject matter have often provoked a lot of emotions and sentiments.

It beats one`s imaginations that this desirable project that is of strategic national value has been left on the drawing board for too long on account of irresponsible politicking and selfish considerations by those oppressors who do not see the location of the proposed bridge as serving their best interests.

There ought not to have been any misgivings or controversies at all over the second Niger Bridge, given its national economic value which cannot be over-emphasized. The bridge, when completed will naturally foster and deepen national integration since it serves as the only link between the South West including Delta and Edo States and the South East and deep South, consisting of Rivers, Akwa Ibom, Bayelsa and Cross River States.

Also, in the light of the on-going dualization of Abuja-Lokoja-Okenne-Auchi-Benin highway, the proposed second Niger Bridge comes in handy as it will now take increased traffic from the Northern parts of the country. What this means essentially is that rather than serve the interests of the old Western and Eastern regions alone, the bridge on completion, will serve the collective interests of the entire people of Nigeria.

In saner societies, where issues are determined on the basis of merit, projects of high national value like the second Niger Bridge ought to have been executed long ago. But the matter has been left to drag for ages because marginalization and official discrimination, contrary to Constitutional provisions have been adopted as a Directive Principle of State Policy by the powers that be in Nigeria.

The issue of the second Niger Bridge at Onitsha had been a longstanding matter in the country. It, however, became pronounced during the regime of President Ibrahim Babangida (1985-1993) who challenged indigenous engineers to put up a design for the bridge. The Nigerian Society of Engineers (NSE) took up the gauntlet and came up with what was considered enduring and competitive. The euphoria that attended that feat soon died down when the Babangida administration failed to award the contract.

Under the civilian administration of former President Olusegun Obasanjo, hope was raised on the construction of the bridge when he made it a major issue in his electioneering campaigns in 1999 and 2003. It later became clear from his lukewarm attitude that he was not interested in the project.

In 2003 when he was seeking re-election, Obasanjo played a fast one on the people of the South East when he went to Onitsha and purportedly flagged off the construction of the bridge under a Public-Private Partnership (PPP) arrangement. It turned out to be a huge fraud as investigations by the National Assembly later revealed that there was no valid contract for the construction of the bridge.

Here we are before fate thrusts Dr. Goodluck Jonathan forward on the national political stage as the President and Commander-in-Chief of the Armed Forces of the Federal Republic of Nigeria. Under his divinely ordained Presidency, the jinx on the second Niger Bridge is about to be broken; in deed, the national conspiracy is being terminated.

Upon the reconstitution of the Executive Council of the Federation (EXCOF) recently, President Jonathan identified the second Niger Bridge as a national priority and mandated the new Minister of Works, Senator Sanusi Daggash to commence immediate action on the project. It is heartwarming and instructive to note that the first official assignment of the Minister outside Abuja was a visitation to and on-the-spot assessment of the project site.

Senator Daggash visited the project site in the company of his Minister of State, Engr. Chris Ogienwonyi to underscore the seriousness attached by the Jonathan administration to the project. He assured the people of South East that accelerated action would be taken on the matter.

Last week, the Minister disclosed that the Federal Government has set aside the sum of N10 billion under the 2010 appropriations for the initial take off of the second Niger Bridge. Senator Daggash was speaking when the Deputy Senate President, Senator Ike Ekweremadu paid him a courtesy call in his office in Abuja.

This is definitely good news for all Nigerians particularly the millions of commuters who ply that bridge on a daily basis. Now that it appears that the second Niger Bridge is a dream come true, we need to see action immediately. We have had enough rhetoric and motion without movement on this matter. Government should begin to match words with action. Nigerians can no longer wait to see actual construction commenced on the bridge. To that extent, the contract should be immediately awarded on selective tendering to competent contractors like Messrs Julius Berger or Fougerolle.

It must however be pointed out that N10 billion cannot be sufficient for the job. In this regard, therefore, adequate financial provisions should be made in the 2011 budget to ensure uninterrupted construction and completion of the bridge on schedule.

The need for the timely execution of the project can hardly be over-emphasized, considering the fact that the existing bridge linking Onitsha to Asaba in Delta State is almost in a state of disrepair occasioned by age. The condition of the bridge, according to experts, is a source of concern, given the fact that it is more than 45 years old.

It is therefore important that the contract be immediately awarded so that work can effectively commence on the project. While that is being done, the existing bridge which is in a bad shape should be strengthened and re-enforced so as to avert any looming human disaster.

ThisDay, June22, 2010

Chapter 56

New Dawn in Abia Politics

For a very long time before now, any perceptive observer of the political developments in Abia State would have known that all was not well, going by the trend of events in the area. The Executive Governor of the State, Chief Theodore Ahamefula Orji who was elected on the platform of the Peoples Progressive Alliance (PPA) in 2007 had been trying, under difficult political circumstances, to shoulder the huge burden of providing democracy dividends in a State that is completely weighed down by local and external debts.

The substantial portions of the debts were said to have been incurred under the administration of late Chief Sam Onunaka Mbakwe in the old Imo State. The present Abia was carved out from the old Imo State in 1991. The Mbakwe administration (1979-83), in a hurry to develop the State, took foreign loans under the guarantee of the Federal Government. The loans were, however, effectively utilized in setting up a lot of infrastructure including roads, hospitals, schools, industries and hotels among which is the prestigious Concorde Hotels, Owerri.

With the creation of Abia State in 1991 by the Babangida regime, the new State inherited a huge debt overhang as part of its liabilities from the mother State. Successive administrations in Abia, whether military or civilian, had battled with the challenges of developing the State under the shadow of the debilitating loans.

While some of the previous administrations in the State made sincere efforts to bring down the debts, others even incurred more debts, further mortgaging the future of the State. The Federal Government that guaranteed the loans had since been deducting the revenue allocations of the State from source to repay the loans. Given this scenario, we now have a situation where some States like Abia cannot meet their statutory obligations to their citizenry because of the huge debts that had accumulated over the years. It is under this kind of situation that Governor T.A. Orji has had to function in the last three years.

Information available to the media indicated that amidst the financial squeeze in the State, Governor T.A. Orji had been subjected to serious pressures by certain vicious and mindless political godfathers and godmothers who believe that the vaults of the State must be surrendered to them to dispense the resources of Abia as they liked.

The cabal which had turned itself into a political dynasty in the State is not bothered in the least about the precarious financial standing of the State. All it wanted at all times was the continuous milking of the State to the detriment of infrastructural development.

Close watchers of political developments knew that it was only a matter of time before the bubble would burst as the Governor had gotten fed up with the unreasonable demands of this cabal which had remained unyielding and undaunting.

Against this background, therefore, the resignation of Governor T. A. Orji from the PPA and subsequent declaration for the All Progressives Grand Alliance (APGA) last week did not come as a surprise. Rather, what came as a surprise was the timing. The dumping of the one man-controlled PPA which had been a bad influence on the social and political values of the State by the Governor had long been expected.

It is in deed unbelievable that one man and his family would hold the rest of the State in such servitude and bondage for this long. Nonetheless, it is better late than never. The decision of T. A. Orji to quit the PPA is a laudable one as it marks the beginning of the total liberation of Abia, God`s own State, from the forces of darkness and retrogression.

We want to commend Governor T. A. Orji for this courageous and pragmatic move which will definitely put an end to the evil empire. By forcing Governor Orji out, the PPA has made the biggest blunder ever. No matter whatever plot the mafia in the party may be hatching, it is yet to be seen how they can rout out the incumbent Governor from office in the 2011 elections.

With the latest developments in Abia State, it has become crystal clear that the current political crisis stems from the inordinate ambition of one man to subjugate, dominate and freely ride roughshod over the South East political landscape. It started first in Imo State where Governor Ikedi Ohakim was compelled by unsavory political circumstances to pull out from the PPA, the platform through which he came to power in spite of threats and acts of intimidation that were directed at him.

The next victim was Chief Clement David Ebri, former Executive Governor of Cross River State, who had to voluntarily quit the PPA as the National Chairman because he could not stomach the nonsense that was going on in the one-man owned enterprise. A highly principled man, Ebri, refused to be used to do any dirty job for anybody. He left with his honour and integrity intact. The members of his National Working Committee including the Deputy National Chairman, Lisa Olu Akerele had to resign in solidarity with Ebri.

Indeed, it must be stated clearly that the departure of Ebri from PPA signaled the beginning of the end for the party. That was a man whose distinguished presence gave the PPA a respectable image. With his exit and replacement with the domestic aides of the founder of the party, it was obvious that the PPA was descending into oblivion.

The resignation of T. A. Orji from the party is definitely the last straw that has broken the back of the camel. Nigerians and Abians are watching to see how the party is going to do the magic of winning back the State.

Now that Governor T. A. Orji has dumped the PPA, all lovers of development and progress in Abia must come together and rally round him to ensure that the liberation of Abia from forces of retrogression which has begun with his declaration for APGA is taken to a logical conclusion. No one should however entertain any illusion that the journey is going to be easy. It is not. Rather, the struggles that lie ahead will be titanic, vicious and even bloody. But at the end of the tunnel, there will be a reassuring light.

Governor T. A. Orji has with his defection to APGA proven beyond any shadows of doubt that he is his own man and therefore capable of placing his political destiny in his own hands. He has confounded his critics by this latest action. I have the feeling that with the assured confidence that comes with the new found freedom, Abia State is going to witness a socio-political and economic rebirth. All patriots in Abia should back the Governor so that he can retain his seat on the platform of APGA. There should be no sitting on the fence. Everyone must rise up to be counted.

ThisDay, July 6, 2010

Chapter 57

Possibility of a New Constitution

Media reports last week indicated that the amendments to the 1999 Constitution proposed by the two chambers of the National Assembly may have run into a cul de sac. The proposed amendments are part of the electoral reforms initiated by the Yar`Adua administration to ensure free, fair and credible elections. President Jonathan has since his assumption of office after the death of Yar`Adua continued with the reforms.

The two chambers of the National Assembly, working separately on the amendments, proposed the alterations of about 50 sections of the Constitution. The amendments, however, were not far-reaching enough as they failed to take into account the key recommendations of the Justice Muhammed Uwais Panel on Electoral Reforms.

One of such recommendations which were rejected by the National Assembly was the appointment of the Chairman and members of the Independent National Electoral Commission (INEC) by the National Judicial Council (NJC) which is considered a neutral and independent body.

In the opinion of the Uwais Panel, the removal of the power to make such appointments from the Presidency and its location in the NJC, would guarantee the independence and autonomy of the electoral body. The entire people of Nigeria tired of elections manipulations and riggings and wanting a fresh air, clamoured for the retention and entrenchment of this proposition. But to their utter disappointment and disbelief, the National Assembly members in their wisdom turned down the recommendation.

What eventually emerged from the harmonized report of the Senate and House of Representatives fell far short of expectations, with most of the proposed alterations considered self serving.

The harmonized version from the National Assembly has since been transmitted to the various State Houses of Assembly in the country for concurrence. Surprisingly and to the delight of Nigerians, the State Assemblies have refused to be used as rubber stamps. They have been very thorough and painstaking in their consideration of the amendments as passed by the National Assembly. Many of the State Assemblies have rejected the self serving provisions and clauses to the bewilderment of the National Assembly leadership.

As at press time, Kogi was the only State in the whole Federation that has adopted the entire harmonized version of the amendments as presented to them by the National Assembly. The Constitution Amendment Bill 2010 containing the harmonized version was handed over to the States through the Chairman of the Conference of Speakers of State Houses of Assembly, Hon. Istifanus Gbana on June 5, 2010 by Senate President, Senator David Mark at a ceremony at the National Assembly, Abuja.

Twenty four State Assemblies, representing two-third of the States of the Federation, need to concur with the Senate and House of Representatives on the amendments before they can become law. Media inquiry showed that about 27 State Assemblies have passed the document and expunging some of the offensive clauses. Nine States were yet to conclude deliberations on the draft amendments.

The States include Lagos, Akwa Ibom, Cross River, Delta, Kano, Kwara, Bauchi, Anambra and Enugu. Media reports showed that the sections mostly rejected by the States included Section 65, which seeks to raise the bar of educational qualification for political office holders from school certificate to diploma.

Another provision that is affected is Section 177 which provides for Independent candidature in future elections and the self-serving Sections 108 and 109, approving cross-carpeting by Federal and State legislators to the parties of their choice without any sanction.

Most of the States also rejected the provision for first line charge on the Consolidated Revenue Fund of the Federation for the State and Federal legislatures. This provision, if it had been adopted, would ensure financial autonomy for the legislature at federal and State levels.

However, many of the State Assemblies approved proposals which empower the Vice-President and Deputy Governors to automatically assume duty in acting capacity once the President and Governors are out of the country beyond 21 days without transmitting letters to the legislature.

They also approved, among others, financial autonomy for the Independent National Electoral Commission (INEC) and first line funding for the judiciary.

Reacting to the developments from the State Assemblies, the Deputy Senate President, Senator Ike Ekweremadu who is the Chairman, Senate Ad-Hoc Committee on Constitution Review said that the State legislatures do not possess the power to alter the draft amendments transmitted to them by the National Assembly. Speaking through his Media Adviser he stated: 'The law does not allow the State legislatures to change anything from the document as handed over to them by way of subtraction or addition'. He however failed to cite the relevant law which denies the State legislatures such powers.

There is no provision any where in the 1999 Constitution that says State House of Assemblies will act as mere rubber stamps in the process of Constitution amendments. Even the framers of the 1999 Constitution could not have imagined that the State Assemblies will act as zombies in matters of such grave national importance. I don't think that Ekweremadu is correct in his position. The State Assemblies are closer to the grassroots. Therefore, their inputs should matter and must be taken into consideration by the National Assembly. It bothers on arrogance for any one to say that all that is required is for State Assemblies to vote 'yes' or 'no'.

For me, what has emerged from the discordant tunes by the National Assembly and State legislatures is that the amendment process suffers from inadequate stakeholders' consultations. If the State Assemblies had been duly taken into confidence at all stages of the amendments, the unfolding scenario would have been avoided.

In the light of the present circumstance, the National Assembly must climb down from its high horse and face reality. The leadership of the National Assembly should go into dialogue with the State Assemblies to resolve all the grey areas. This is the only way the amendment process could be saved from a sure atrophy. Otherwise, the impending 2011 elections may be in jeopardy given the fact that time is actually running out.

ThisDay, July 13, 2010

Chapter 58

Towards a Crisis-free and Credible Election

In the past few weeks, the nation has been inundated with reports of violent political clashes as rival political gladiators engage one another in supremacy contest. The political prize is the tickets to stand for elections on the party platforms. The desire to secure party nominations at all costs has led to a situation where political aspirants are ready to deploy violence at the least opportunity.

This negative social conduct borders on high level political intolerance and desperation. If the reports of the violent clashes within and among parties involving rival political contestants are anything to go by, then there are definitely genuine fears for the 2011 General Elections. What the evolving scenarios signpost is that grave danger lies ahead in the coming months.

In Zamfara State, for instance, eight political operatives were reportedly killed last week in an inter-party clash involving the supporters of former Governor Sani Yarima of All Nigerian Peoples Party (ANPP) and the incumbent Governor, Alhaji Mahmud Aliyu Shinkafi, previously of the ANPP but now a stalwart of the ruling Peoples Democratic Party (PDP) at the center.

Similarly, in Edo State, an aspirant to the House of Representatives on the platform of Action Congress of Nigeria, Mr. Oghogho Ayo Omoregbe was assassinated after conducting a rally in Benin City where he declared his intention to seek the ticket of his party for the position. The aspirant was trailed home by gun men who defied all pleas by the wife and members of the aspirant`s family and killed him in what was clearly seen as a politically instigated assassination.

Also in Ilawe Ekiti, Ekiti State recently, a political aspirant and some unfortunate indigenes of the area were brutally killed in what the community called "externally instigated violence".

It is in deed frightening to note that this wave of violence is being unleashed on the polity even when the Independent National Electoral Commission (INEC) was yet to release the time table for the commencement of the processes leading to the 2011General Elections.

What the present turn of events suggests is that we have learnt nothing and we have forgotten nothing from the previous sham elections.

Up till this moment many aggrieved Nigerians are still lamenting the 2007 elections conducted by the former Chairman of INEC, Professor Maurice Iwu as the worst in Nigeria's political history. The outcome of the elections was condemned locally and internationally as lacking in credibility and transparency on account of State-sponsored riggings and massive violence that characterized the conduct of the polls nationwide.

The current militarization of the polity in which armed militants, kidnappers and various hoodlums have taken the nation hostage is widely seen as fallout of the electoral heist of 2007. The desperate and unscrupulous politicians who armed these bad boys to rig the elections could not retrieve the guns and ammunitions from them after failing to settle them for the assignments they executed. The illegal weapons in the hands of these hoodlums, today, constitute a direct threat to national security and well being of the society.

Some urgent and concerted actions need to be taken now to nip in the bud the incipient culture of violence and hooliganism which is fast becoming the electoral norm in our land. It is not enough to reconstitute INEC with men of impeccable integrity and unimpeachable character like Professor Jega and co. What is needed is complete sanitization of the political process to rid it of all the bad elements in low and high places that make election conduct in Nigeria a lamentable experience.

In this regard, the security agents, civil society and in deed all Nigerians have a role to play in breathing a fresh air of hope into the system. The assignment cannot be left to INEC alone. To start with, the security agencies in Nigeria at all levels should be empowered by Government to launch a nationwide operation to retrieve illegal armaments circulating in the country.

It is widely believed from intelligence sources that a lot of light arms which many politicians brought into the country for the prosecution of the 2007 elections are still very much in circulation. The truth of the matter is that until the circulation is drastically curtailed, a free, fair and credible election may be impossible in 2011.

If the security agents are encouraged to work, they can break some new grounds. They have successfully done that before. And I don't see any reason why they cannot do it again. I am aware that in the aftermath of the Nigeria-Biafra war, a nationwide operation was launched by the military authorities to retrieve all the illegal arms that were in circulation then.

A similar operation was launched in Kano during the Gen. Sani Abacha regime following a bloody clash between some religious fanatics and non-indigenes in the State. Undertaking such a move will be the first step towards making the coming 2011 polls crisis-free.

This should be followed up with serious public enlightenment campaign and voter education across the country. This responsibility should not be left to INEC and other statutory agencies of government like National Orientation Agency (NOA) alone. The organized civil society and other agents of socialization in our polity must be brought in to assist in the sensitization and re-orientation of the citizenry, particularly the youths on the need to shun violence, thuggery, and other acts of impunity and embrace peace, orderliness and Godliness in their conduct.

All these efforts, however, will come to naught, if no credible voter register is provided by INEC before the 2011 elections. The old register used in the 2007 election has been discredited as it contains many fake names and names of under-aged voters which were used in the massive riggings of that election. Besides, some new voters who have attained the voting age of 18 would need to be accommodated. And also the names of voters that have died since 2007 would need to be expunged from the register. This makes a new voters` register imperative.

Against this background, therefore, it is heartwarming to note that the National Assembly has approved the request of INEC for the whooping sum of N87.7 billion to carry out fresh voter registration. The data arising from the new voter registration will form a valid basis for a reliable conduct of the 2011 General Elections. The country has a golden opportunity to get it right this time. All hands must, therefore, be on the deck to ensure that the 2011 election is free from violence and manipulations. The votes must be made to count.

_____

ThisDay, August 24, 2010

Chapter 59

The Crisis of Presidential Rotation

As the various political parties gear up for their primaries and conventions, there appears to be palpable tension in the air particularly within the ranks of the ruling Peoples Democratic Party (PDP).

As at press time, there is still confusion and anxiety as to which zone of the country its presidential ticket would go.

The PDP in its Constitution has a provision for the zoning and rotation of power between the North and South. This principle of rotation which is seen as an article of faith by the founding leaders of the party is what probably has made the party what it has become in Nigeria-a formidable and all-conquering political machine.

The founding fathers of the party, of which the incumbent National Chairman, Dr. Okwesilieze Nwodo is one, in their wisdom adopted the principle with a view to ensuring that all parts of Nigeria were given equal opportunities to effectively participate in power at the highest level of political governance; the ultimate goal being to ensure and guarantee the unity and stability of our fragile polity.

In recent times, a crisis of confidence has been building up as a result of the different interpretations and colourings being given to the rotational principle by many vested interests in the party. The resultant tension thrown up by these developments has turned the contest for the presidential ticket into a desperate situation.

The matter is even worsened by the ambiguous and duplicitous decision of the last meeting of the National Executive Committee of the party to uphold the principle of zoning and rotation as enshrined in its Constitution, which meant that the presidential ticket would remain in the North, and at the same time endorsing President Jonathan to run on the ground that he is a beneficiary of a joint and inseparable mandate with the late President Umar Musa Yar`Adua.

With that dubious decision, the PDP has created room for an inevitable crisis, which if not creatively managed would lead to conflicts of unimaginable proportions. But it is not late in the day for the party to save Nigerians such dastardly consequences by resolving the crisis and allowing greater wisdom to prevail.

Nigeria is a country that has seen a lot of tragedies and calamities in its history. And these problems have always revolved around the struggle for the control of political power and scarce socio-economic resources amongst the contending ethno-religious groups in the country.

The inter-ethnic struggles for power have often been very bitter and vicious. The series of tragedies which this country has gone through from the pre-colonial era through the post-colonial period to the present find explanation in this bitter contest for political control of Nigeria by the major ethnic groups in the country.

The Nigeria-Biafra Civil War (1967-1970) which pitted the Igbo-dominated Eastern Region against the rest of Nigeria is unarguably a direct consequence of the vicious power struggle for political control by the different factions of the political elite in the country.

The political distortions occasioned by that crisis and other upheavals that have continued to impede national progress in deed informed the national consensus reached on power sharing amongst the different regions of Nigeria in the 1994/95 National Constitutional Conference moderated by the General Sani Abacha regime.

At the historic conference, the South led by former Vice President Alex Ekwueme, against formidable odds was able to convince the North led by General Shehu Musa Yar`Adua to accept that the only guarantee for a stable and united Nigeria lay in an equitable formula for power sharing among the constituent geo-political zones of Nigeria. Dr. Ekwueme proposed to the conference the current six geo-political zones as we have them today. The proposal was unanimously adopted.

Accordingly, the six geo-political zones as presently constituted were accepted as the minimum basis for power sharing in the country. However, the delegates to that conference in their wisdom decided that instead of rotating power among the six zones, it should be between the North and the South.

This historical account is important for a proper appreciation of the on-going debate on zoning and rotation. The PDP did not wake up overnight to enshrine and adopt rotation as a cardinal principle in its Constitution. The decision of the founding leaders of the PDP to enshrine the principle of zoning and rotation in the Constitution of the party was a logical fall-out from the 1994/95 Constitutional Conference. That decision could hardly be faulted in the light of our national trajectory since independence.

Without any fear of contradiction or equivocation, that decision still remains a potent instrument for guaranteeing the unity and stability of Nigeria in perpetuity. Any action, therefore, that that has the potential of eroding the values of rotation and zoning as envisioned by the founding fathers of the PDP must be totally avoided because of the devastating consequences such an action may visit on our fragile polity.

The Statesmen who negotiated the consensus on zoning and rotation at the conference and who are still alive today include the likes of Ekwueme, Adamu Ciroma, Emeka Odimegwu Ojukwu, Atiku Abubakar, Tanko Yakassai, Barnabas Gemade, Olusola Saraki, Ebenezer Babatope, Dr. Josiah Odunna, and Dr. Uzodinma Nwala. Other key players who are no longer here with us include Gen. Yar`Adua, Dr. Sam Mbakwe, Dr. Chuba Okadigbo, Sunday Awoniyi and Dr. Ibrahim Tahir.

It will be a great disservice to the memories of these late elder statesmen and those still living if the PDP on the basis of political expediency decide to throw over board the principle of zoning and rotation.

It will be totally unfair and at the same time fraudulent for people who are favoured by current political realities in the country today, no matter how ephemeral the situation may seem, to begin to derogate zoning and rotation. In the final analysis, such unprincipled stance cannot enhance the process of nation building. Rather, it will truncate it.

Zoning and rotation are the only panacea, in the circumstance, for the unity and stability of Nigeria. It is therefore in the interest of the country for this ingenious device to be maintained until power rotates around all the six geo-political zones of the country.

It is important to state here that zoning and rotation as a power sharing principle was conceived as a transitional arrangement that would last for 30 years with the initial understanding that each zone would take the slot for 5 years.

Since President Obasanjo commenced the arrangement by doing 8 years, it is only meet and proper that power would rotate between the

North and South along the identified six geo-political zones for 8 years each accordingly. Anything to the contrary, in my view, is an invitation to chaos and anarchy which may not augur well for our nation.

ThisDay, September 14, 2010

Chapter 60

Place of South East in the Unfolding Political Scenario

As the various political parties commence their primaries and conventions for the purpose of nominating the candidates that would fly their flags at various levels of electoral contests, the political stakes are getting higher and higher. It is therefore instructive that several meetings and rallies are being held in different parts of the country by different socio-political groups with a view to articulating and aggregating their interests for bargaining with the presidential frontrunners.

In the last couple of weeks, I have participated in some of these meetings called by some Igbo interest groups with the sole agenda being the place of Ndigbo in the forthcoming 2011 presidential elections. The questions on the lips of every one at these meetings are: What direction should the South East geo-political zone go? Which of the identified presidential aspirants would best serve the interests of Ndigbo if elected into power? What is the strategic interest of Ndigbo in the 2011 elections? Can we achieve power in 2015 or 2019? If we must get power by 2015 which of the candidates is in a position to guarantee this? Is it Jonathan, Babangida, Atiku, Buhari or Saraki?

These are critical and hard questions which require dispassionate analyses and considerations before a conclusive and definitive position can be taken by Ndigbo. In arriving at what may be considered a rational and meaningful position, the dictum that in politics what matters is permanent interest, must be taken into serious consideration.

By sheer divine providence, Dr. Goodluck Jonathan, a minority from the Ijaw ethnic nationality is currently the President and Commander-in-Chief of the Armed Forces of the Federal Republic of Nigeria. It is a welcomed development which has been widely hailed by well-meaning Nigerians. By May 29, 2011, President Jonathan would have spent almost one year and four months in office. This is no mean feat in a country where primordial factors still define our politics and way of life.

At these Igbo forums, opinions have been sharply divided over whether Jonathan or a Northern candidate should be supported in 2011 or not. But it is pertinent to observe that some Igbos are hardly bothered about what constitutes the strategic interest of Ndigbo in the 2011 presidential. In this group are people who subscribe to the view that Jonathan should continue in office till 2015. This same people also believe that by 2015 when Jonathan would have done more than five years as President, he would hand over to an Igbo man .

It is a possibility, no doubt. But it is certainly a remote possibility that power will still be retained in the South after Jonathan and Obasanjo had jointly done more than thirteen years compared to only less than three years of late President Umar Musa Yar`Adua who held the position in the name of the North. It amounts to an act of serious political naivety for any one, especially an Igbo to think that against the spirit of power sharing and federal character arrangement as provided in our constitution that the North would allow itself to be shortchanged.

As I argued last week on this page, the principle of zoning and rotation was conceived and adopted by Nigerian leaders in 1994 to ensure equity, unity and stability of the country against the tragedies and calamities of the past that put to task the continued peaceful coexistence of the nation. The decision thus was clearly informed by these unsavoury incidents of the past.

The political fault lines in our country still exist. It is in the bid to moderate the centrifugal forces that feed on the divisive tendencies in our polity and guarantee a sense of belonging to all sections of Nigeria that the principle of zoning and rotation was devised. And it has since been accepted as the most potent and ingenious instrument for holding the country together. We must therefore run away from any scheme that is aimed at truncating the principle.

It is against this background that the Igbo nation must begin to reappraise its chances and opportunities vis-à-vis its role in a post Jonathan era commencing from either 2011 or 2015.

Without beating about the bush, the strategic Igbo interest is to attain political power in the shortest possible time having been kept out of political governance at the highest level through acts of conspiracy by certain entrenched interests in Nigeria since 1966 in spite of the frontline role played by her leading lights in the struggle for Nigeria`s independence. The average Igbo man is also of the view that the political marginalization of Ndigbo arising from the loss of the civil war in 1970 will be seen to have ended the very day an Igbo is elected to the position of the President of the country; a country in which they have labored perhaps more than any other group in building up.

In politics what matters is permanent interest. The permanent interest of Ndigbo cannot be best served by our neighbor or friend no matter how benevolent. Our destiny lies in our own hands. Our interest will best be served by the Igbo giving Jonathan all the support he needs to complete his tenure in 2011, and in the spirit of zoning support a candidate from the North with a commitment and guarantee to cede power to the South East in 2015. By that date, the other two zones in the South, that is South West and South South, would have taken their turns, leaving only the South East as the only zone in the South to produce a democratically elected President.

And like Dr. Jideofor Adibe, a columnist with the Trust newspapers argued recently, "a Jonathan candidacy in the current politics of zoning strongly conflicts with Igbos` own interest because they are the only major ethnic group which has not produced an elected President of this country, and 2015 is their best chance of doing so". I also concur with him that "the PDP`s zoning arrangement, as imperfect as it is, presents perhaps the best opportunity for a president of Igbo extraction in 2015".

In the light of what constitutes the strategic interest of Ndigbo in the current political calculations, a Jonathan presidency in 2011 is a huge setback to the political aspiration of Ndigbo. The implication is that the Igbos will have to wait till 2023 before they can bid for power. What that means is that the Igbo presidency may not happen within the lifetime of the generation of the Igbos that witnessed the horrendous civil war.

An Igbo presidency in 2015 will permanently heal the wounds of the civil war and bring that dark chapter of our history to a close.

ThisDay, Septemer 21, 2010

Chapter 61

INEC's Request for Time Extension

The leadership of the Independent National Electoral Commission (INEC) held a crucial meeting last week with the National Chairmen of the existing political parties in Nigeria over the Commission's guidelines and preparations for the 2011 general elections. Key on the agenda was the timelines for the elections which the INEC Chairman; Professor Attahiru Jega explained were too tight for the Commission to make any meaningful headway with the preparations for a successful polls conduct in 2011.

By virtue of the relevant provisions of the newly amended Constitution and the Electoral Act recently passed by the National Assembly, the 2011 general elections are to be held within the month of January of that year, which by implication means that INEC and the participating political parties have barely three months from now to prepare for the polls.

For INEC specifically, it has only three months from now to acquire and deploy 120, 000 units of Direct Data Capture (DDC) machines required for the voter registration, train the staff that will man the machines, compile the register, display the register for claims and objections, train the ad-hoc staff and other officials that would administer the actual elections, embark on voter and civic education etc. All these activities are expected to take place in the next three months before the elections.

The Commission, realizing that the time frame was too short for it to deliver free, fair and credible elections, initiated the consultative meeting with the leadership of the political parties with a view to seeking their support for the extension and realignment of the electoral time table.

Speaking on the occasion, Prof. Jega said that INEC needed two additional months and would prefer an extension up to April 2011 to enable the Commission do a good job. "If we have sufficient time up to April to do a good job, the result is that there would be no need for politicians to go to court. If we get enough time, we shall do a Grade A job", he noted.

The request, understandably, has generated some mixed reactions. Many groups including a majority of the political parties have risen in support of INEC, noting that the time frame as contained in the electoral guidelines were far too short for INEC to meet up with the tight schedules.

They are therefore agreed that for INEC to deliver on its promise of a free and fair election, it must be granted time extension.   However, there is a school of thought which believes that the tampering of the election schedule so early in the day will be sending wrong signals on what is to come.

For this group, any such alteration now may create doubts and lead to possible erosion of public confidence in the widely acclaimed leadership of Prof. Jega. There is a lot of merit in this. However, it is said that he who wears the shoe knows where it pinches. Jega and his Commissioners are at the driving seat. They know where they are taking the country to.

He has repeatedly promised to organize a free, fair and credible election for which the nation would be very proud. Anything that would make him to give us excuses for failure must be done away with out rightly. That is why I am aligning myself with those who are rooting for time extension for INEC.

A critical look at the electoral time table as it exists clearly shows that INEC is seriously constrained by time. It will be sheer magic if it can pull the election within the time available to it.

For instance the Commission had fixed September 23, 2010 as the deadline for the training of the trainers on the DDC machines to be used in the voter registration. That date has passed, yet INEC is to take delivery of the machines. Of what use would the training have been when the machines the trainees are to use in the voter registration are not available. Expatiating on the time challenges, Prof. Jega stated: "The award of contract for the acquisition of the DDC machines was to take place in early August and the delivery of the first 15, 000 units of the machines was to be in early September and training of registration officers by early to middle of September. It has since become clear that we have missed some of these time lines".

Again, INEC had slated the voter registration to last for only two weeks because of the tight time schedule. We know that it would be impossible to compile the register nationwide and display same for claims and objections within two weeks.

The foregoing illustrations clearly show that the extension and adjustment of the electoral time table is inevitable. However, such an extension cannot be possible without effecting necessary amendments to both the recently amended Constitution and the Electoral Act 2010.

The crux of the matter now is can the National Assembly and the 36 State Houses of the Assembly in the country be able to pull the amendments between now and March next year given the laborious and cumbersome processes that are involved in the passage of legislations, particularly constitutional amendments?

The Federal Government will have to quickly come in to the rescue. It must immediately engage the leadership of the National Assembly and the State Governors, who obviously are in control of the State Assemblies, to prepare the groundwork for the amendments. And this will be followed with an Executive Bill which should be transmitted to the National Assembly for speedy consideration. Securing the understanding of the National Assembly and the State Houses of Assembly is very necessary to ensure that the amendments which will involve first reading, public hearings, second and third readings and passage are carried out with minimum delay.

If eventually the amendments are effected, the proposal to conduct all elections in the month of January as contained in the recently amended Constitution should be retained. The commencement date should however be shifted to 2015 as that provision may no longer be applicable in 2011. The January date is still very important as it would make room for the resolution of disputes arising from the conduct of elections before the swearing in and oath taking on May 29.

The political class and in deed every Nigerian owes it as a responsibility to ensure that INEC this time does not have any cause to fail the nation. If the extension of time and adjustment of the electoral calendar is the sacrifice we need to make for INEC to get it right, let's do it. The future of Nigeria is inexorably tied to the fortunes of the 2011 elections. We must get it right or say bye bye to democracy.

ThisDay, September 28, 2010

Chapter 62

Nigeria @ 50: Failed or Endangered?

Many Nigerians had looked forward to celebrating Nigeria's golden jubilee on 1st October with pomp and pageantry ostensibly because fifty years in the life of a nation represent a milestone. It did not really matter whether Nigeria within this period has performed or underperformed. The fact that the country has remained intact in spite of several travails and difficulties that have dogged her path all this while, in deed calls for thanksgiving.

It is against this background that Nigerians in their good number trooped out across the entire Federation to celebrate 50 years of nationhood and freedom from British colonial domination. A whooping sum of N10 billion was set aside by the Federal Government to bankroll all the activities that were planned for the golden jubilee anniversary.

Critics had berated the Dr. Goodluck Jonathan-led Federal Government for being utterly wasteful and extravagant with such prohibitive expenditure profile on the jubilee celebrations particularly against the background that Jonathan's predecessor, the late President Umar Musa Yar'Adua had budgeted only N100 million for the same event before he was snatched away by the cold hands of death in May this year.

The central thesis in the arguments of the critics is that there is nothing really worth celebrating about Nigeria in the last fifty years. For this group, the fact that the country had remained together in spite of centrifugal forces that had been pulling at her from different directions is not a sufficient reason to roll out the drums in sumptuous celebrations. The country with all her potentials and promises, compared to her contemporaries at independence in 1960 and their present level of development, in their view, could be considered as a failed or failing State.

Such countries that were on the same pedestal of development with Nigeria and which today have left Nigeria behind in a state of underdevelopment include Singapore, Malaysia, Indonesia, South Korea and nearer home, Uganda, Botswana and Ghana amongst many other less endowed countries within our sub-region. At 50, Nigeria is yet to have stable electricity which constitutes the basic foundation for industrial and technological development.

A far less endowed country like Bourkina Faso was reported by the great Chinua Achebe in his political treatise, The Trouble with Nigeria, as one country within the West Africa sub-region that had made an encouraging progress particularly with regard to the stability of electricity supply compared to the so-called giant of Africa. He recalled with nostalgia how he spent over one week in Ouagadougou, the country`s capital city without experiencing any power outages. It is instructive to note that Achebe`s book was written over 20 years ago. Several years after, Nigeria was yet to make any difference in the lives of her citizenry.

The golden jubilee celebrations in Abuja were however marred by incidents of bomb blasts which left in their wake destructions, deaths and blood of innocent Nigerians. It is in deed difficult to believe that such dastardly acts could happen in the nation`s capital brimming with all kinds of security outfits including the army, police and state security services.

It was a big blow and blight which took the shine off the celebrations. Media reports indicated that 16 casualties were recorded while scores of other victims suffered varying degrees of injuries and are currently being hospitalized in different Clinics in Abuja.

It was a sad day for the country. The timing of the bombs by those who planted them was intended to achieve a maximum effect especially when foreign dignitaries including visiting Heads of States had already gathered at the Eagle Square, the venue of the golden jubilee celebrations.

This is sheer terrorism on our soil and it stands condemned by all well meaning Nigerians and people of good conscience. There is no justifiable reason that may be advanced for such a heinous crime against humanity. The terrorists and their sponsors must be fished out and given the maximum punishment. The Movement for the Emancipation of the Niger Delta (MEND), a rebel group within the oil-rich Niger Delta region of the country had claimed responsibility for the bombing and their reason is that "for 50 years the people of Niger Delta have had their land and resources stolen from them" and that "there is nothing worth celebrating".

The irony is that the sitting President, Goodluck Jonathan is from the Niger Delta. If as the President he cannot protect and advance the interests of the region, who else can? Although Government has doubted the involvement of MEND in the bombing, claiming that it had information which suggested that some highly placed Nigerians were involved in the plot, it is yet to be seen how the bombing of innocent and ordinary Nigerian citizens would be the solution to the problems of the Niger Delta.

Beyond the bombings and the claims and counter claims is a common realization that at 50 all is not well with Nigeria. Some scholars are still strongly of the view that the country is a failed or failing state. For them the indices are there for every one to see: insecurity of lives and property, massive corruption in high and low places, excruciating poverty in the land, absence of rule of law, weak democratic institutions, pliant or in some cases compromised judiciary, urban terrorism, lawlessness, rising waves of kidnappings and armed robbery and total devaluation in national life.

When a State has failed or is failing, one thing that is apparent and obvious is that governance in such a State has gone into retreat. The rule of the mob takes over. From the Niger Delta through South East to South West and the Far North, criminal gangs and cult groups prowl the land, violating its innocence and holding the populace hostage. In Nigeria today, the jury is out on whether governance has gone into retreat or not.

Nigeria may not have degenerated to the level and status of Somalia and Sudan which are classical examples of failed and failing States in Africa, but the prevailing regime of fear and insecurity in the land today strongly suggests that we are on a steady descent into anarchy. With the evidence available, can Nigeria be said to have failed?

We are not far from being classified as a failing State on the account of the indices that we have identified. But I think it is apposite to classify Nigeria as an endangered State. The incumbent regime of Jonathan has a bounden responsibility to bail the cat. Nigeria is not a hopeless case. Our present predicament can be reversed once the political will and determination exists.

It is hard to believe that at the celebrations of the nation's golden jubilee anniversary, terrorists would choose to strike deep at the heart of Nigeria. It is also unspeakable that on the eve of the anniversary, heartless kidnapping gangs seized and held in their captivity 15 innocent kids of a nursery and primary school in Aba, the diminishing commercial capital of Abia State.

A few weeks earlier a criminal sectarian group in the North known as Boko Haram had taken security agencies in Bauchi by surprise and striking at the Bauchi prisons in the heart of Bauchi State and freeing all the inmates numbering over 700 and leaving in their trail several casualties including prison warders and other security personnel.

In a commando-like operation that lasted a few hours, these religious terrorists overwhelmed security agents by deploying bombs, grenades and other superior weapons. It was an exercise that exposed the underbelly and the state of readiness of our security forces.

Several months earlier, we had seen how some innocent villagers were massacred in their sleep in Plateau State in a dispute that was inspired by sectarian and ethnic hatred.

Now, the 2011 elections are around the corner and politically instigated killings are being witnessed in several parts of the country. Fear and insecurity rule the land. The Abuja bomb blasts represent the high point in the unfolding saga of violence and intolerance in the land. All these unsavoury experiences clearly show that Nigeria today stands at the cross road as an endangered State.

Every hand must be on the deck to save the ship of State from sinking. The emerging signs are ominous. The tension is building up rapidly. With the mass of angry and unemployed youths, many of them graduates, idling away across the length and breadth of Nigeria, we have a time bomb on our hands. Government must evolve some remedial measures in the interim to meaningfully engage these youths as they are available for recruitment for evil causes. The time to act is now. Tomorrow may be too late.

_____

ThisDay, October 12, 2010

Chapter 63

Ironsi: Humility in Greatness

B arely five days after the country's golden jubilee anniversary which was tragically marred by bomb blasts that killed over a dozen innocent Nigerians in Abuja, my friend and media guru, Uche Ezechukwu had asked me to accompany him to honour an invitation to the home of Ambassador Tom I. Aguiyi-Ironsi, who was marking his 57th birthday anniversary.

I did not hesitate in acceding to the request because I felt it would be a welcomed opportunity for closer and intimate interactions with someone whose noble carriage I had been admiring from a distance. I happen to come from the same town, Umuahia, like Ironsi. At home, he holds a lot of attraction to the people for attaining great heights in his career without courting or getting involved in any needless controversy either at the State or national levels.

I have never had any personal encounter with him or any other member of the Ironsi family except his sister, Louisa, a professional journalist whom I met when she was practicing with Newswatch in the 1990s in Ikeja. I had followed Austen Oghuma, a colleague of Louisa at Newswatch to a party organized by the late Group Captain Brian Ayonote, Louisa's husband at their Ikeja GRA residence in honour of his wife. I was then the Political Editor of the Daily Times.

It was at that event that I came closest to the Ironsi family members. Her other siblings and their mother were in attendance. I came out from the event with an impression of the Ironsis as a closely knit family. From there I got to know that the eldest of the Ironsi children, Tom, who shares the same name with the former military Head of State, was in the diplomatic service.

It was therefore a hearty development, when the opportunity presented itself, for me to meet one on one with this scion of Major General JTU Aguiyi-Ironsi, the first indigenous Commander of the Nigerian Military and first Military Head of State of the country who was brutally assassinated in the counter coup of July 1966. When we were ushered into his modest home in the city centre, I was disarmed by his humility, simplicity, infectious personality and extreme courteousness (his being a trained diplomat notwithstanding). He was very delighted to meet with us and particularly pleased to learn that I am from the same town with him.

My impressions of the man from the close encounter in deed provided the impetus and motivation for this piece. The birthday celebration was very low-keyed with only his children, mother, Lady Victoria Aguiyi Ironsi and very few close relations in attendance.

I was surprised that a man of such immense stature (in real and metaphorical sense) would be having what may pass for an austere celebration. He said he was not a noisy person and beside, the nation was in a mourning mood following the bombing incident few days earlier; and as such the situation in the country only called for sober reflections and deep national introspection.

The mother, looking very regal and graceful at her age had journeyed to Abuja the previous day on the invitation of the First Lady, Dame Patience Jonathan to be part of the 50th Independence anniversary programmes organized by the Government. She took time off her schedule to pray with her son on his 57th birthday. It was quite moving seeing the former First Lady sharing intimate moments with her son and grand children. The bonding and love were very visible.

In course of our discussions I saw a man with a large heart who does not habour any ill feelings towards his enemies including those who were implicated in the gruesome murder of his father. He disclosed how not quite long ago at a social function up North he came face to face with those that masterminded the killing. And true to the nobility of his character and upbringing, he was charitable to them all. It takes a man with such generosity of heart and forgiving spirit like Ambassador Tom not to betray any emotions on an occasion like that.

For him, the nation must not be allowed to be held hostage by the ugly incidents and bitterness of the past, but rather a new vista should be opened to reposition the country for greatness and prosperity. For Ambassador Tom who is the first Igbo man to date to serve as the Minister of Defence, the country must move on.

He was appointed into that position which is considered very strategic and sensitive in January 2007 by former President Olusegun Obasanjo. He had previously served as Minister of State in the same Ministry of Defence.

As a career diplomat he had served in several countries and in different capacities. Some of the Missions include Switzerland, Niger Republic, Ireland, Scotland, Pakistan, and Bangladesh. In May 2004, he was appointed the Ambassador of Nigeria to Togo, a position he held until he was made a Minister of State in 2006.

One would have expected a man of such robust pedigree to be loud and very visible as the average Nigerian politician is wont to. But not for Ambassador Tom! He remains very self-effacing and unobtrusive in spite of his several accomplishments in national service. He believes that a leader can still make his contributions without necessarily being overbearing and noisy.

It is perhaps because of his cultured disposition and self-effacing nature that the great strides he recorded while he was serving as Nigeria's envoy in Togo were not known to many. When the security of Nigerians and other ECOWAS nationals was threatened in the 2005 presidential election in that country, it was Ambassador Tom Ironsi who deployed all his diplomatic skills to ensure that no harm came the way of Nigerian residents.

He also used his clout to ensure that the Togolese borders which were closed at the time and which caused concerns in ECOWAS were promptly re-opened without any eruptions in the existing good bilateral relationship between Nigeria and Togo. For his efforts, the country rewarded him with it's highest national award.

He noted that he joined the diplomatic service to serve Nigeria and that serving the country was the legacy he inherited from his late father who was also the first UN Military Commander in Congo. The father by that role had the distinction of being the first Commander of UN Peace keeping force anywhere in the world.

He could not be drawn into any discussions on whether the successive administrations in the country had been fair to the memory of his late father who died in active national service. Only recently, the Federal Government reeled out names of 50 eminent Nigerians including some past political leaders who had distinguished themselves in the service of their fatherland and accorded them national recognitions. General Ironsi's name was conspicuously omitted.

From the attitude of previous governments in the country, there appears to be a national conspiracy to deny Ironsi his appropriate place in nation building. It took an exception in General Sani Abacha to acknowledge Ironsi`s contributions by naming a major street and military cantonment in Abuja after the slain General. We still believe that in the shortness of time General Ironsi will be properly appreciated for the sacrifices he made to unify the country, even though his intentions were greatly misunderstood.

As for Ambassador Tom, he can no longer continue to hide in his cocoon. It is said that a golden fish has no hiding place. Only a few people in this country possess the kind of credentials he has. He must be ready to put his rich and varied experiences at the disposal of his people either at the State or national levels. We cannot have such great minds and the ship of state continues to flounder. Tom must step out from his comfort zone and bring his wealth of ideas to bear on the management of his society.

From his home State, Abia, things have gone terribly wrong. Kidnappers and sundry criminals have seized the land. At the national level, the unity of the country faces continuous threats. It is in times of such grave national emergency that good men must step out to be counted.

In the words of Alighieri Dante, an Italian philosopher of old, "the hottest part of hell is reserved for those men who keep silent in times of moral crisis". The likes of Tom can no longer continue to shy away from the current crisis of governance ravaging the country. He should be part of the rescue mission.

ThisDay, October 19, 2010

Chapter 64

Enugu Airport in Perspective

It is no longer news that the Federal Government has approved the upgrading of the Akanu Ibiam Airport in Enugu to an international status. The welcomed development came a few weeks ago when the current Minister of Aviation, Mrs. Fidelia Njeze, after a meeting of the Federal Executive Council in Abuja, informed the nation on the Government`s decision which delighted many Nigerians, particularly the long deprived people of the South East.

In announcing the approval, the hard working Minister disclosed that the Dr. Goodluck Jonathan-led Federal Government has set aside N90 billion naira to expand and improve existing facilities in Enugu airport alongside the other International airports at Lagos, Abuja, Kano and Port Harcourt. Njeze explained that as part of the efforts to lift up the Enugu airport, which at the moment is undergoing some renovation, the existing run ways are to be expanded and increased to accommodate bigger aircrafts. She also disclosed that the upgrading included the construction of a new and befitting terminal building.

When the airport comes on stream, the people of the South East who are mainly engaged in commerce, trading and industrial activities would fly direct from Enugu to any part of the world to conduct their businesses without the inconvenience of going through any of the other airports in the country. What this also means is that the teeming number of Igbos in the Diaspora can also fly straight to Enugu from their different locations.

This development, predictably, has gladdened the hearts of Ndigbo who have been effusive with praises to the Government for finally hearing their prayers. In demonstration of their gratitude, the Deputy Senate President, Chief Ike Ekweremadu has led a delegation of Igbo legislators in the National Assembly to commend President Jonathan for making the Enugu International airport a reality at last.

There is no doubt that the step which the government has taken will go a long way in boosting the economy of the South East, given the multiplier effects which the heightened tempo of activities at the airport will have in the area whose people are widely noted for their industry and hard work.

Ordinarily, the news of the long awaited upgrading of the Enugu airport should be a matter for celebration for what is considered a wise decision that is of national strategic value; especially for a zone that has remained economically depressed since after the Civil War. But it does not seem to appear so for some ethnic jingoists who always read primordial meanings into every actions of government that do not personally favour them.

How else does one react to a provocative and jaundiced report by one Wole Shadare in the 1st October, 2010 edition of the Guardian questioning the wisdom in upgrading the Enugu airport into an international status? In his words: "The news that the Federal Government has approved the upgrade of the Akanu Ibiam Airport, Enugu to international status came as a shock. The decision was shocking; in the sense that the government has taken a rather dangerous path without understanding what it takes to do so".

If one may ask, what is dangerous in upgrading an existing airport in Nigeria like the Enugu airport with very great economic potentials to an international airport? I went through the entire hogwash by Mr. Shadare to see his evidence which makes the government decision dangerous. He did not provide any.

To show his deep seated ethnic bias he went further to insinuate that political rather than commercial considerations may have informed the decision on the Enugu airport. He asked: "Is it a case of politics where every State must have an airport, not based on commercial considerations but for the simple fact that we just need an airport?" It is very clear that Mr. Shadare is being mischievous.

In order to achieve his predetermined and hideous agenda, he deliberately glossed over the fact that the Enugu airport is the fourth busiest airport in the country after Murtala Muhammed International Airport, Lagos; Nnamdi Azikiwe International Airport, Abuja; and Port Harcourt International Airport, Omagwa. He also failed to disclose that the Enugu airport currently accounts for annual passenger traffic of 30 percent of the total national passenger traffic.

With these incontrovertible facts, it is not in contention that the Enugu airport, on merit, more than deserves to be upgraded into an international status. The airport is assured of high passenger patronage given the teeming number of business men and industrialists that abound in the area. The airport is sure to benefit from the support of millions of Ndigbo and their friends in the Diaspora who will henceforth not experience any difficulties in connecting their flights direct to Enugu from their various bases.

It is gratuitous insults for Shadare and his ilk to question the viability of Enugu International Airport in the face of unassailable facts to the contrary. The economic benefits of the airport cannot be overemphasized. There is no doubt that the opportunities which the upgrading of the airport will throw up may go a long way in addressing the problem of youth unemployment in the area. It will further stimulate other small scale economic activities which will also help to improve the living standards of the people.

Aviation Minister, Njeze, similarly highlighted the advantages derivable from the new status of the Enugu airport and also underscored the significance of the airport to the economy of the South East geo-political zone which has witnessed remarkable economic growth in recent years. She correctly noted that "a large proportion of businesses in the region are of international dimension", adding that with the upgrade, "international travelers will be saved the added cost of going to Lagos or Port Harcourt to travel".

The clamor for the upgrading of the Enugu airport had been on for quite a long time. Successive governments at the center have had to make promises on the matter without fulfilling same.

ThisDay, October 26, 2010

Chapter 65

The Bickering in Governors' Forum

W hat used to be a very cohesive and all powerful lobby group in the body politics of the country is at the verge of losing relevance in the light of the brewing crisis of succession within the organization. The Nigerian Governors' Forum (NGF), an exclusive platform of all the elected governors of the 36 States of the Nigerian Federation, until the recent cracks within its fold is a very potent and influential lobby group within the nation's political system that is seriously reckoned with.

Even though the body is unknown to the Constitution of the land, it has become one of the key players in our current democratic dispensation that can only be ignored by our policy makers at their own peril.

Given the vantage position which the Executive governors enjoy in their various States, the NGF has grown to acquire enormous clout, strength and resilience. The Forum had been in existence since the nation's return to civil democratic rule in 1999. The group is so powerful that the high and mighty in our society cultivates and romances with it. In deed in 2003 the body demonstrated its power and relevance when it stood against the second term aspiration of President Olusegun Obasanjo.

Obasanjo, in his holier than thou attitude, had before his re-election in 2003, been using the security apparatus of the State including the Economic and Financial Crimes Commission (EFCC) and Independent Corrupt Practices and other related offences Commission (ICPC) to persecute, harass and intimidate some of the governors who were not in his good books. So, the presidential primaries of the party in 2003 which pitched Obasanjo against his deputy, Alhaji Atiku Abubakar, was for the governors a pay back time. Most of them being known allies and loyalists of Atiku, rallied round the Turaki Adamawa, as Atiku is popularly known, to stop Obasanjo in his tracks.

The imperial Obasanjo was so rattled that he had to climb down from his high horse, as it were, to submit to the will of the governors.

Sources close to the NGF then confirmed that Obasanjo had to grovel, genuflect and even prostrate before Vice President Atiku Abubakar before he could get any reassurance of support from the all powerful governors' forum. That was the measure of clout and power wielded by the forum. It will not be an exaggeration, however, to say that the NGF became more powerful under the chairmanship of Governor Abubakar Bukola Saraki of Kwara State who is currently in the race for the presidential ticket of the ruling Peoples Democratic Party (PDP).

As an outgoing chairman, it is the scheming to find a suitable replacement, at a time the governors have become divided over the ambitions of the various presidential aspirants particularly on the platform of the PDP that is causing the current crisis within the forum.

The NGF has suddenly and understandably become politicized. The incumbent President, Dr. Goodluck Jonathan may not have forgotten in a hurry how the NGF stood between him and the presidency during the period his former boss and the immediate past President, Alhaji Umar Musa Yar'Adua disappeared from the public scene on account of his prolonged hospitalization in far away Saudi Arabia without handing over power to Jonathan. Even up to the time the doctrine of necessity was invoked by the National Assembly to break the logjam, the NGF was still adamant in its trenchant opposition to the transfer of power to Jonathan in acting capacity. Against this background it is quite understandable why the current bitter struggles for the control of the NGF.

But what sparked off the current problem was the ill-advised decision of a section of the governors to foist the Ogun State governor, Otunba Gbenga Daniel on the NGF, apparently acting a script in lieu of the 2011 presidential elections. It was reported that the action was the handiwork of only about eleven PDP governors who are staunch loyalists of Jonathan. They were said to have proclaimed Governor Daniel chairman after attending the fund raising event at the International Conference Center, Abuja in aid of the presidential aspiration of Dr. Jonathan.

The arrow heads of the 'coup' which purportedly unseated Saraki were Gabriel Suswam and Godswill Akpabio, the governors of Benue and Akwa Ibom respectively. Their argument was that since Saraki was involved in the presidential race, the NGF was no longer living up to expectations. They even cited the bomb blast incident in Abuja which allegedly did not elicit any reaction from the forum as one of the main reasons why they moved for the ouster of Saraki.

Their action however backfired as several of the governors reacted with rage over the purported election of Daniel as the new chairman of NGF. Governors from the opposition parties like Adams Oshiomhole,

Babatunde Fashola and Kayode Fayemi all of the Action Congress of Nigeria (ACN) and Ibrahim Shekarau of All Nigerian Peoples Party (ANPP) condemned the so-called election of Daniel as undemocratic, warning that the misadventure casts a huge cloud of doubts on the commitment of President Jonathan to conduct a free and fair election in 2011. Even the PDP governors from the North did not spare the master minders of the 'coup'. In deed, the governor of Niger State, Dr. Babangida Aliyu, the chairman of the Northern Governors Forum, on behalf of his colleagues from the North, fired the first salvo by disowning Daniel. The development necessitated an emergency meeting of the NGF in which the succession crisis was discussed and resolved.

At the meeting, the 'coup plotters' were seriously tongue lashed and compelled to recant. They reportedly apologized for their misdemeanor and asked for forgiveness. Saraki was retained while a succession panel headed by Governor Fashola was set up to shop for a new chairman who would take over from Saraki in accordance with rules of the NGF.

What has emerged from the unfolding scenario is a desperate bid by some desperate political forces to hijack the NGF and use same for the advancement of the presidential aspiration of one of the desperate contenders to the PDP ticket. The failure of the 'coup plotters' to have their way is another glaring indication that a big hurdle lies ahead. It further shows that incumbency factor may not play much role in determining who picks the prized ticket.

Such underhand tactics like smuggling in toxic clauses into the Electoral Act, setting EFCC and other security agents after perceived political opponents or in this instant case, hijacking a democratic institution like the NGF for ulterior motives will not work. Aspirants should move into the field and sell their manifestoes and programmes to the people. Anything short of this may prove disastrous in the final analysis.

ThisDay, November 9, 2010

Chapter 66

Resurgence of Criminality in Niger Delta

It was widely believed that the amnesty programme instituted by the late President Umar Musa Yar'Adua in 2008 in which all former militant leaders and their army of supporters in the Niger Delta were granted free pardon would bring lasting peace and stability to the region. With the recent turn of events in the area today, the expressed optimism appears to have been misplaced.

Rather than the crises abating, tension is gradually building up again following the ill-advised decision of some of the ex-militants and some budding warlords to spurn the amnesty programme and return to the creeks.

Hostilities, of late have resumed in the volatile region after some long spell of calm and quiet that were the immediate spin-off of the amnesty programme in which the militants surrendered their deadly weapons in exchange for rehabilitation and empowerment by the Federal Government.

Intelligence reports indicate that the unrepentant militants have started setting up camps in some of the communities in Niger Delta particularly Bayelsa, Delta and Akwa Ibom State from where they set out to take oil workers hostage and inflict damages to oil and gas installations.

As at press time, the eight oil workers abducted from Exxon Mobil facilities at Ibeno in Akwa Ibom including some Americans were yet to be released by the militants operating in the name of Movement for the Emancipation of the Niger Delta (MEND). One of the criminal elements who goes by the name "General Togo" is said to be the brain behind the current wave of criminality in the region.

In Bayelsa too about 19 foreign oil workers including some Nigerians were similarly abducted and held in custody for over a week by some of the criminal gangs operating along the creeks and water ways. Following the international outrage that greeted the events, the Joint Military

Taskforce in the Niger Delta had to launch massive rescue efforts which resulted in the successful release of the hostages.

It was also in the same Bayelsa that the home of Chief Timi Alaibe, the presidential coordinator of the amnesty programme was recently bombed by suspected militants. In that unconscionable attack, one of the security guards of Alaibe was killed.

How did we get to this faux pass? What really went wrong? The country was already counting her gains in the increased oil revenue she was now earning following the cessation of hostilities in the troubled region which ensured uninterrupted pumping of crude oil.

With the recent turn of events in the area, the question is what has really gone amiss with the amnesty programme? If we relate the current crisis with the Independence Day twin-bombings in Abuja which MEND claimed responsibility, it may be rightly concluded that the amnesty programme has broken down or the implementation is faltering.

Whatever interpretation that may be offered, the truth of the matter is that we have a national emergency on our hands. The Federal Government must rise quickly to the occasion. If the amnesty requires some fine tuning or adjustment to accommodate some disgruntled or grumbling militants that may have been inadvertently excluded, that should be done with a sense of urgency.

When this happens, the so-called militants who presently constitute a big nuisance along the creeks and water ways should be isolated and treated as common criminals; for that is what they are. They cannot continue to deceive the people, claiming to be freedom fighters when they are in actual fact armed marauders and economic saboteurs.

The amnesty programme was well conceived by the late President Yar'Adua who as a humanist was genuinely concerned about the deep-seated poverty and degraded environmental conditions of the Niger Delta. The programme which is in stages has the ultimate goal of transforming the Niger Delta from a zone of crises and conflicts to a region of sustainable peace and development.

It is in keeping with this vision that the government, right from Yar'Adua's presidency, proposed the Petroleum Industry Bill (PIB) which is to confer on host oil producing communities fuller participation in the management of the oil industry. The allocation of ten percent equity stakes in oil production to the host communities was intended to assist development in those communities and mitigate the incidents of restiveness.

This milestone, even if it has not meaningfully addressed the agitations for resource control, it is definitely a huge step forward in the economic emancipation of the Niger Delta region.

All well meaning Nigerians and particularly those residing in the Niger Delta are worried on this latest resurgence of violence and instability in the area more than two years after the widely acclaimed amnesty programme had come into force.

The security agencies in Nigeria particularly the JTF operating in the Niger Delta must begin to articulate effective strategies on how to rid the area of all the loafers, pirates, oil thieves, rapists and kidnappers who parade themselves as militants. They must be made to realize that the period of militancy was over with the declaration of the amnesty.

These criminal elements who do not want to give peace a chance must be fished out and made to face the full wrath of the law. Since they have decided, out of selfish economic reasons, to hold the nation hostage, there should be no hiding place for these destructive agents. An all-out war must be declared against them in order to give the law-abiding people of the Niger Delta an opportunity to live in peace and harmony.

Government must also make strenuous efforts, using its vast intelligence networks, to identify and fish out the sponsors of the criminal activities in the region, particularly the 'big men' who are behind the illegal oil bunkering in the area and similarly bring them to justice.

Government must demonstrate the resolve to make an example out of these highly placed people who are benefitting from the chaos and instability in the region. With that, a strong signal would have been sent that it can no longer be business as usual. This has to be done in order to bring sanity into the place and secure the fragile peace which the amnesty programme has succeeded in enthroning before the current relapse.

It is against this background that the decision of the Nigerian Navy and other security agencies to launch a holistic operation to flush out all criminal elements from their hideouts in the creeks must be applauded.

The Chief of Training and Operations, Naval Headquarters, Rear Admiral Ben Acholonu had told news men in Abuja after a brain storming session by the Naval authorities that the nation`s armed forces have concluded plans for a joint military exercise code named 'Operation Nemo' to curb kidnapping and other criminal activities in the Niger Delta.

Although he was tactical with the use of language when he stated the objectives of the military exercise, it was, however, imperative that the armed forces have declared war against the criminal gangs in the area. He said the objectives "are to assess the operational state of the naval ships, air access and the logistics support the navy could give to its ships in sustained operations at sea".

The operations must be sustained until the region is rid of the menace of all the criminals that have made peace impossible in the Niger Delta.

ThisDay, November 30, 2010

Chapter 67

Triumph of Legislative Independence

The leadership of the two chambers of National Assembly was formally constituted last week, thus ending many weeks of tension, anxiety and high-pitched horse trading that attended the scramble for the top most positions in the national legislature.

Never in the legislative history of the country have we witnessed such high wired and fierce politicking that presaged the election of the leadership of the National Assembly, particularly the House of Representatives. Against all odds, majority of House members, acting independently and in total defiance of the ruling Peoples Democratic Party (PDP), voted for the leaders of their choice.

The candidates that were anointed by the Presidency and PDP were roundly defeated by the legislators who had to defy all manner of threats, intimidation and blackmail from the party hierarchy and foot soldiers of the presidency to ensure that the will of the majority prevailed.

The independent action of the House members ensured that Hon. Aminu Waziri Tambuwal (Sokoto State) and Hon. Emeka Ihedioha (Imo State) were overwhelmingly elected as the Speaker and Deputy Speaker respectively. The candidate backed by the PDP hierarchy and President Goodluck Jonathan in the person of Hon. (Mrs) Mulikat Akande-Adeola (Oyo State), was completely rejected by the House members.

Akande-Adeola who hails from the South West where the party had zoned the Speakership polled miserable 90 votes while her opponent, Tambuwal from the North West scored 252 votes to clinch the coveted trophy. Ihedioha from the South East, on his part, was returned unopposed. Thus the massive endorsement of the duo of Tambuwal and Ihedioha by the House members ended the long running game of intrigues and the strenuous but futile efforts made by the PDP hierarchy to impose their lackeys on the leadership saddle of the House.

This remarkable development in the House has been widely hailed by well-meaning patriots as one of the best things that have happened to our democracy in recent times. By refusing to toe the path of officialdom which would have compromised its independence and render it impotent, the House of Representatives has given a strong signal to serve only the best interests of the nation.

The former military President, General Ibrahim Babangida, leading the pack, commended the House members for the courage of their conviction, arguing that the development would strengthen our democratic practice and safeguard the principle of separation of powers.

His words: "The bold moves of the Federal House of Representatives will further strengthen our democratic structures and entrench a culture of separation of powers with its manifest checks and balances for a people-driven democracy. It is a wake-up call and the earlier the polity allowed this culture of separation of powers to flourish, the better it would be for participatory democracy…The example that the Federal House has shown would go a long way to eliminate culture of impunity and executive interference into the internal operations and workings of the legislature".

It is against this background that political observers have condemned in strongest terms the arm-twisting tactics and intimidation employed by the PDP leadership to cow the House members and prevent them from acting in accordance with their individual conscience. Democracy is all about freedom of choice, expression and association.

These are fundamental freedoms that are firmly guaranteed by the Constitution of the land. Whatever reasons the PDP may have for seeking to subvert these freedoms, in my view, constitute an affront on the Constitution. It is regrettable to observe that the top echelons of the party including the likes of the Acting Chairman, Dr. Mohammed Haliru Bello, former Chairman of PDP Board of Trustees, Chief Tony Anenih and the Secretary to the Government of the Federation (SGF) Senator Anyim Pius Anyim were at the National Assembly to coerce the members to toe the official line. This in deed is a sad commentary on our political development which should be of serious concern to all lovers of democracy.

The reality on the ground is that the members of the House of Representatives have, in their own accord, freely chosen their leadership based on the credentials, antecedents, pedigree and integrity of the candidates. That choice, even if it breaches the official position of the ruling party, should be respected because the mandate given to Tambuwal and Ihedioha transcended partisan lines as lawmakers from the opposition parties unanimously endorsed the new leadership.

The new found unity and nationalist fervor in the House as evident in the historic decision of the members should be sustained as it will go a long way in cementing the existing bonds of ethnic fraternity which in recent times have come under strains by centrifugal forces in the country. The decision of the National Working Committee (NWC) of the PDP to oppose the new leadership in the House after they had emerged through what may be regarded as national consensus is in bitter taste. It will not serve the nation any useful purpose. Rather it will amount to sowing the seeds of instability with far-reaching consequences for the polity.

That the majority of the House members from both the ruling party and the opposition defied the zoning formula of the PDP to enthrone the leaders of their choice shows clearly that there was something basically wrong with the application of the zoning principle by the PDP hierarchy. Instead of the party threatening sanctions against the new leadership, it should embark on deep self-introspection with a view to finding where the party got it wrong and subsequently make amends.

The truth is that it is the same forces in the PDP who are now insisting on the strict application of zoning that unwittingly created the precedent conditions for the so-called rebellion in the House. The double speak and duplicitous position of the party leadership on the issues of zoning and rotation when the debate on these matters was raging on in the party prior to its presidential primaries have dimmed and diminished whatever moral authority the party possesses to call the 'errant' legislators to order.

The best path for the PDP hierarchy to toe now is that of conciliation and reconciliation. The resort to any underhand tactics with a view to emasculating the House leadership can only aggravate the existing tension in the polity and rupture the cordiality that was witnessed in the relationship between the Presidency and the legislature in the Sixth National Assembly.

Conclusion

The Path to a New Nigeria

W hen the British colonial authorities came into Nigeria at the turn of the 19th century on their "civilizing mission", they met a vast country of diverse people and cultures. A country of very heterogeneous populations at varying levels of human civilization.

Although the colonialists pretended to have come on a civilizing mission, they barely concealed their economic objectives. There is no doubt that their political intervention caused some setback to the orderly development of the natives.

The President of Uganda, Yoweri Museveni captured this clearly when he noted: "When the European exploiters first set foot in Africa.....the natural process of growth and advancement towards higher forms of civilization was interrupted and distorted. This affected both the economies and the people of Africa. The dominant exploitative relations in production, distribution and exchange were imperialist/capitalist ones which have always worked to the detriment of the African people" (Museveni; 1997:34).

The colonialists were confronted with a hard task of aggregating and articulating the huge diversities under a common administrative framework. It was a daunting mission which clearly tasked the administrative ingenuity and diplomatic acumen of the colonial overlords.

Bringing the people of such great diversities under a common political and administrative umbrella in deed proved a herculean task as the 'meddlesome interlopers' encountered fierce resistance in a number of places. In the so-called British expedition in the country, the invading colonial authorities resorted to the policy of 'pacification' in which maximum force was employed to subdue recalcitrant and belligerent indigenous communities and kingdoms.

The resistance to colonial domination was fiercest in the southern parts of Nigeria especially the Bini Kingdom in the present day Edo State and Arochuku society in the current Abia State.

Similar resistance to colonialism by indigenous Nigerian populations was also witnessed in some of the Yoruba speaking communities of the

South Western axis of the country which at the time included parts of former Dahomey, known today as the Republic of Benin.

Indirect Rule

After the pacification of the South, the British colonial authorities instituted the system of indirect rule; a programme through which existing traditional institutions were used to administer the people on behalf of the colonial powers. In other words, the newly empowered traditional institutions became the instrument through which the colonialists ensured public order and the exploitation of the people and their God-given resources.

In the Northern parts of Nigeria, particularly the Hausa-Fulani emirates where through the Islamic Jihad of 1804 led by Sheik Usman Dan Fodio, the people had put in place elaborate centralized political and administrative structures, the Indirect Rule system worked very well.

The invading colonial forces subdued the jihadists but reached a mutual understanding not to interfere in the culture and religion of the people. The British authorities were content with using the traditional institutions in administering the affairs of the vast geographical space of Northern Nigeria. Of course, it suited their political and economic designs perfectly well.

In the South, the Indirect Rule system succeeded partially because the traditional institutions on which the colonialists relied upon were not as well established as in the North. But in those areas in South West where the Obaship system was well rooted, the Indirect Rule also largely succeeded.

But in the South East with a highly reputed republican tradition, the Indirect Rule was a complete failure. In the absence of any existing centralized political or traditional authorities, except in a few places like Onitsha, Arochuku and Nri, the colonial authorities resorted to enthroning warrant chiefs to act as their political and administrative agents.

The system was met with stiff resistance as the warrant chiefs were lacking clearly in legitimacy and popular acceptance. The Aba Women Riots of 1929 was a practical demonstration of the people's indignation and rejection of external imposition.

This account is corroborated by Ellen Thorp. He wrote: "In 1914, when the Protectorate of Northern Nigeria was amalgamated with the colony (Lagos) and Protectorate of Southern Nigeria, the system known as "Indirect Rule" which Sir Frederick Lugard had instituted in the North was introduced into the South. Under Lugard`s inspiring direction the system was working well in the North......In the Yoruba countries of Southern Nigeria, whose people have for centuries acknowledged the authority of tribal chiefs, the system of indirect rule worked as successfully as it did in the North. In many parts of Eastern Nigeria, however, where traditional Chiefs were unknown, and where people were divided into small village units each with its own headman, the system was to prove less adaptable".

The foregoing historical background is very important in understanding the evolution of Nigeria as a nation state. Any objective analysis of the Nigerian condition today must of necessity take into account our past trajectories and current realities for us to be able to achieve national reconstruction.

The varying levels of challenges encountered by the British colonial authorities in different parts of Nigeria and their patterns of responses contributed greatly to the skewed political structure they bequeathed to us as an independent nation on 1st October, 1960.

It is also important to note that Nigeria was administered as two separate political entities from 1900 to 1914 when Lord Frederick Lugard through the Act of Amalgamation brought the Northern and Southern Protectorates under one political and administrative unit without the consent of the natives.

The Amalgamation though desirable to the British for effective and efficient political and administrative control, did not factor the varying levels of the socio-cultural development of the disparate ethnic groups in the North and South into any consideration. That singular error of commission or omission has continued to haunt Nigeria even till today.

An American journalist, Blaine Harden, who was for many years, the Africa Bureau Chief for the Washington Post acknowledged this pattern of colonial intervention in Africa and noted that the countries forged out of many rival ethnic groups within the continent by the colonial powers were artificial creations.

"Like most of the countries carved out of colonial Africa, Nigeria was a geographical and historical fluke. It was created by Lord Frederick Lugard, a British colonial governor-general and named after the Niger River by a foreign correspondent from the Times of London (a woman who married Lugard). Nigeria roped together three huge and highly developed tribes. They each had rich cultural traditions reaching a thousand years. Predictably, they did not like each other much" (Harden;1993:283).

Structural Imbalance

The three huge tribes in Nigeria which Harden was referring to are the Hausa-Fulani in the North, the Igbo in the East and the Yoruba in the West. Prior to the coming of the colonialists, there were no records of any meaningful interactions or exchanges of any type amongst these dominant groups that were separated by great distances in geography, religion, language and culture.

The American Jewish Congress in a Memorandum it issued on December 27, 1968 in New York City pointedly acknowledged the vastness of these three major contending groups in Nigeria, their diversity and distinctiveness as rival nationalities with capacity to lead independent political existence. In the memo prepared in the heat of the Nigeria-Biafra war, the American Jewish Congress wrote:

"More than fifty years ago, Great Britain artificially carved an area out of West Africa containing hundreds of different groups and arbitrarily unified it, calling it Nigeria. Although the area contained many different groups, three were predominant: the Hausa-Fulani, which formed about 65% of the peoples in the northern part of the territory; the Yoruba, which formed about 75% of the population in the southwestern part; and the Ibo, which formed between 60-65% of the population in the southeast

Each of these groups was so distinctive politically, religiously, culturally, and socially, as to constitute what in Europe in most circumstances would be thought of as a separate nation. The profound differences between them account, in a large sense, for the disintegration of the Nigerian Federation during the past several years.

The semi-feudal and Islamic Hausa-Fulani in the North were traditionally ruled by an autocratic, conservative Islamic hierarchy consisting of some thirty-odd Emirs who, in turn, owed their allegiance to a supreme Sultan. This Sultan was regarded as the source of all political power and religious authority.

The Yoruba political system in the southwest, like that of the Hausa-Fulani, also consisted of a series of monarchs. The Yoruba monarchs, however, were less autocratic than those in the North, and the political and social system of the Yoruba accordingly allowed for greater upward mobility based on acquired rather than inherited wealth and title.

The Ibo in the southeast, in contrast to the two other groups, lived in some six hundred autonomous, democratically-organized villages. Decisions among the Ibo were made by a general assembly in which every man could participate.

The different political systems among these three peoples produced highly divergent sets of customs and values. The Hausa-Fulani commoners, having contact with the political system only through their village head who was designated by the Emir or one of his subordinates, did not view political leaders as amenable to influence. Political decisions were to be obeyed without question. This highly centralized and authoritarian political system elevated to positions of leadership persons willing to be subservient and loyal to superiors, the same virtues required by Islam for eternal salvation. One of the chief functions of the traditional political system was to maintain the Islamic religion. Hostility to economic and social innovation was therefore deeply rooted.

In contrast to the Hausa-Fulani, the Ibo often participated directly in the decisions which affected their lives. They had a lively awareness of the political system and regarded it as an instrument for achieving their own personal goals. Status was acquired through the ability to arbitrate disputes that might arise in the village, and through acquiring rather than inheriting wealth. With their emphasis upon achievement, individual choice, and democratic decision-making, the challenges of modernization for the Ibos entailed responding to new opportunities in traditional ways. For the Hausa-Fulani, however, modernization required and still does a complete change in values and ways of life. The Yoruba were somewhere between the Hausa-Fulani and the Ibos regarding their need for achievement and emphasis upon individual choice".

It is not often for nothing that in the last two decades of our national existence there has been intermittent calls from several quarters for the convening of a Sovereign National Conference for the purpose of re-negotiating the basis of the Nigerian Federation. The nature of federalism which the British colonial powers bequeathed to Nigeria had in-built contradictions which would later lead to distortions in the system.

And as the late Senator Francis Ellah who represented Port Harcourt Senatorial District in the country's National Assembly during the Second Republic strongly observed in his book, The Unfinished Motion, a political or democratic set-up that has an in-built imbalance only breeds instability and restiveness. He noted as follows: "Once imbalance is installed in a system or the framework of a State becomes lopsided in favour of a visible majority ethnic group and against all other groups combined, then the political air is ominously fouled up and the hell of tribal hostility is let loose on all fronts upon the State and the nation". (Ellah, 1982:48)

The Nigerian federation was that of unequalled parts in which one of the federating units, the Northern region was larger in geographical size than the two other regions in the South namely, East and West, put together. This detracted sharply from the norm, as in any normal federation no federating unit should be in a position as to dominate the rest of the constituent units.

But in the case of Nigeria, the Northern region was twice the size of the South and was also given a democratic advantage over the two regions in the South combined together. There was genuine need to establish the North Central zone of the country otherwise known as the Middle Belt as a separate region from the North. The people of the area led by the late Dr. Joseph Tarka, the leader of the United Middle Belt Congress (UMBC) agitated for it, but the colonialists refused to accede to the request.

As the nation went for the first parliamentary elections in 1959 on the eve of independence, we had an unbalanced federation in which the North had half of the seats in parliament allocated to it. The new Nigerian federation was thus confronted with what was clearly a 'fait accompli'; a situation in which the North already had majority seats in the parliament even without undertaking any electioneering. This was a dangerous development; a faulty foundation on which the emergent State, Nigeria, was laid.

The implication of such a skewed federal structure was that the leadership of the country was deliberately handed over to the North by the colonial authorities to do as it pleases. With such a disingenuous arrangement, the North was meant to hold on to power in perpetuity.

The in-built contradictions in the system would sooner than later manifest as the other regions being excluded from power were naturally to mount a challenge to such a political arrangement that consigned them to a state of irrelevance. The crisis of nation building in Nigeria logically finds explanation within this context.

The bitter inter-ethnic struggles in Nigeria for the control of power at the center which had often seen some of the competing social groups seeking to wrest power from the hegemonic control of the Hausa-Fulani oligarchy would seem to be informed by the need to ensure equitable distribution of power and the associated privileges. A cursory study of the socio-political crises we have had in this country, including the unfortunate Civil War (1967-1970) had their immediate and remote causes in the big scramble for the control of the reins of power at the center.

Until the imbalance in the political structure is satisfactorily addressed, the notion of Nigeria as one indivisible and indissoluble political entity may not endure with time. There are cries of marginalization issuing out from different regions of the country, arising from obvious frustrations embedded in the system.

It is perhaps, the need to address the question of imbalance in any federal set-up that the duo of Kunle Amuwo and Georges Herault acknowledged the desirability of political restructuring in such situations.

They wrote: "Notwithstanding the existence of other forms of logic, the main drive towards institutional reforms in a federal system is the recognition, however arrived at, that existing state institutions, particularly at the centre, are inadequate to apprehend, comprehend and resolve immediate and new challenges" (Kunle Amuwo et al; 1998:6).

The National Question

These issues which border on the National Question must be sincerely and mutually resolved by all the ethnic nationalities in Nigeria if we are to enjoy inter-ethnic and religious harmony on a sustainable basis.

The current fierce debate over the place of zoning and rotation in the allocation of power and scarce national resources has once again brought to the fore the unending quest for the equitable restructuring of the Nigerian federation. As the nation plans to go into General Elections in April 2011, the arguments on the zoning and rotation of the presidency have drowned any other discussions on the preparations by the Independent National Electoral Commission (INEC) concerning the elections.

What is of paramount interest to many Nigerians who have bothered to join the debate is the geo-ethnic region to which the office of the president has been zoned by the contending political parties, particularly the ruling Peoples Democratic Party (PDP). Not many people are bothered in the least about the credentials and competence of the several aspirants that are in the race.

Even the aspirants themselves have not helped matters by their continuous engagement with the question of zoning and rotation as the basis for power sharing. This in itself is a tacit admission of the problems that are inherent in our federal structure.

For instance, four leading presidential aspirants of northern extraction, namely former military president, General Ibrahim Babangida, former Vice President, Alhaji Atiku Abubakar, former National Security Adviser, General Muhammed Aliyu Gusau and the governor of Kwara State, Dr. Abubakar Bukola Saraki, have been stoutly opposed to the candidacy of President Goodluck Jonathan on the ground that he was ineligible to contest for the presidency on the platform of the PDP because zoning and rotation policy of the party rules Jonathan out of the contest.

Atiku Abubakar was later adopted as the consensus choice of the Northern Political Leaders Forum led by veteran politician, Mallam Adamu Ciroma. The other aspirants, in agreement with the consensus choice collapsed their individual campaign structures into the Atiku Campaign Organization.

Goodluck Jonathan from the south was the Vice President under the late President Umar Musa Yar'Adua from the north. Yar'Adua was barely three years in office when he died in May 2010. His death paved way for Jonathan's ascendancy to the presidency. It was the decision of Jonathan to present himself for election that compelled the northern presidential aspirants to come together to ensure that the presidency is retained in the north till 2015.

For these Northern elements, Jonathan's decision was seen as a breach of the subsisting policy of zoning and rotation within the PDP. However, Jonathan and his supporters were of the view that as a sitting President he had the constitutional right to contest irrespective of the party's position on zoning. A High Court in Abuja presided over by the Chief Judge of the Federal Capital Territory (FCT) Justice Lawal Gummi however ruled that Jonathan had the right to run as the issue of zoning was the internal affair of the party.

With the ruling, the legal impediments on the way of Jonathan were cleared for him to contest. This set the stage for the titanic battle in the

PDP presidential primaries held in Abuja on 13th January, 2011 in which Jonathan emerged victorious ahead of the General Elections in April 2011.

He went ahead to win the presidential elections held on April 16, 2011, defeating his main opponent, General Muhammadu Buhari of Congress for Progressive Change (CPC) with a wide margin.

The fact that Nigerians are still talking about the zoning and rotation of the highest office in the land fifty years after the nation's existence as an independent political entity shows that the Nigerian federation is very defective and therefore requires some tinkering.

In Search of National Consensus

But having interacted together with one another these past fifty years, the various social groups in Nigeria have no choice but to work in unison in the search for enduring solutions to the challenges of nation building.

By the act of destiny, through the instrumentality of colonialism, the over three hundred ethnic nationalities in Nigeria have come to share a common political heritage. It is therefore important that they accommodate each other's differences and chart a common front for the survival of the country as one harmonious nation state.

In this regard, there should be less emphasis on those things that tend to pronounce our differences. Rather, every conceivable effort must be made to emphasize those things that unite and bind us together as a people of common destiny. If we shall ever make it as a nation, the Hausa-Fulani, Igbo, Yoruba and all the various ethnic groups in Nigeria must come together with the singleness of purpose and vision. No individual ethnic group can go it alone. There is a lot of sense in the saying that unity is strength. And in deed, it is not for nothing that the founding fathers of Nigeria referred to the country at independence as a country of unity in diversity.

For example, the greatest strength of the United States, the most powerful country in the world today lies in its diversity; a nation of many races bound together by a common dream and shared vision. It remains a country where no structural limitations are placed in the aspirations of the citizenry irrespective of colour, creed, sex, or race.

It is true that the enviable status of the US was not attained over night. Like our country, Nigeria, she even had to fight a civil war to cement her unity and launch her on the path of liberty and freedom. We definitely have a lot to borrow from the American experience to assist our efforts at national integration. It is not just enough to adopt the American model of presidential democracy; we must however make some adaptations to suit our own peculiar cultural circumstances.

In the American situation, there are constitutional provisions for affirmative actions which seek special protection for the weak and minorities including women. In her search for national consensus, Nigeria can take a cue from there by introducing and entrenching affirmative clauses into her constitution with a view to safeguarding and protecting the interests of the vulnerable members of the society.

The United Nations in its 2004 Human Development Report acknowledged the need for institutional measures to protect marginalized groups in culturally diverse societies.

"Constitutions and legislations that provide protection and guarantees for minorities, indigenous people and other groups are a critical foundation for broader freedoms....unless citizens come to think, feel and act in ways that genuinely accommodate the needs and aspirations of others, real change will not happen" (HDR;2004:V).

While I am not opposed to the borrowing of ideas from outside to add value to our system, I still believe that in doing so we must take into consideration our own peculiar local environment. This is where the question of zoning and rotation as a basis for power sharing amongst the constituent geo-political regions in Nigeria becomes germane.

A peculiar problem requires peculiar solution. Attaining national integration in Nigeria in the last five decades of her existence has been particularly tasking and difficult. Since, at the centre of the National Question, is the problem of power sharing amongst the competing ethnic groups in Nigeria, it makes sense to put in place a political system in which no group is excluded from the power configuration of the State

The frustrations that often result from the policy of exclusion and marginalization are at the roots of several ethno-religious and socio-political conflicts in many plural societies particularly in Africa including Nigeria. In our search for national consensus, deliberate State Directive policies must be evolved to accommodate and balance the interests of all the ethnic groups in the power arrangement of the country.

This is where those who fault the principles of zoning and rotation as an equitable basis for power sharing in Nigeria miss the point. In the light of experience and reason, the zoning and rotation of power amongst the six geo-political zones, even if it is a transitional arrangement, in my view, holds very bright prospects of deepening national integration and guaranteeing national consensus.

It is even gratifying to note that the nation has come to realize that the only way forward in the pursuit of political stability and social cohesion is the adoption of an arrangement in which power would rotate amongst the six geo-political zones. The national consensus on power rotation was reached at the 1994/95 National Constitutional Conference in Abuja under the auspices of the regime of late General Sani Abacha.

At the conference which was convened to chart a way forward for the country and avert a possible disintegration, the delegates unanimously agreed on the rotation of power between the North and South along six geo-political zones. That decision was clearly informed by the crises arising from the illegal annulment by the military of the June 12, 1993 presidential election widely believed to have been won by a wealthy Southern business man, Chief MKO Abiola.

The delegates in their wisdom conceived the rotational principle as a transitional arrangement that would be in place for thirty years; the period within which each of the six geo-political zones would have had its turn in power. This was considered a fair deal, considering that the ethnic monopolization of power had been at the root of all the political conflicts in many African societies.

Sufficient examples abound in such countries as Burundi, Rwanda, Democratic Republic of Congo, Uganda, Sudan, Cote d'Ivoire, Angola, Liberia and Nigeria in which the inter-ethnic struggles for control of power resulted into civil wars.

It is, perhaps, in recognition of this fact that Wale Olaitan wrote: "The virtual collapse of the state machinery in the context of the June 12, 1993 presidential election debacle arose out of a contention on the basis of distribution and control of important state offices as many segments complained of persistent marginalization and a deliberate ploy to keep them out of such control. This means that deft moves were required to organize state-building efforts in the direction of working out acceptable basis of sharing and guaranteeing access to state offices in order to assure the Nigerian state of continued existence" (in Kunle Amuwo et al:144).

Against this background, any policy device that can guarantee social inclusiveness must be welcomed and embraced as it would help to steer the ship of state away from conflicts and crises.

References

1. **Abubakar, Jamila J.** et al, Conflict of Securities: Reflections on State and Human Security in Africa; Adonis and Abbey Publishers Ltd, London, 2010.

2. **Achebe, Chinua,** The Trouble with Nigeria, Heinemann, London, 1983.

3. **Amuwo, Kunle** et al, Federalism and Political Restructuring in Nigeria; Spectrum   Books Ltd, Ibadan, 1998.

4. **Baum, Phil,** "Memorandum from American Jewish Congress", 15 East 84th Street, New York, 1968.

5. **Ellah Francis J,** The Unfinished Motion on Creation of States in Nigeria; Chief J. W. Ellah Sons & Co. Ltd, Port Harcourt, Nigeria, 1982.

6. **Harden, Blaine,** Africa: Dispatches from a Fragile Continent; Harper Collins Publishers, London, 1993.

7. **Meredith, Martin,** The State of Africa: A History of Fifty Years of Independence; The Free Press, United Kingdom, 2006.

8. **Museveni, Yoweri Kaguta,** Sowing the Mustard Seed: The Struggle for Freedom and Democracy in Uganda; Macmillan Publishers Limited, Oxford, 1997.

9. **Nwosu, Humphrey,** Laying the Foundation for Nigeria`s Democracy: My Account of June 12, 1993 Presidential Election and Its Annulment; Macmillan Nigeria Publishers Limited, Ilupeju, Lagos, 2008.

10. **Olive, David,** Barrack Obama's Great Speeches, Beulahland Publications, 10 Owoseni Street, off Mission Road, Benin City, Edo State, 2008

11. The Constitution of the Federal Republic of Nigeria, 1999.
12. **Thorp, Ellen,** Ladder of Bones; Spectrum Books Limited, Ibadan, 1956.
13. **UNDP Human Development Report, 2004,** Cultural Liberty in Today`s Diverse World

Index

Switzerland, 251

T

Tarka, Joseph, 271
Thorp, Ellen, 16, 267, 279
Tofa, Bashir, 197
Turaki, Saminu, iv, 26, 27, 28, 29, 256

U

Uganda, 18, 27, 100, 176, 208, 246, 266, 276, 278
Ukachukwu, Nicholas, 93, 168, 169, 170, 171
Umuahia, xi, xv, 56, 62, 122, 142, 150, 157, 164, 165, 166, 196, 206, 218, 249
Unfinished Motion, 270, 278
Union Bank, 59
University of Nigeria, Nsukka, vii, 34, 43, 106, 170, 188
Utomi, Pat, 55

Uwais Committee, 195, 196, 198

V

Vatsa, Mamman, 23
Vision 2020, 26

W

West African Pilot, 46

X

Xavier Communications Ltd, xi

Y

Yemen, 161, 162
Yoruba., 16

Z

Zamfara State, 74, 75, 77, 232
Ziks Flats, 189, 190
Zimbabwe, 18, 40, 100, 101, 111

www.ingramcontent.com/pod-product-compliance
Lightning Source LLC
Chambersburg PA
CBHW070610270326
41926CB00013B/2489